INDUSTRIAL INCENTIVES

Competition among American States and Cities

Peter S. Fisher
Alan H. Peters

1998

W.E. Upjohn Institute for Employment Research
Kalamazoo, Michigan

Library of Congress Cataloging-in-Publication Data

Fisher, Peter S.
  Industrial incentives : competition among American states and
cities / Peter S. Fisher, Alan H. Peters.
    p. cm.
  Includes bibliographical references and index.
  ISBN 0–88099–184–4 (hardcover : alk. paper). — ISBN 0–88099–183–6
(pbk. : alk. paper)
  1. Incentives in industry—United States.   2. Industrial
promotion—United States.   3. Competition—United States.
I.   Peters, Alan H.   II. Title.
HF5549.5.I5F57   1998
338.9734—dc21   98–18002
                                                                                      CIP

The facts presented in this study and the observations and viewpoints expressed are
the sole responsibility of the authors. They do not necessarily represent positions of
the W. E. Upjohn Institute for Employment Research.

Cover design by J. R. Underhill
Index prepared by Leoni Z. McVey.
Printed in the United States of America.

CONTENTS

Acknowledgments   xi
The Authors   xiii

1 State and Local Incentive Competition for New Investment   1
  The Expansion of and Justification for State and Local Incentives   5
  Criticisms of Incentive Competition   7
  Why Economic Development Incentives May Be
    Useful: Revisionist Research   10
  Issue 1: Can Incentives Reasonably Be Expected
    to Influence Business Location Decisions?   13
    The Survey Technique   14
    The Case Study Technique   15
    The Econometric Technique   15
    The General Equilibrium Technique   17
    The Hypothetical Firm Technique   18
    Conclusions: How We Propose to Deal with the
      Incentive Question   19
  Issue 2: The Spatial Distribution of Incentives   20
  Measuring Incentives and the Standing Offer   24
  The Structure of the Book   26
  Notes   27

2 An Overview of Method   31
  What Are Competitive Economic Development Incentives?   31
  Taxes and Tax Incentives   33
    Corporate Income Tax   35
    The Sales Tax   36
    The Property Tax   38
  Non-Tax Incentives   39
    General-Purpose Financing Programs   40
    Customized Job Training and Wage Subsidies   40
    Infrastructure Subsidies   42
    Other Incentive Programs Not Included   43
  The Hypothetical Firm Method: An Introduction   45
  Extensions to the Hypothetical Firm Method to Include
    Non-Tax Incentives   49
  Selection of the State and City Samples   50
  Notes   52

3 The Hypothetical Firm Method Extended   55
Alternative Approaches   56
    Aggregate Tax Measures   56
    Program Counting   57
    Program or Tax Expenditures   58
The Hypothetical Firm Method   58
Which Industries and Firm Sizes?   63
Firm, Plant, and Headquarters Location   70
How Are the Firm's Sales Distributed among States?   72
Interstate or Interlocal Competition?   75
Measuring Effects over Time   78
Disaggregating the Results   82
Simulating the Worth of Non-Tax Incentives   83
    Infrastructure Incentives   87
    Wage Subsidy and Worker Training Incentives   89
    General-Use Grants, Loans, Loan Guarantees, and Related
      Debt Instruments   90
    Generating Incentive Amounts and Incentive Terms   91
    Distributing Incentives across Asset Classes   95
    Awarding Grants, Loans, and Loan Guarantees   95
    Adding State and City Incentives   98
Limitations of the Analysis I: The Administration of Incentives
    Alters Their Worth   98
Limitation of the Analysis II: Completeness of the Non-Tax
    Portion of TAIM   103
Limitations of the Analysis III: Targeting Geography   104
Conclusions   105
Notes   106

4 Tax Systems and Incentive Programs in States and Cities   109
Variation in Taxes and Tax Incentives   110
    Sales Taxes   110
    Corporate Income Taxes and Credits   113
    Property Taxes   118
    Targeted Tax Incentives   118
Basic Tax Systems versus Tax Incentives   119
The Importance of State versus Local Taxes and Tax Incentives   129
Non-Tax Incentive Programs and Their Value to the Firm   134
The Spatial Pattern of Taxes and Incentives   142
Conclusions   171
Notes   173

5 The Effects of Taxes and Incentives on the Spatial Distribution of Investment Returns   175
   The Pattern of Returns among States   176
   The Pattern of Returns among Cities   186
   The Effects of Enterprise Zones   190
   Conclusions   200
   Notes   201

6 Incentive Competition and Public Policy   203
   Are Tax and Incentive Differences Important?   203
   The Spatial Pattern of Incentives and the National Benefits
     of Competitive Economic Development Policy   211
   Taxes, Incentives, and Efficiency   213
   Incentive Competition and Equity   218
   Can and Should Incentive Competition Be Curbed?   219
   Notes   221

Appendix A Characteristics of the Sample States and Cities   223

Appendix B The Hypothetical Firm Model: Assumptions and Details of Operation   237

Appendix C Computational Structure of TAIM   247

Appendix D Additional Results on the Worth and Spatial Distribution of Taxes and Incentives   253

Appendix E Detailed Results: Correlations between Project Returns and Unemployment Rates for States and Cities   265

References   277

Author Index   289

Subject Index   293

LIST OF TABLES

2.1 Sample of Cities 51

3.1 Characteristics of the 16 Hypothetical Firms, by Industry,
SIC Code, and Size 66
3.2 How Firm Characteristics Affect Rankings of Investment
Returns for Selected Multistate Firms 69
3.3 Selected Cities Ranked by Returns on Investment for Multistate
and Single-Location Firms 73

4.1 State Sales Taxes on Business Purchases as of 1992 111
4.2 State Corporate Income and Net Worth Taxes as of 1992 114
4.3 Property Tax Base, Effective Property Tax Rates, and
Abatements Offered, by State, 1992 120
4.4 State Tax Incentives Available Statewide and in Enterprise
Zones for Distressed Areas, 1992 122
4.5 Value to the Firm of Selected Features of State and Local
Taxes: % Reduction in Tax Burden 125
4.6 Effective Tax Rates in a Representative City in Each State 131
4.7 Effective Tax Incentive Rates in a Representative City in
Each State 135
4.8 State Non-Tax Incentive Programs That Were Simulated 138
4.9 Composition of Incentives 141
4.10 Project Returns after All Taxes and Incentives for
16 Multistate Firms Locating in 112 Cities 144
4.11 The Impact of Taxes and Incentives on Project Returns
for Small Drug Firms, 112 Cities 158
4.12 The Impact of Taxes and Incentives on Project Returns
for Large Drug Firms, 112 Cities 158
4.13 The Impact of Taxes and Incentives on Project Returns
for Small Soap Firms, 112 Cities 159
4.14 The Impact of Taxes and Incentives on Project Returns
for Large Plastics Firms, 112 Cities 159

5.1 Correlation between State Average 1992 Unemployment Rate
and Firm's Net Return on New Plant Investment in Each State 178
5.2 Correlation between State Employment Growth and Poverty
Rates and Firm's Net Return on New Plant Investment in
Each State in 1992 182

5.3 Correlations of Effective Tax and Incentive Rates in a
     Representative City in Each State with State Unemployment,
     Job Growth, and Poverty Rates   185
5.4 Correlation between City 1992 Unemployment Rate and
     Firm's Net Returns from New Plant Investment in Each City   187
5.5 Correlation between City 1990 Poverty Rate and Firm's
     Net Returns from New Plant Investment in Each City:
     Multistate Firms Only   189
5.6 Characteristics of Cities with and without Enterprise
     Zones, 1992   191
5.7 The Importance of Enterprise Zone Incentives: Average Value
     among Cities of 25,000 or More for Selected Multistate Firms 193
5.8 Correlation between City Unemployment Rate and Value
     of Incentives: Enterprise Zone versus Other Incentives   195
5.9 Correlation between City Poverty Rate and Value
  . of Incentives: Enterprise Zone versus Other Incentives   199

6.1 The Subsidy Package for the Mercedes-Benz Auto
     Assembly Plant: Gross Value versus Value to the Firm
     in Alternative Locations   209

A.1 Characteristics of the 24 Sample States   225
A.2 City Sample: Demographic Characteristics and Taxes   227
A.3 Average Effective Local Property Tax Rates by State   234

B.1 Assumed Cost of Equity for Hypothetical Firms   241
B.2 Interest Rate and Loan Term Assumptions   242
B.3 Unemployment and Residence Assumptions for Enterprise
     Zone Incentives   246

D.1 The Impact of Taxes and Incentives on Project Returns, Small
     Furniture and Fixtures Firms, 112 Cities   255
D.2 The Impact of Taxes and Incentives on Project Returns, Large
     Furniture and Fixtures Firms, 112 Cities   255
D.3 The Impact of Taxes and Incentives on Project Returns, Large
     Soap Firms, 112 Cities   256
D.4 The Impact of Taxes and Incentives on Project Returns, Small
     Plastics Firms, 112 Cities   256
D.5 The Impact of Taxes and Incentives on Project Returns, Small
     Industrial Machinery Firms, 112 Cities   257

D.6   The Impact of Taxes and Incentives on Project Returns, Large
       Industrial Machinery Firms, 112 Cities   257
D.7   The Impact of Taxes and Incentives on Project Returns, Small
       Electronic Components Firms, 112 Cities   258
D.8   The Impact of Taxes and Incentives on Project Returns, Large
       Electronic Components Firms, 112 Cities   258
D.9   The Impact of Taxes and Incentives on Project Returns, Small
       Auto/Auto Parts Firms, 112 Cities   259
D.10 The Impact of Taxes and Incentives on Project Returns, Large
       Auto/Auto Parts Firms, 112 Cities   259
D.11 The Impact of Taxes and Incentives on Project Returns, Small
       Instruments Firms, 112 Cities   260
D.12 The Impact of Taxes and Incentives on Project Returns, Large
       Instruments Firms, 112 Cities   260
D.13 Average Value of Incentives, Multistate Firms   261

E.1   Correlation between State Average 1992 Unemployment
       Rate and Firm's Net Return on New Plant Investment in
       Each State   267
E.2   Correlation between State Average Unemployment Rate
       1989–1993 and Firm's Net Return on New Plant Investment
       in Each State   268
E.3   Correlation between City 1992 Unemployment Rate and
       Firm's Net Returns from New Plant Investment in Each
       City: Selected Multistate Firms, by City Size Class   269
E.4   Correlation between City 1992 Unemployment Rate and
       Firm's Net Returns from New Plant Investment in Each
       City: Average for All City Sizes by Firm   271
E.5   Effective Tax and Tax Incentive Rates in a Representative
       City in Each State: Correlations with State Unemployment,
       Job Growth, and Poverty Rates   274

LIST OF FIGURES

3.1 TAIM Extended to Include Non-Tax Incentives   86

4.1 Small Multistate Drug Firms, Project Returns after
      All Incentives, 112 Cities   146
4.2 Large Multistate Drug Firms, Project Returns after
      All Incentives, 112 Cities   147
4.3. Small Multistate Soap Firms, Project Returns after
      All Incentives, 112 Cities   148
4.4 Large Multistate Plastics Firms, Project Returns after
      All Incentives, 112 Cities   149
4.5 Small Multistate Drug Firms Investing in a $50 Million
      Plant, Project Returns after Taxes and All Incentives
      in the Top 20 Cities   150
4.6 Large Multistate Drug Firms Investing in a $470 Million
      Plant, Project Returns after Taxes and All Incentives
      in the Top 20 Cities   151
4.7 Small Multistate Soap Firms Investing in a $20 Million
      Plant, Project Returns after Taxes and All Incentives
      in the Top 20 Cities   152
4.8 Large Multistate Plastics Firms Investing in a $70 Million
      Plant, Project Returns after Taxes and All Incentives
      in the Top 20 Cities   153
4.9 Project Returns after Taxes and All Incentives in the
      Worst 20 Cities for Small Multistate Soap Firms Investing
      in a $20 Million Plant   155

4.10 Range of Project Returns within States, Small Multistate
      Drug Firms   164
4.11 Project Returns Rank Position over 112 Locations, Small
      Multistate Drug Firms   165

5.1 Rate of Return on New Plant Investment in Top 25 Cities:
      Multistate Instruments Manufacturer, $180 Million Plant   197

C.1 Computational Structure of TAIM   251

D.1 Project Returns Rank Position over 112 Locations, Large
      Multistate Drug Firms   262
D.2 Project Returns Rank Position over 112 Locations, Small
      Multistate Soap Firms   263
D.3 Project Returns Rank Position over 112 Locations, Large
      Multistate Plastics Firms   264

LIST OF MAPS

2.1 Geographic Distribution of States and Cities Included
      in the Analysis   47

4.1 Best and Worst Locations for Small Multistate Drug Firms   163
4.2 Small Multistate Drug Firms, TIN Digital Elevation Model
      of Project Returns   167
4.3 TAIM Simulation of Best and Worst Locations for Large
      Multistate Drug Firms   168
4.4 TAIM Simulation of Best and Worst 20 Locations
      for Small Multistate Soap Firms   169
4.5 TAIM Simulation of Best and Worst Locations
      for Large Multistate Plastics Firms   170

Acknowledgments

This book has been a long time in the making. The original research, funded by the W.E. Upjohn Institute for Employment Research, began in 1992. We had proposed looking at what sort of places offer the biggest business incentives. It was soon obvious that if we were really going to measure the generosity of economic development incentives, a lot more work would have to go into building an entirely new hypothetical firm model. Building this model soon became an all-consuming task. For close to 18 months, the focus of the research was on how to solve the problems we saw with existing models and how to incorporate discretionary incentives into our own evolving model. Concurrently, we had to collect enough detailed information on discretionary incentives from states and cities that our model would have a good database with which to work. Although the vast majority of state and local officials were incredibly helpful and went out of their way to provide us with the necessary information, assembling the database was a slow and tedious exercise taking well over two years.

Along the way we accumulated many debts. Our first is to the W.E Upjohn Institute, for providing the original funding. At Upjohn, Tim Bartik oversaw the project. His work on the impact of economic development policy had inspired our own, and it was wonderful to have him as the first external resource for our research. Others at Upjohn, especially Randy Eberts and Allan Hunt, also provided very helpful comments and publicized our work widely. One result of their effort was that we were asked to present our research at a number of conferences and meetings. Of these, the comments and suggestions we received at three symposia on economic development policy, organized by the Federal Reserve Banks of Minneapolis, Chicago, and Boston respectively, proved immensely useful. Bob Tannenwald, at the Boston Fed, has continued to be a great help and supporter. Comments received at other conferences (both academic and professional) have also been helpful. There are many colleagues to whom we are very grateful; special mention must be made of Ned Hill, who has seen and made comments on the work since its earliest days. We have also benefited greatly from careful comments made by the reviewers of the earlier version of this manuscript, as well as the reviewers of the various technical papers we published on methodology.

The University of Iowa provided support for this project. During the early stages of the research, both of us were given sabbaticals during which we were Fellows at the Obermann Center for Advanced Studies at the University of Iowa. The Director, Jay Semel, provided a wonderful intellectual environment that encouraged scholarly productivity. Our home department, the Graduate

Program in Urban and Regional Planning, provided a number of research assistants to whom we owe an enormous debt. Kala Sridhar and Lisa Schweitzer worked with us over a long period and were crucial in developing the discretionary incentive database. Roxanne Addink, Tyler Deke, Ray Keller, Richard Ray, Chris Mefford, Chris Kivett, and Lynn Rose also worked on this database. We thank them all. We would also like to thank the hundreds of state and local officials without whose help and generosity the research could not have progressed.

Moving from research to producing a book has involved huge effort. Again, it was made that much easier by the people at the Upjohn Institute. We owe a special debt to Susan Friedman, who edited the manuscript and, in so doing, managed to turn our sentences into "English." Natalie Lagoni did the typesetting and page layout of this often complex manuscript. Richard Wyrwa worked with us on publicity. David Nadziejka oversaw much of the production of the manuscript. We thank them all.

Finally, but probably most importantly, we are grateful to our families. For about three years we were obsessed with the work on which this book is based. Although, as enlightened males, it is embarrassing to have to admit this, our families usually ended up taking up the slack. Alan thanks his wife, who cooked dinner many times too often and with whom he discussed most of the work. Peter thanks his wife and his children, who found him poor company those many evenings he spent muttering at his computer.

Although we have many debts to others, the errors and omissions in the book are ours alone.

The Authors

Peter Fisher is Professor of Urban and Regional Planning at the University of Iowa. He holds a bachelor's degree from Haverford College and received a Ph.D. in economics from the University of Wisconsin–Madison in 1978, where he majored in public finance. At the University of Iowa, his research and teaching has focused on state and local government finance and economic development policy. He has served as a consultant on a variety of finance and policy issues for state government agencies and nonprofit organizations.

His recent publications, both with Alan Peters, include "Measuring Tax and Incentive Competition: What is the Best Yardstick?" in *Regional Studies*, and "Tax and Spending Incentives and Enterprise Zones" in the *New England Economic Review*.

Alan Peters is an Associate Professor in the Graduate Program in Urban and Regional Planning at the University of Iowa. He received his Ph.D. from Rutgers University in 1989. Over the past few years his research has focused on measuring the effectiveness of state and local economic development policy. He has also done research on the administration of economic development policy and the impact of commuting behavior on the employment opportunities of low-income workers. Currently, he is writing a book (with Peter Fisher) on the usefulness of enterprise zones in promoting growth in declining areas. Prior to coming to the United States, he worked on economic development policy issues in southern Africa.

1 State and Local Incentive Competition for New Investment

Over the past decade and a half, "economic development" has become entrenched as an important function of state and city government. Unlike much of the other, more hidden, work undertaken by states and cities, the special economic development deals offered by local officials to lure new investment are often covered prominently in the press. Few have been unimpressed by the $250 million Alabama reputedly gave Mercedes-Benz or by the estimated $130 million South Carolina gave BMW (Council of State Governments 1994, p. 12). Possibly as a result of such eye-grabbing deals, it has become commonplace, not only in the press but among policymakers and academics, to characterize the current level of economic development effort as too highly competitive and probably detrimental to sound fiscal policy. State and local competition for new industrial investment has been widely criticized for being a zero-sum, or worse, a negative-sum game—in other words, providing no national benefits—and for being potentially harmful to economic growth because it reduces the ability of state and local governments to finance investments in education and infrastructure. Indeed the subtext of much popular reporting and even academic discussion is that states and cities have become imprudently generous to private investment while cutting back on more typical governmental activities. It is unsurprising then that some prominent researchers have called for the federal government to severely limit state and local economic development efforts (Burstein and Rolnick 1996; Rolnick and Burstein 1996; Schweke, Rist, and Dabson 1994) or for a major reorientation of the state and local economic development effort (LeRoy 1994; Smith and Fox 1990).

Notwithstanding the existence of both this sort of criticism of economic development policy and a number of academic and policy journals dedicated to the issue of state and local economic development policy, very little is known about the size of the economic development effort. We have some idea of the staff size at state development agencies and of the budgets of those agencies (although for reasons that will

1

become clear, it is most unlikely that these budget numbers say much about the size of the state economic development effort), and we have some knowledge of what economic development instruments states are able to use (although there are important discrepancies among the various directories of state instruments). However, there is virtually no reliable information on the really important questions: How much are states willing to provide to a firm? What are state incentives actually worth to a firm? What sort of places offer the biggest incentives? At the city level, the situation is that much worse; here there is not even a reliable directory of instruments or budgets. One result is that public and even academic debate on economic development issues is often seriously flawed.

Possibly two of the most crucial issues for economic development concern are 1) measuring the worth *to the firm* of incentives offered and 2) identifying the spatial pattern of incentives (in other words, determining which communities offer the largest and smallest incentives). These issues are important because almost all economic development policy is based on the idea—emanating from modern location theory—that the purpose of incentives is to influence business location decisions by improving the relative profitability of investing at a particular site (Blair and Premus 1987; Chapman and Walker 1990). Unfortunately, the academic and policy literature on economic development has tended to focus on other issues, usually the cost of incentive programs to government or the nominal size of incentive deals. The Alabama incentive package to Mercedes-Benz was reported by one source to be composed of $112 million in infrastructure improvements, $30 million to build a training facility, $60 million for training, $8.7 million for tax abatements on machinery and construction materials, and $39 million in other incentives (Council of State Governments 1994, p. 12). What is unclear is the extent to which Mercedes-Benz benefits from each dollar of public money spent. Is Mercedes-Benz able to capture the full $30 million in state funds spent on the training facility or the $112 million spent on infrastructure? These problems are even more stark in the BMW deal. Fifty million dollars of BMW's $130 million package was for expansion of the Greenville-Spartanburg airport. It seems unreasonable to assume that BMW will be able to capture all of the benefits of airport expansion; airports are public facilities, and it is much more likely that many (if not most) of the airport's improvements will be captured by other individual and corporate business users, not BMW. Much of the economic development literature ignores this problem.

More generally, the literature has mostly failed to distinguish between the nominal value of incentive awards and their actual value to the firm. For instance, the 1980s saw considerable Japanese auto plant investment in the United States. In a widely quoted article looking at this issue, Milward and Newman (1989) claimed that Mazda had received state incentives worth around $15,000 per employee for its investment in Flat Rock, Michigan. This figure included $19 million in worker training, $5 million in road improvements, $3 million in on-site railroad improvements, $21 million in an economic development loan to be recaptured, and $5 million in water system improvements. This gives a total of $53 million for what was then projected to be 3,500 employees at the new plant. In the same article, various other Japanese auto manufacturers were reported to be receiving vast incentive deals. Similar claims about the nominal value of economic development deals are commonly made in the press and in the academic and policy literature. However, there are problems with such measures beyond the matter of a firm's ability to capture directly the benefits of an incentive. Consider the case of Mazda just cited. The costs and benefits associated with various types of economic development incentives vary greatly; adding up nominal awards across different programs has the effect of comparing apples with oranges. Most obviously, a $1 million capital on-site railroad improvement award is likely to be much more costly for government, and much more beneficial to the recipient firm, than a $1 million capital loan. In the Mazda case, consider the $19 million worker training award. If this award provides workers with general and transferable skills, then it is unlikely that it was worth the full $19 million to Mazda, but if the training were highly customized to Mazda's special needs, then it may indeed have replaced $19 million in expenses that Mazda would otherwise have incurred.

So, the question remains, How should the worth of incentives be measured? The first concern of this book is to measure, from the point of view of the firm, the true benefits of state and city incentives. A cogent answer to this question is a prerequisite to any sensible debate on the impact of incentives on a firm's investment decisions. Moreover, an answer also allows us to begin to provide innovative and useful responses to a related issue that has dogged the economic development literature: can development incentives reasonably be expected to influence a firm's location decisions? In all of this, our purpose is not to add to the already extensive econometric and survey literature on whether economic development incentives measurably affect the location decisions of firms. While our results do complement this research, our purpose is limited to measuring the worth of incentives to the firm.

Unfortunately, providing a comprehensive and cogent measurement of the worth of economic development incentives to firms is a dauntingly complex task. A vast proportion of the work going into the answers provided in this book is methodological. As a result, much of the book is itself devoted to methodology (although more technical discussions are segregated into Chapter 3 and Appendixes B and C and may be avoided by readers not interested in such issues). Simply put, the answers we give in this book derive from the output of a very large computer simulation model (the Tax and Incentive Model, or TAIM). It has been our experience that the answers provided by TAIM—and equally by competing models—are often crucially dependent on the assumptions incorporated into the model. Understanding the assumptions is an important part of understanding the answers themselves. One of the criticisms we have of some—although certainly not all—of the work done in the same tradition as ours (researchers using the hypothetical firm method) is that public policy conclusions are made on the basis of data and assumptions the underpinnings of which are inadequately discussed.

The second concern we focus on is the spatial pattern of economic development incentives. In particular, do poorer, more distressed places tend to offer bigger incentives than wealthier, less distressed places? We believe this matter has received insufficient attention in the literature. An answer to this question is crucial; if *competitive* state and local economic development policy is to provide net benefits for the nation, then it should, we believe, tend to promote the redistribution of employment from areas of low economic distress.[1] For this to occur, economic development efforts should be concentrated or more active in poorer, economically troubled places.

Although our research concentrates on these two issues—the worth and spatial pattern of incentives—our results also shed light on a set of related, secondary questions:

- Would it be feasible for the federal government to limit the state and local economic development effort?

- What is the role of enterprise zones in delivering incentives to firms?

- What proportion of the total incentive package is a tax-based entitlement and what proportion derives from non-tax awards (such as grants, loans, and loan guarantees)?

Here we focus on taxes and incentives across the 24 most important industrial states and a sample of 112 cities within those states. We measure the value of incentives available in these states and municipalities from the standpoint of a business.[2] That is, we assess the after-tax income effects of state and local tax and incentive regimes. This enables us to explore the size and redistributional impacts of state and local incentive programs in considerable detail.

THE EXPANSION OF AND JUSTIFICATION
FOR STATE AND LOCAL INCENTIVES

Although states were subsidizing private industry with public money over a century and a half ago, and although explicit "smokestack chasing" began nearly 60 years ago with Mississippi's "Balance Agriculture with Industry" program, it is only over the past two decades that there has been explosive growth in state and local economic development activity (McCraw 1986; Netzer 1991). Many, if not the majority of, state-level economic development agencies were established during this period, and although no accurate historical census of municipal economic development agencies exists, it is likely that the majority of local economic development departments were either established or greatly increased over the past 20 years (Eisinger 1988, pp. 16–17). So too, the instruments of economic development have expanded rapidly, and the use made of any single instrument has intensified. Eisinger (1988), using data from the annual survey of economic development incentives by *Site Selection and Industrial Development* (and the magazine's precursors), developed a measure of state-level policy penetration that assesses the use by states of economic development instruments available at a particular time period. He found that from the mid 1960s to the mid 1980s there were large increases both in the variety of instruments available to state officials and in the use made of any particular instrument. Eisinger (1995) claims that there is some evidence of a slowdown in the economic development effort during the early 1990s, and data from the Council of State Governments suggest that this is indeed the case (Council of State Governments 1994, pp. 4–6). What limited information we have on the expenditures of state and local economic development agencies suggests a substantial increase in spending during the 1980s (Fisher 1990) but some "state fiscal crisis-induced" cutbacks during the early 1990s (Bradshaw, Nishikawa, and Blakely 1992). State appropriations for state economic development agencies rose from $255 million in 1982 to $999 million in 1988 (National Association of State Development Agencies 1988) but declined somewhat in the early 1990s (although these figures are far from being unambiguous indicators of the development effort). The net result is that both relocating and new plants in the United States now appear to regularly receive incentive packages consisting of various combinations of federal, state, and locally financed subsidies. These can include a mix of property tax abatements, sundry tax credits and exemptions for such things as investment in plant and machinery or research and development, job training credits and wage subsidies, road and other infrastructure improvement incentives, and various sorts of capital grants, loans, and loan guarantees.

The usual justification for these types of incentives is that they are necessary for the local expansion of employment opportunities, given the competitive investment environment in which states and municipalities currently exist. In other words, a locality usually finds itself competing for new private investment with other similarly endowed localities; in order to "capture" a relocating firm, the locality must ensure that it offers, other things being equal, the "least cost" site. This understanding of the role of economic development policy is based explicitly on traditional industrial location theory. Here, firms are held to be profit maximizers that evaluate alternative business sites based on product demand and the costs of production at various sites (Wasylenko 1981). Localities having high product demand (or at least good and cheap access to areas of high demand) and low costs for primary inputs (such as wages, land, energy, and capital) and processing costs (such as taxes and general regulations) will be most attractive to firms. From the viewpoint of city or state government, the argument in favor of economic development incentives is that they might be able to reduce the cost structure of a potential plant just enough to induce relocation from the maximum-profit site to the incentive-offering site (Blair and Premus 1987; Chapman and Walker 1990). Although the range of incentive instruments is extraordinarily diverse, "all focus on reducing the costs of doing business" at a particular site (Gerking and Morgan 1991, p. 34).[3]

This raises a more basic question: Why should states and localities want to use scarce revenues to encourage new industrial investment? The political justification is almost always that, since states and municipalities are part of a competitive interjurisdictional locality market, incentives are necessary to lure new investment and the jobs (for residents of the state or municipality) and the taxes resulting from that investment. Consequently, incentive programs are usually judged—in the popular media, by politicians, and very often by development officials—on their ability to retain or generate new employment. The central financial justification is that new investment, and its resultant direct, indirect, and induced jobs and spending, will help maintain or expand the state or local government's revenue base and presumably improve the government's ability to provide its residents with services (or reduce the per-capita costs of providing the current level of services). The principal economic justification is that the new investment and its associated multiplier will enhance the income of the locality's residents.[4]

CRITICISMS OF INCENTIVE COMPETITION

A number of criticisms have been leveled at incentive competition. Some individuals have worried about the effects on the ability of state and local government to provide services. Without proper analysis and administration, incentives may become overly generous, resulting in a net drain on a local government's revenue base. Incentive competition could, in fact, divert resources from state and local programs, such as investments in education, that in the long run are important contributors to economic growth, locally and nationally. As a corollary of this argument that the net fiscal impact of incentives could be negative, some have noted that the economic growth sought by development officials can in the long run raise the costs of providing municipal services. There is evidence that larger city size is associated with higher per-capita costs of supplying city services to residents (Muller 1975, pp. 3–19; Ladd and Yinger 1991, pp. 83–85). Thus, leaving aside the issue of the direct costs and benefits of an incentive regime itself, incentive-induced development may result in fewer or more costly public services for a locality's residents.

Others have argued that, without a commitment to the long-term management of incentives, job creation may never materialize or may materialize only at the expense of job loss elsewhere in the state, municipality, or metropolitan area. Indeed, the professional economic development literature is littered with stories in which incentives did not produce the requisite revenue or job benefits (Glickman and Woodward 1989; Guskind 1990; Hovey 1986). Related to these issues is a much broader concern that states and municipalities often provide incentive packages based more on politics and perceptions than on a formal consideration of either the local costs and benefits or of the optimal size of the incentive package necessary to induce relocation. Certainly, this has been a constant theme in the coverage by the popular press of the various deals for foreign auto manufacturers. Nevertheless, the focus of scholarly criticism has not been on these practical issues of program administration but on the economic justification for development incentives. Indeed, criticisms of the economic justification raise fundamental questions about the merit of locational subsidies.

Since American labor is highly mobile—over 13 percent of the metropolitan population moves across metropolitan areas in any given four-year period—some economists have argued that, at least in the long run, labor will tend to move from areas of high unemployment to areas of low unemployment (Marston 1985).[5] Job-creating incentives in a single locality are therefore unnecessary and probably counterproductive. Without the incentives, unemployed or underemployed workers in a locality would eventually find jobs elsewhere. If government were genuinely concerned with the welfare of its citizens, it would more logically spend revenues not on locational incentives to encourage investment, but on increasing the mobility of the unemployed so that these individuals would benefit from the work opportunities in more vigorous labor markets elsewhere.

Moreover, if workers are mobile, using incentives to create jobs in one location merely provides inducement for job-seekers from elsewhere to move into that location (Logan and Molotch 1987). Thus, the original unemployed inhabitants of that locality may benefit very little, if at all, from incentive-induced new investments. By extension, in the long run, such investment may have little or no positive effect on the locality's unemployment or labor force participation rates. This sort of argument has led others to claim that while the public rhetoric of incentives is always couched in language focusing on the job gains for unemployed and underemployed locals, the true beneficiaries of incentive-induced growth are not local job-seekers but the owners of that immobile and scarce resource, land (Logan and Molotch 1987). Therefore, economic development policy is likely to have a regressive impact on the local distribution of income.

Rubin and Zorn (1985) have argued that, because state and local programs tend to be competitive and therefore merely encourage the movement of employment opportunities from one place to another but do not actually result in net national job creation, the overall benefits to the nation of state and local incentive programs are close to nil. Incentives merely result in the spatial reshuffling of investment, which would, *sans* incentives, have occurred *somewhere* anyway. Borrowing a term from game theory, a number of critics have characterized state and local incentive competition as essentially a zero-sum game.[6]

Insofar as the incentive-induced reshuffling of investment results in a spatial pattern less efficient than the pattern would have been without such incentives, it is plausible to argue that state and local incentives produce net economic welfare losses for the national economy and thus may more usefully be characterized as negative-sum.[7] The contention here is that incentive competition induces firms to choose locations based on their tax consequences rather than on the basis of real resource cost differentials (such as the price and productivity of land and labor, transportation costs, and so on). Taken together, these criticisms present a damning picture of economic development practice in the United States. However, there is reason to believe that many of the criticisms are misplaced.

WHY ECONOMIC DEVELOPMENT INCENTIVES MAY BE USEFUL: REVISIONIST RESEARCH

There is an expanding body of research suggesting that the preceding arguments against the use of incentives are misplaced. For instance, there is evidence that some groups of people, especially older, less-skilled, or minority workers, are relatively nonmobile, and that even for skilled, younger, or nonminority workers, spatial mobility is quite limited in the short run. Moreover, a number of economists have argued that interjurisdictional competition for investment may be 1) economically efficient, 2) have a much smaller negative impact than has been claimed, or 3) have effects not nearly as strong as assumed in the literature. Given some assumptions about the nature of competition among localities,[8] Oates and Schwab (1991) contend that, in equilibrium, business taxes become true benefits taxes in that they equal the value businesses place on the government services they receive. In these circumstances, interjurisdictional competition fosters economic efficiency. Netzer, while disagreeing with Oates and Schwab about the efficiency of local taxes, nevertheless argues that incentive competition does not have the negative impacts claimed by its critics: "If markets are not functioning perfectly, economic development policy instruments that offset the imperfections can move toward, rather than away from, efficiency in resource allocation" (Netzer 1991, p. 230). Thus,

> economic development incentives are . . . neither very good nor very bad from the standpoint of efficient resource allocation in the economy. With all the imperfections, the offering of incentives does not represent a fall from grace, but neither does competition in this form operate in ways that truly parallel the efficiency-creating operations of private competitive markets. Given the low cost-effectiveness of most instruments, there is little national impact, only a waste of local resources in most instances. (Netzer 1991, pp. 239–240)

Netzer also maintains that the supposed zero-sum nature of American economic development policy rests on an implausible assumption: that the American economy is closed. Although the proportion of foreign direct investment (FDI) in the United States (measured as a share of total employment or assets) is still much smaller than in a number of European countries, foreign investment has become an increasingly important part of the American economy, and states and localities very often target their incentives to encourage FDI (Glickman and Woodward 1989). In fact, a large number of American states have overseas offices chartered specifically to encourage such investment (Archer and Maser 1989; Kudrle and Kite 1989). Thus, incentives do not merely move a set number of jobs around the United States; they may also serve to encourage new investment from abroad. Other critics have shown that the level of interjurisdictional competition is much more limited than had previously been thought (Hanson 1993). Indeed, Hanson argues that there is inertia in the economic development efforts of states and cities; for example, the best predictor of what a locality will offer this year is what it offered last year.

Insofar as state and local economic development programs are concerned, some of the most interesting recent empirical work has suggested that incentives might be beneficial both to localities and to the nation. Bartik (1991b) claims that incentive-induced employment growth might have advantageous long-term effects on a locality's labor force participation and unemployment rates. Moreover, incentive competition may have significant benefits from the national perspective.[9]

Bartik's argument, backed by various empirical results, is that incentive-induced employment growth in a locality's labor market may be long-term, progressive, and salutary. Employment growth in a metropolitan area will lead to a permanent drop in the area's unemployment rate and to an increase in its labor force participation rate. In percentage terms, the real earnings effects of incentive-induced job growth are greater for black and less-educated workers than for white or more educated workers, and greater for lower-earning males than for higher-earning males (Bartik 1991b, pp. 184–185). As a result, the impact of employment growth on income distribution may be modestly progressive. Based on these results and on a speculative benefit-cost analysis, Bartik goes on to make two major claims:

- In places of high unemployment, economic development incentives are more likely to be cost-effective.

- From the national standpoint, to the extent that incentives are concentrated in places of high unemployment, economic development policy may tend to be positive-sum.

Translated crudely, economic development policy is likely, all else being equal, to be more beneficial if pursued more vigorously by poorer places and to be less so if pursued more vigorously by wealthier places. The reason for both of Bartik's claims is that the wage level necessary to induce movement of unemployed individuals into jobs (the reservation wage) is likely to be lower in high-unemployment areas than in low-unemployment areas. Thus, the true benefits of employment—the wage offer made to the individual minus his or her reservation wage—are greater from a benefit-cost viewpoint in locations with high unemployment than in those with low unemployment. To the extent that areas with a low reservation wage are net investment recipients, reshuffling of jobs may produce net national benefits. These findings and claims clearly challenge much of the traditional scholarly wisdom about the local and national impact of spatially competitive economic development incentives, and they set the stage for the argument of this monograph.

Bartik's positive scenario rests on three critical and logically sequential arguments:

- Economic development incentives probably can influence firm location and expansion decisions and thus can result in shocks (sudden growth) to local labor demand.

- Reservation wages are indeed higher in low-unemployment areas and lower in high-unemployment areas.

- The pattern of incentives at the state and local level tends to result in the relocation of investment from areas of low unemployment to areas of high unemployment.

Most of the rest of this book focuses on the first and third arguments. We ignore the second because providing a cogent answer would take us much too far from the central focus of our research and because the academic literature on the issue, while quite thin, is generally supportive of Bartik's position.[10] In the case of the first argument, the literature is massive but still inconclusive; in the case of the third, the literature is small and contradictory.

ISSUE 1: CAN INCENTIVES REASONABLY BE EXPECTED TO INFLUENCE BUSINESS LOCATION DECISIONS?

It should be obvious that to claim any benefits from economic development policy we must be reasonably sure that it works—that incentives can reasonably be expected to influence the investment behavior of expanding and relocating firms. From a theoretical perspective, taxes and incentives are a locationally variable business cost, and thus, at the margin, will influence location and investment decisions. At the same time, the costs of locally supplied labor are about 14 times state and local business tax costs, and regional variations in construction,[11] energy, and labor costs are often larger than variations in state and local taxes (and incentives). Small differences in labor costs can outweigh quite large differences in tax costs. Cornia, Testa, and Stocker found that "a mere 2 percent difference in wages could offset as much as 40 percent in taxes" (1978, p. 2). Thus, some have claimed that where taxes and incentives do influence location decisions, it is largely as tie-breakers between essentially similar locations (Schneider 1985).

Unfortunately, measuring the impact of taxes and incentives on growth is extremely complex. It is very difficult to evaluate the achievements of economic development policy, because it is hard to know what industrial investment would have occurred in its absence (Diamond and Spence 1983).[12] Our practicable ability to model and predict accurately changes to a local economy, a task necessary if we are to measure the precise impact of an incentive program, is quite limited. Moreover, our ability to measure cause and effect is circumscribed by often significant (and variable) time lags between the introduction of a policy instrument, spending allocations to that instrument, offers to individual firms, investment decisions on the part of a particular firm, the actual construction of a factory by the investing firm, and the achievement of a normal employment level at the factory site.[13] Nevertheless, there is a vast literature on the economic impact of development incentives. Because there are a number of recent comprehensive reviews, we will merely provide a summary of the literature.

In the United States, five basic methods of evaluating the impact of incentives have been developed. Considerable work has been done using two of these methods. Unfortunately, the results of this research effort cannot be said to support any strong statements on the impact of incentives on firm investment and location behavior.

The Survey Technique

In a number of studies, researchers have surveyed executives to determine what role incentives (and other locational factors) play in a firm's relocation and expansion decisions. The surveys often distinguish between "must have" location factors and merely "desirable" factors. There is evidence that the location choice of large manufacturing firms tends to be based on a sequential evaluation of factors at successively narrower spatial scales, with decisions first on a broad geographic region, then a state, a metropolitan area (or county), a city, and, finally, a plant site. Therefore, some surveys have attempted to distinguish the impact of incentives (and other locational factors) at various spatial scales (Schmenner 1982).

The advantages and disadvantages of the survey technique are well known (Calzonetti and Walker 1991). At their best, surveys provide direct information about the actual siting decisions made by executives. Also, the more complex statistical assumptions that beset econometric analyses can be avoided. Unfortunately, survey researchers often have difficulty finding the cohort of individuals within a corporation who were responsible for a particular location decision. Moreover, executives may have a direct interest in saying that incentives were important even if they were not—admitting that an incentive had little effect in one's location decision might cause later political problems—although, given the findings of the literature, this problem may have been exaggerated. Finally, while surveys may rank the importance of various locational factors, they do not provide a precise measure of the impact of each locational factor on local growth. In fact, the results from the survey-based literature are unclear, with some research indicating incentives are indeed important to location decisions (Premus 1982; Walker and Greenstreet 1989; Calzonetti and Walker 1991;

Rubin 1991), and other work indicating the opposite (Morgan 1964; Stafford 1974; Schmenner 1982).[14]

The Case Study Technique

Other researchers have taken a different tack and, using variations on the case study method, have evaluated the impact of specific economic development programs. The advantage of this method is that the work has covered a variety of different incentive instruments, from enterprise zones, research parks, and property tax abatements to export promotion schemes. Unfortunately, there are also major problems with this approach. In the first place, incentive programs are often very small relative to the local economy in which they operate. Thus, even where subsidies are effective, measuring their impact on a local economy is rendered difficult by economic white noise, by the other local factors that influence growth. Moreover, impact evaluations need to establish some sort of comparative control economy in order to measure precisely the effect of incentives. In the best of all worlds, the control economy would be identical to the economy receiving the incentive except that the control would not receive the incentive, but choosing a control is itself fraught with practical methodological and political difficulties. Unsurprisingly, given the range of programs covered, the published research using the single program approach is as contradictory, in terms of both detailed method and results, as the survey-based literature.[15] However, even work focusing on broadly similar types of programs shows discrepant results. For instance, in a recent widely quoted volume on enterprise zones, one study found clear evidence of impact success (Rubin 1991), while studies reported in two other papers found little or none (Elling and Sheldon 1991; Grasso and Crosse 1991).

The Econometric Technique

A third strategy has been to use econometric techniques to measure the impact of incentives on state and local growth. At the outset it should be noted that, although the econometric literature is large, nearly all published models concern taxes. There is very little work on non-tax incentives, and most of this research focuses on infrastructure programs.[16] Moreover, of the tax models, very few have data on local abatements or on the various tax credits commonly in use at the state level. Most merely use effective tax rates (ETRs)[17] as the exogenous (independent) tax and incentive variable within the location equation. For reasons we discuss in Chapter 3, we doubt very much that traditional ETR measures provide an accurate depiction of the tax liability faced by firms. In fact, we believe the econometric literature would be much improved if greater use were made of more defensible measures of tax and incentive incidence.

Econometric models have been developed for various spatial scales and for a number of different state and local taxes. State and local growth measures have included "levels of" or "changes in" indicators such as employment, gross state product, per-capita personal income, number of new plant openings, and small-firm birth rates. The models also range widely in their technical sophistication, from simple regressions with poorly specified locality growth variables and with no treatment of time lags in the growth variable or of endogeneity in the explanatory variables, to considerably more complex models that address most, if not all, of these issues. Almost all develop equations that use variables such as local labor costs, transportation costs, energy costs, infrastructure provision, and tax costs to explain (predict) local growth.

Since impressive reviews of this literature have been published recently, we will not repeat that work. Nevertheless, a number of points should be noted. No definite conclusions can be reached on the basis of the published research. Even the reviews seem to disagree about the impact of (tax) incentives on economic growth. Eisinger (1988), in an admittedly partial assessment of both the econometric and survey evidence, suggests that the majority of work still indicates that state and local taxes have little or no influence on economic growth. Nevertheless, also in 1988, Newman and Sullivan, in a much more involved review, wrote, "The most recent studies, employing more detailed data sets and more refined econometric techniques, have generated results which cast some doubt on the received conclusion that tax effects are generally negligible" (Newman and Sullivan 1988, p. 232). Bartik, in what is probably the most comprehensive assessment of recent research to date, takes Newman and Sullivan's conclusions a step further:

> The most important conclusion . . . is that most recent business location studies have found some evidence of significant negative effects of state and local taxes on regional business growth. The findings of recent studies differ from those in the 1950s, 1960s, and early and mid-1970s, which generally did not find statistically significant and negative effects of taxes on state and local growth. (Bartik 1991b, pp. 38–39)

The reason for this change is that the newer work is technically more sophisticated and thus better able to describe the relationship between incentives and growth.

However, there have been other dissenting voices. In a review of Bartik's summary of the literature, McGuire (1992), who has herself produced important work indicating that taxes do influence growth (Wasylenko and McGuire 1985), argues that Bartik claims too much. In particular, McGuire is concerned that some studies that did find a significant effect of state taxes on job growth have not been replicable and are not robust to changes in specification or time period.[18] She argues that the recent literature is as contradictory and inconclusive as the earlier literature. Our own sense is that there is a pressing need in econometric studies for a better measure of state and local tax and incentive policy. Underlying all of the econometric literature is the assumption that firms select locations so as to maximize their income. Thus, taxes and incentives should not be evaluated from the point of view of government—receipts or spending—but from the point of view of the firm's income. We provide such a firm-oriented measure later in this book.

The General Equilibrium Technique

A fourth and quite recent strategy has been to use applied general equilibrium models to measure the impact of tax policy, for example, on the location of economic activity (Morgan, Mutti, and Partridge 1990). General equilibrium models have an advantage over econometric models in that they specify the structural relationships, and thus interactions, between the economic variables in the model. Unfortunately, the work in this area is still too new to draw definite conclusions about the impact of taxes on local growth.

The Hypothetical Firm Technique

Given the difficulties of drawing any solid conclusions based on the existing literature, a few researchers have opted for an entirely different approach to the problem of taxes, incentives, and growth. This solution involves looking at the impact local taxes and incentives have on a firm's actual income. In order to accomplish this, researchers build models that replicate the operating ratios, balance sheets, income, and tax statements of real (or, at least, potentially real) firms; this technique is sometimes called the "hypothetical firm," or "representative firm," method. It allows researchers to calculate exactly what impact a state's or city's taxes would have on a firm's income. Almost all of the work in this tradition has looked at comparative tax burdens.[19] Very little research has used hypothetical firm results within an explicit economic development framework. Bartik et al. (1987) analyzed the location of the General Motors Saturn plant. Using realistic simulations of transportation, labor, and tax costs, they calculated that the best location for the new plant would be Nashville, Tennessee, about 30 miles from Spring Hill, the actual site chosen by the company. However, as yet, no hypothetical firm models have explicitly incorporated economic development incentives such as grants, loans, and training awards.[20] All current models remain essentially tools for calculating comparative tax burdens.

Hypothetical firm models, because they focus directly on the income effects of taxes, have tended to show that state and local taxes can and do have an important influence on the returns on investment of the firm. Few studies, on the other hand, have directly compared the impact of spatial variation in taxes with spatial variation in, for example, the costs of labor, transportation, or infrastructure. Those that have appear to suggest that in some circumstances taxes (and other incentives) may have a major impact on the profitability of various investment locations (Bartik et al. 1987; Peters and Fisher 1996).

We will not pursue the hypothetical firm literature here, since most of the rest of the book is taken up with our extension of the hypothetical firm technique to include most major economic development incentives. However, a few points are worth noting right away. There is increasing policy interest in using the hypothetical firm approach to look at the relationship between incentives and growth. Recently, a number of states (and quasi-government organizations) have commissioned hypothetical firm studies (Brooks et al. 1986; Laughlin 1993; Wisconsin Department of Revenue 1995).[21] We believe part of the reason for this movement is disappointment that the other techniques, those that are generally much simpler to implement, have failed to provide clear prescriptive answers on the question of taxes and growth. Another factor is that recent developments in computer technology have made hypothetical firm models much easier to build. Finally, there also is the misguided belief that the hypothetical firm technique does not suffer from the ambiguities (particularly the statistical ambiguities) that beset the other methods, that the effect of two competing states' tax regimes on a firm's income can indeed be calculated directly.

In a few cases, the results of hypothetical firm studies have been included in econometric analyses of the relationship between taxes and growth (or, at least, taxes and investment). Industry-specific measures of the burden of taxes deriving from the hypothetical firm model replace ETRs as one of the dependent variables in the econometric equation (Steinnes 1984; L. Papke 1987, 1991; Tannenwald and Kendrick 1995; Tannenwald 1996). Obviously, none of these studies was able to include non-tax incentives. Nevertheless, we believe that in general this is the right way to measure taxes (and incentives) within econometric models of the impact of state and local policy on growth.

Conclusions: How We Propose to Deal with the Incentive Question

Leaving aside work in the hypothetical firm tradition, solid conclusions about the broad impact of business incentives on the locational decisions of firms cannot be drawn from the existing academic literature. As it now stands, the published research is contradictory on many of the most important issues. Although we are inclined to believe that taxes and incentives have major impacts on some locational decisions, we are also bound to admit that the scholarly literature—again excluding research in the hypothetical firm tradition—does not necessarily support or contradict our position.

Part of the confusion in the literature is a consequence of the way in which taxes and incentives have been assessed. This appears to be particularly true for the econometric studies that have relied on averaged tax measures (in other words, ETRs) or simple tax rates as the "incentive." As noted, very few econometric (or other) studies have taken the results of detailed tax impact models as their "incentive measure," although it is clear that doing so would provide a vastly more accurate picture of the influence of taxes and incentives on firm investment and location behavior. A major move forward in the econometric literature would seem to be unlikely without first having a rigorous implementation of the hypothetical firm technique to cover both taxes and non-tax economic development incentives. We believe that our work with the hypothetical firm method, discussed in Chapters 2 and 3, provides such a step. The incorporation of the results of this model may give future researchers a much more accurate picture of taxes and incentives, and thus could bring about a more reliable measure of the impact of taxes and incentives on location decisions.[22]

ISSUE 2: THE SPATIAL DISTRIBUTION OF INCENTIVES

The second issue we consider refers to Bartik's *minimum requirement* that state and local incentive programs must meet if they, taken together, have the potential to produce net national benefits. It is the requirement that the spatial pattern of incentives offered by states and localities does not run counter to the need to promote the redistribution of jobs from places with lower unemployment to places with higher unemployment. In practical terms, if state and local incentives do produce national net benefits, we should expect, *at the very least*, that places with higher unemployment would offer greater incentives than places with lower unemployment. As indicated earlier, from the national perspective the point of redistributing employment (even the identical number of jobs paying identical wages) from places of low unemployment to places of high unemployment is to exploit the differential between offered wages and reservation wages. Most of this book contains our empirical evaluation of the spatial distribution of incentives. We now turn to the extant literature on this distribution. We look at the research in some detail because it has not been recently reviewed.

Do poorer places provide more in the way of incentives? It is reasonable to assume that the states and municipalities with the highest unemployment face the greatest political pressure to create jobs, and thus one might expect them to offer the largest incentives. On the other hand, high unemployment and slow job growth are likely to coincide with state and local fiscal distress, a declining tax base, and a reduced capacity to support new expenditure initiatives (Guskind 1990). Furthermore, many of these programs are tax expenditures and thus escape scrutiny during the annual budget process; once enacted, during a recession perhaps, they will tend to persist long after their political, no less economic, rationale has disappeared. Indeed, Hanson (1993) found that there is considerable long-term inertia in state-level economic development policy-making. Also, it is hard to imagine a state official who would not believe that having more jobs is always a good thing. Given the tendency of states to imitate one another and their fear of appearing antibusiness by not having a decent menu of financial inducements to offer prospective businesses,[23] there is every reason to suppose that economic development incentives will become quite widespread and may end up bearing little or no relationship to state and local economic conditions.

The empirical work on this question is sketchy and contradictory. At the broadest level, Fosler (1988) has claimed that, historically, states experiencing economic distress have tended to be the ones adopting new economic development instruments and institutionalizing the economic development process. According to Eisinger (1988), the expansion in economic development incentives in the Northeast and Midwest during the 1970s and 1980s was a direct result of deindustrialization in those regions. At the local level, Fainstein (1991) has argued that the administrative switch from regulating growth (with zoning and other growth management instruments) to promoting growth (through incentives) was a direct result of economic restructuring in the United States. All three writers have supported these claims with simple historical data showing policy adoption following economic decline.

It is true that, in a number of states, severe economic decline did prompt the development of new and powerful instruments. For example, the combined impact of severe employment loss in Iowa's biggest manufacturing sector and the farm crisis provided the political impetus for the development, in the mid 1980s, of the state's flagship economic development program, the Community Economic Betterment Account (CEBA). It is also true, however, that this program continues today, at a time when Iowa's unemployment rate is between 2 and 3 percentage points *below* the national average.

Clarke's (1986) more detailed study of state governments, conducted for the National Governors' Association, suggests that recession and industrial restructuring, and the gubernatorial initiatives they trigger, are important catalysts for expansion of the state economic development effort. Of recent statistical analyses undertaken, Lugar (1987) developed models predicting state economic development policy adoption in eight categories (plus a summary category). He found that "overall state effort in industrial development is associated with lower wages and higher unemployment" (p. 47). Gray and Lowery (1990) ran regressions on the adoption of 43 state-level economic development instruments (and on two subsets of these 43). According to their results, the level of economic distress (measured by 1982 per-capita manufacturing income and by the 1983 unemployment rate) was an important motive for policy adoption.

At the city level, Clingermayer and Feiock (1990) ran separate regression models for five different categories of economic development instruments: industrial revenue bonds (IRBs), Urban Development Action Grants, abatements, national advertising, and business assistance centers. Their economic need variables (measured by city per-capita personal income and the city bond rating) were positively related to policy adoption in all five policy categories. On the other hand, the local development of pro-growth coalitions and various local institutional arrangements, such as a mayor-council form of government, accounted for far more of the adoption of highly visible economic development instruments than did the level of local economic distress. Green and Fleischman (1991) compared policy adoption by central cities, suburbs, and nonmetropolitan communities. They found that in suburban communities the 1980 poverty rate was positively and significantly related to the development effort, but this was not the case in central cities or nonmetropolitan communities. However, their other "economic need" measures—the percentage of the population minority and the percentage of jobs in manufacturing—were not statistically significant in any of the models they developed.

Other studies broadly support these results. Bowman (1987), Rubin and Rubin (1987), and Feiock and Clingermayer (1986) found that more distressed localities tended to use a wider set of economic development tools or to spend more on incentives.[24] For economic development policy that targeted high technology, Atkinson (1991) found greater political and administrative commitment to policy instruments in states that perceived economic distress.

In contrast, Grady (1987) found little correlation at the state level between changes in the level of economic distress and expanded use of economic development incentives. Hanson (1993) found that the state unemployment rate did not account for much variation in economic development policy choices in two of his four broad state policy categories. Interestingly, he found considerable policy inertia; states modified incrementally what they had already been doing. Confirming Brierly's (1986) earlier work, Reese (1991) found in a study of tax abatements in Michigan that wealthier cities and cities with growing economies abated more.

Two recent pieces, which pay much more attention than do other studies to defining how policy expenditures vary spatially, have also demonstrated little positive correlation between the amount of incentives offered by and the economic distress of a locality. Fisher's (1991) simulation of the impact of investment and job creation tax credits, and of sales tax exemptions for manufacturing machinery and equipment, on the cost structure of two hypothetical firms found little evidence to suggest that the spatial pattern of incentives favored states and cities with high unemployment. "Competition does not appear to be perverse in its effects, [by] redistributing jobs away from distressed states; the pattern simply shows no consistent relation between a state's economic distress . . . and the magnitude of the state tax incentives offered . . ." (Fisher 1991, p. 20). Sridhar's (1996) study of the distribution of spending in the Illinois Enterprise Zone program uncovered no clear link between the intensity of incentives offered and the local unemployment rate.

Overall, the literature is inconclusive about whether incentives are concentrated in more distressed localities. Four factors account for the inconclusiveness: 1) varying methodological approaches, with some researchers using broad historical analyses and others using statistical ones; 2) varying levels of sophistication, even within the body of statistical research; 3) model misspecification, especially the failure to include measures of the impact of locality competition on policy adoption (Feiock 1989, p. 267),[25] and 4) disparate independent and dependent variables. The dependent variable issue requires special consideration. In other words, the problem is similar to that of the econometric literature on taxes, incentives, and growth. Not enough effort has been put into accurately measuring taxes and incentives.

MEASURING INCENTIVES AND THE STANDING OFFER

Most studies measure the economic development effort in ways that lack a sound theoretical basis for comparing variations in incentive levels across localities. For instance, the increase in the number of programs offered by a state or locality says nothing about the increase in spending on those incentives. In fact, states often have incentives on their books that are essentially unfunded.[26] Conceivably, the size of the economic development staff might say a lot about the proper management of the locality's economic development instruments (although we doubt it), but it says nothing of how much money is available for subsidizing individual firms. Similarly, total spending ignores the discrepancies in the size of states. A $10 million program in Wisconsin shows a very different economic development effort than a similarly sized program in California. Spending per capita solves this latter problem but raises a yet more fundamental one. If two states both spend an identical per-capita amount on a particular sort of economic development instrument and if, in the first state, the program funds a much larger number of plants (again on a per-capita basis) than in the second state, then at least from the point of view of the firm, the second state would be offering a larger locational incentive than the first. Thus per-capita expenditure differences among localities ignore the way localities see fit to distribute their funds. Spending per job created or retained has more intuitive appeal for measuring policy concentration because it provides a seemingly clear (and comparative) measure of the actual value that the locality puts on each new or retained job. It indicates how much the locality is willing to give to create 50 or 100 or 200 jobs. This can be compared to spending on a similar number of jobs in other programs and other localities (the method has been used in a number of federal programs to indicate something of incentive costliness). Nevertheless, this approach has severe methodological problems.

Different sectors, and even different plants within the same sector, operate at different levels of capital intensity. Identical incentive expenditures per job might result in disparate levels of total investment. Moreover, per-job data are not available for many programs, especially those that are part of state tax codes. There are also very important conceptual and administrative difficulties involved in using jobs created or retained as an outcome measure (these are discussed in Chapter 3). The most important objection is that, if incentives do influence a firm's location decision, it is only because the incentives alter the relative costs associated with operating at a particular site. Per-job incentive expenditures fail to capture this notion. Except for job training grants and loans and jobs tax credits, almost all incentives lower the cost of capital, not labor, so incentive dollars per job will not reflect the incentive amount per dollar of capital. Although there may be some, presumably sector- and asset-size-specific, relationship between the reduction in plant (establishment or operating) costs associated with an incentive and actual spending on the incentive (measured on a per-job basis), as far as we are aware no empirical test of this relationship exists. We also do not believe that the empirical data for such a test are available.

Thus, it turns out that the answers to two of the most important questions facing economic development policy suffer from the same sort of problem. On the issue of whether taxes and incentives significantly affect growth, almost all work has used inferior measures of state and local taxes and—where indeed researchers have been concerned with non-tax subsidies—incentives. On the issue of what causes localities to offer higher or lower levels of incentives, the identical problem arises, but now in a more pronounced form, because much of this literature has been concerned with non-tax subsidies rather than taxes. No logically and empirically coherent measure of the economic development effort exists.

The intensity of a locality's tax and non-tax incentive effort is best measured not by incentive spending per job, but by the locality's *standing incentive offer* to the individual firm. The standing offer is obtained from the standard menu of taxes and incentives applicable to a firm locating at a particular site; it is the dollar value of the income deriving from that tax and incentive package available to the firm at that site. In this book, a comparison of spatial variation in the size of the standing offer to spatial variation in wage rates is used to assess the impact of taxes and incentives on firm investment and location behavior. The relationship between the size of this standing offer and the economic health (especially the unemployment rate) of the locality making the offer is used to assess whether economically distressed places pursue development policy more vigorously.

In this study, we analyze spatial variations in state and city standing offers and then correlate the standing offer of each state and city in our sample with the unemployment rates of those states and cities. We find that there are large differences among the standing offers of various states and cities. Indeed, in some cases the standing offer differences between two sites are larger than the labor costs differences. This suggests to us that taxes and incentives may have an important impact on firm investment and location decisions.

With regard to the overall pattern of standing offers, we find a somewhat distressing pattern. There is little reason to believe that higher unemployment states and cities provide the largest standing offers. This suggests that the antecedent condition for Bartik's argument that incentives may have net national benefits is not true: the spatial pattern of taxes and incentives in America is not likely to promote the redistribution of jobs from places of low unemployment to places of high unemployment.

THE STRUCTURE OF THE BOOK

This book is divided into six chapters. Chapter 2 covers some basic, albeit important, empirical issues, such as our choice of states, cities, incentives, and industrial sectors, and briefly describes our implementation of the hypothetical firm method. The methodological descriptions in Chapter 2 are restricted to a few sets of issues crucial to understanding our results; a much more comprehensive discussion is in Chapter 3, which covers most of the questions that readers familiar with the hypothetical firm method will want answered. (Readers with less interest in these technical issues may want to pass over this chapter and proceed directly to Chapter 4.) The substantive focus in Chapter 3 is on two separate sets of concerns: 1) the traditional methodology of hypothetical firm simulations and our extensions of this methodology and 2) our technique for the inclusion of non-tax incentives into the traditional hypothetical firm framework. The chapter, especially the second part, provides a very extensive discussion of a range of quite practical modeling issues. The reason for this detail is that because we are the first to incorporate non-tax incentives comprehensively, on many technical issues there was no established literature to guide our decisions. Methodological assumptions play an important role in determining the results of hypothetical firm simulations; consequently, transparency of method is crucial.

In Chapters 4 and 5 we present our substantive results. Chapter 4 looks at the menu of incentives that states and cities offer and the differences these incentives make to a firm's income. Chapter 5 considers the spatial pattern of the standing offer. It focuses on whether poorer places actually offer larger incentives. The conclusion, Chapter 6, summarizes our findings and defines a future research agenda for economic development in the United States. We also discuss briefly a number of economic development policy issues for which our results have some bearing.

NOTES

1. Our interest is in competitive economic development policy, in other words, policy instruments that encourage the relocation of investment within the United States. We are not concerned here with those economic development tools meant to increase productivity, such as industrial extension services, or those tools meant to promote exports or encourage entrepreneurship.

2. In a manner similar to that advocated by Rasmussen, Bendick, and Ledebur (1984).

3. Unfortunately for policymakers, there is evidence from the survey literature that businesses often make location decisions on the basis of non-economic factors, such as a good climate. Statistical models of the growth of high-technology industries routinely include climate indexes, not because of the "least cost" issue of plant heating costs but because it is believed that high-technology engineers prefer to work in places with attributes such as sunshine (Markusen et al. 1986). Opportunities for good golfing were a claimed reason Scotland was the recipient of such a large proportion of Japanese and American high-technology inward investment during the 1980s. There is a range of evidence that locational behavior is influenced in a manner not obvious from traditional location theory. For instance, geographical models of corporate growth have indicated a distance-decay relationship in the establishment of branch plants. Ray (1971) found that American branch plants operating in Canada were much more likely to be controlled by headquarters in Chicago, Detroit, or New York, while those in Mexico were more likely to be con-

trolled by headquarters in Los Angeles. Models of corporate expansion developed by Taylor (1975) and Watts (1980) also support the idea of limited spatial searches.

However, neither the use of non-economic factors nor the spatial restriction of search behavior necessarily undermines the general appropriateness of traditional location theory. Non-economic factors may have a clear economic impact on the availability of inputs; for instance, if an important cohort of a firm's employees values sunshine and other amenities highly, then the provision of these through appropriate location may be considered part of the employee's competitive benefit package. A more general point should also be made: personal factors may enter location decisions, "but to the extent that firm's profit-maximizing location is altered by personal preferences, the firm will trade off profits for personal factors" (Wasylenko 1981, p. 160). With regard to the spatial search issue, traditional location theory can be expanded to take into account factors such as the costs of locational information and the friction of distance.

4. This is the central "positive" justification for economic development policy. It is true that there are a number of other important justifications. Kieschnick (1981, p. 26) discusses five:

- equalizing interstate tax differentials, which may serve as an inducement for a firm to select an alternative business location;
- serving as a wage subsidy to offset the effects of wage rigidity or labor immobility;
- lowering the costs of capital to induce greater overall capital formation, independent of location choices;
- serving to redistribute income from labor to capital under the politically acceptable guise of providing development incentives; and
- serving as a "signal" to out-of-state businesses that the state has "pro-business" regulatory and spending policies.

5. For a statement of this argument in the context of infrastructural incentives, see Foster, Forkenbrock, and Pogue (1991).

6. For restatements of the zero-sum position, see Glickman and Woodward (1989) and Rubin and Zorn (1985). For an early discussion of the zero-sum aspect of economic development policy, see Rinehart and Laird (1972). Interestingly, Rinehart and Laird argue that there may be national benefits from state and local competition for jobs. Wolkoff (1990) believes that critics who have described economic development policy in zero-sum terms have tended to misuse or, at least, to overly simplify game theory.

7. This would be true until a locality market equilibrium were reached and all localities provided an equivalent level of incentives. At this point, the impact of incentives might be zero-sum. Of course, equilibrium will not be a normal condition of the market because it will always be in the interest of a locality to provide some new incentive to gain some short-term advantage over all other localities (Netzer 1991, p. 225). However, even at the equilibrium point there may be negative economic consequences for the nation through a misallocation of resources. Most obviously, capital subsidies would lead to excessive national capital intensity (with potentially negative consequences for jobs).

The problem with this latter argument, as Netzer fully admits, is that its assumptions cannot be sustained: there already exist significant imperfections in the locality market; the United States is not a closed economy, and incentives could attract investment from other countries; jurisdictional spillover effects exist; and state and local governments already levy an inefficient system of taxes. Incentives do not necessarily increase these inefficiencies.

Some researchers do not put much store in the misallocation of resources argument and claim that insofar as various incentives work to lower the cost of capital, they induce greater overall capital formation, independent of location factors. They may therefore be "good" from the national perspective (Kieschnick 1981, p. 26).

8. These are as follows: 1) jurisdictions compete for business investment by lowering their taxes and by providing the services needed by business; 2) there are no interjurisdictional spillover effects; and 3) there are sufficient jurisdictions to approximate a competitive market.

9. Underlying Bartik's results is a theory of skill acquisition, the "hysteresis effect." Essentially, migration towards places that have experienced demand-induced job shocks will take place over a period of time because people are not perfectly mobile. Original residents of the place undergoing growth will therefore receive some short-term labor market advantages: for instance, some residents who would otherwise not have jobs will be employed. The human capital resources of these workers will improve, and they will thus be better able to compete with new immigrants when the latter finally arrive. Thus, a temporary labor market advantage will have longer-term effects.

10. Job search theory suggests that the optimal search strategy for the job seeker is to accept the first job offer that exceeds the seeker's reservation wage (Zuckerman 1984). The reservation wage is the lowest wage at which the worker would be willing to accept a job offer and is usually interpreted as a measure of the benefits, psychic and otherwise, that the individual places on leisure time. Bartik (1991b) argues that, on average, the local reservation wage will vary inversely with the local unemployment rate. The reason for this is that in low-unemployment localities, where obtaining a job is relatively easy, individuals who place a high value on getting a job would tend to find work, while those who do not clearly place a high value on their leisure time. On the other hand, in high-unemployment localities, where finding a job is relatively difficult, individuals tend to be willing to work for low wages. As indicated, this purported relationship between the local unemployment rate and the reservation wage is crucial for Bartik's broader argument about the potential positive net national benefits of state and local incentives. It also underpins the research presented in this book: if incentives do tend to promote the redistribution of investment (and therefore jobs) to places of high unemployment, this is beneficial only to the extent that the benefits of employment are greater in high-unemployment localities than in low-unemployment localities.

Unfortunately, only one published study has looked directly at the relationship between the local unemployment rate and the reservation wage. This study was conducted on British data and found that for every 1 percentage point increase in the local unemployment rate, the average reservation wage of the unemployed declined by £0.012, or 1.6 percent (Jones 1989). Sridhar (1996) replicated, as closely as possible, Jones's model using U.S. data from the 1987 Panel Study of Income Dynamics (PSID) established at the University of Michigan. Sridhar's results generally accord with Jones's: she found that for every 1 percentage point increase in the unemployment rate, there was a 10 cent decrease in the reservation wage. This is the first clear U.S. evidence of an inverse relationship between the local unemployment rate and the reservation wage of the unemployed.

11. These estimates are from Bartik (1991b, p. 61). As our work and that of others show (see, for example, Papke 1995), this number varies considerably across sectors.

12. Diamond and Spence (1983) are referring to the evaluation of British regional policy. In fact, many of the instruments, goals, outcomes, and problems of British and European "regional policy" are reflected in U.S. "economic development policy." Both have focused on promoting job growth within subnational regions. Very often, grants, municipal loans, and labor subsidies have been used to encourage relocation (or "inward investment," to use the British euphemism) of firms from other regions. In this book, where appropriate, we treat regional policy and economic development policy as essentially equivalent and make use of the regional policy literature.

Nevertheless, it should be noted that there are some important differences between "economic development policy" and "regional policy." Regional policy is generally financed and directed by central government; for instance, Regional Selective Assistance (a major British subsidy provided during the 1980s) was funded and managed by the London-based Department of Trade and Industry. Economic development policy in the United States is directed by, and very often financed by, state and local government. As a result, central control of regional competition, and thus restrictions on that competition, are clear with most regional policy instruments, but less so with economic development policy.

13. This fact poses considerable problems for the administration of policy incentives as well as for research on policy effectiveness (Peters 1993).

14. For recent reviews of the survey literature, see Calzonetti and Walker (1991), Eisinger (1988), and Blair and Premus (1987).

15. Bartik (1991b) has also provided a recent review of this literature and finds that it is generally supportive of the concept that incentives influence the locational behavior of firms.

16. Recent exceptions include Goss (1994), Goss and Phillips (1994), and Spiegel and de Bartolome (forthcoming), all of whom looked at the impact of economic development agency spending in their models. As indicated in the text, the relationship between infrastructure and growth has been studied in some detail. See Singletary et al. (1995) for recent evidence from the infrastructure literature. There is also a limited amount of work that considers other incentives. See Loh (1995) for a very useful recent study of jobs-targeted development incentives. Marlin (1990), for instance, has looked at the relationship between the issue of IDBs and gross state product. Krmenec (1990) has investigated the relationship between IDBs and employment growth.

17. Effective tax rates are usually calculated by dividing regional gross tax receipts (from all taxes or from particular taxes such as corporate income taxes) by some base, usually employment or population.

18. This refers to a comparison of the results in Wasylenko and McGuire (1985) to those in McGuire and Wasylenko (1987), Carroll and Wasylenko (1990), and Carroll and Wasylenko (1991).

19. This literature is covered comprehensively in Chapter 3. For two recent implementations of this method by the scholar most closely associated with the method, see J. Papke (1995, 1996).

20. This would mean to endogenously incorporate economic development incentives into the financial statements of the firm.

21. A review of this literature is provided in Chapter 3.

22. Until now, hypothetical firm simulations have not included modeling of non-tax incentives such as grants, loans, and loan guarantees (although there has been one very limited attempt). Moreover, the hypothetical firm simulations have suffered from problems of spatial and sectoral scale. These are discussed more fully in Chapter 3.

23. Discussions of business climate surveys certainly bear this out; see Eisinger (1988) and Skoro (1988).

24. See also Hanson (1985), Sharp (1986), Swanstrom (1985), and Young and Mason (1983).

25. Hanson (1993) presents the most sophisticated attempt at including variables for policy competition between states.

26. Also, the directories on which incentive counts are based are sometimes seriously unreliable.

2 An Overview of Method

In this book, we investigate the variation in the provision of economic development incentives (as measured by the standing offer) across the 24 largest manufacturing states in the nation and a random sample of 112 cities within those states. We measure the magnitude of tax differences and the value of the standing incentive offer and its components in each state and city. We then relate the value of the business incentive package available in a state or city to various indicators of economic distress for that state or locality. This study focuses on the year 1992.

In this chapter, we provide an overview of the research method employed to accomplish these tasks: how we selected the incentive programs to include in the analysis, which taxes we modeled, how we chose states and cities, and how we developed a hypothetical firm model to measure the effects of taxes and the value of incentive programs. We have included here only those details essential to an understanding of our study and to interpretation of the results; a more technical and complete discussion of methodology follows in Chapter 3.

WHAT ARE COMPETITIVE ECONOMIC
DEVELOPMENT INCENTIVES?

Since this is a study of state and local government competition for jobs, we focus our analysis on competitive incentives over which state and local governments have some direct control. But what is a competitive economic development incentive? One could argue that nearly everything that state and local governments do has at least an indirect effect on economic activity. Infrastructure, which provides services used directly by businesses, obviously supports production in the private sector, while certain taxes directly reduce business profits. Furthermore, a whole range of services to households arguably increases the productivity of local labor or facilitates the assembling of a labor force, and so has indirect (though often incidental) effects on economic development. Moreover, lawmakers feel compelled to package spending—whether on basic education, higher education, infrastructure, or the arts—on the merits of its ability to improve the state or local climate for growth. Political leaders in Oregon went so far as to campaign for a sales tax on the basis of its economic development purpose: a sales tax would allow a reduction in corporate and some personal taxes and thus improve the state's development prospects (Hovey 1986, pp. 90–91).

Nonetheless, it is useful to identify a subset of state and local policies with an *explicit* economic development objective, programs that would in all likelihood not exist but for the public concern with promoting job creation and economic growth. Since this research is concerned with the effects of intergovernmental competition for jobs and capital, it is this set of overtly development-focused programs that is of interest.

As we are dealing only with competitive incentives, we exclude "new wave" or "demand side" programs, which are aimed at stimulating entrepreneurship, subsidizing research and development, promoting technology transfer or the commercialization of university research, providing venture capital, stimulating exports, or facilitating the incubation of new small businesses. Such programs tend not to be used as relocation incentives for mobile firms; instead, they are usually designed to stimulate the generation of new indigenous technologies or new indigenous firms or to open new markets.

We also exclude those incentives, almost all of which are federally financed, that are offered in a standard format across most localities in the nation, such as industrial revenue bond (IRB) financing and federal programs that operate outside the control of state and local government or that focus on rural areas. The latter incentives include, for example, most Small Business Administration programs, all Department of Agriculture programs, and all Bureau of Indian Affairs programs.

We distinguish between tax and non-tax incentives.[1] The majority of tax subsidies are provided automatically. That is, if a firm meets certain criteria specified in the tax code and makes an investment of the specified sort (a new industrial building, for example) or hires some category of worker, then the firm will receive the incentive. The government unit provides the incentive in an all-or-nothing fashion; it is not possible to focus the incentive program on only those firms that "need" (however this is construed) the subsidy to survive or to enable them to relocate. (The exception is local property tax abatements; for the most part, the cities in our sample offered standard abatement terms for all industrial investments, but in many instances there was some discretion exercised.) Non-tax incentives are usually discretionary; they tend to be negotiated between governmental units and prospective firms. Firms that meet program requirements do not automatically receive a subsidy but must compete with other prospective firms for incentives. In this case, the incentive program might be thought of as an investment vehicle for public funds: program managers should invest only in those projects where the expected rate of return (broadly conceived to include returns on certain social goals) is sufficient.

The distinction between tax and non-tax programs is important in building the simulation model and in interpreting the results. Within clearly definable limits, we know that a firm of a designated asset and employment size in a particular sector making a specific new investment will receive a certain level of tax incentives (negotiated abatements being an exception). However, we can only determine the most likely non-tax award. It should be noted that there is evidence from regional incentive programs in Great Britain that firms are more likely to take into account automatic rather than discretionary incentives when making locational decisions, presumably because automatic incentives are certain and can be incorporated early into the firm's planning process (Swales 1989).[2]

TAXES AND TAX INCENTIVES

One can make a distinction between the effects of competition on overall spending or tax levels and the effects of competition on the creation of particular programs (or tax laws) with an explicit development purpose. This research focuses on *economic development tax expenditures,* credits or exemptions that represent departures from the normal tax base and that are aimed at stimulating private investment. Three kinds of incentives fall clearly into this category: investment and job creation credits against the corporate income or franchise tax, sales tax exemptions provided only to firms locating in enterprise zones, and property tax abatements for new business investment. The investment and jobs tax credits, the sales tax exemptions, and, in many cases, the property tax abatements differ in one significant respect from the other competitive incentives discussed: they are entitlements, provided automatically to any firm meeting the qualifications in the law.

In the area of tax policy, it is more difficult to draw the line between explicit economic development tax laws and general tax policy changes adopted with an eye to their economic development implications. John Shannon has argued that the competition for jobs has led states to become concerned with their overall business tax climate and that they have taken steps to avoid having any of the tax "sore thumbs" that are thought to be trouble signs to potential investors. Shannon identifies the six most often cited "sore thumbs" as 1) a high overall tax burden, 2) a heavy and progressive individual income tax, 3) business taxes (corporate income tax, workers' compensation tax, or unemployment insurance tax) that are clearly out of line with those of other states, 4) heavy property taxes on business realty (land and buildings), 5) any property tax on business personal property (machinery or inventories), and 6) a sales tax on a substantial share of business purchases (such as machinery or fuels and utilities). He then asserts that "the more 'sore thumbs' a jurisdiction exhibits, the greater the likelihood that its policymakers will resort to a wide variety of temporary painkillers—business tax concessions—as the most expedient way to deal with these competitive problems" (Shannon 1991, p. 118).

If Shannon's observation is accurate, then it could be quite misleading to measure only the three clear economic development tax incentives identified at the beginning of this section. It could be that the states that do not provide such incentives, or do so at a very low level, are precisely the ones that have responded to competitive pressures by adopting more general tax policies favorable to business and thus see no need for the explicit investment incentives. Furthermore, economic development concerns have undoubtedly played a significant role in the past 20 years in the decisions by many states to exempt business inventories from the property tax; to exempt machinery and equipment purchases, fuels, and utilities from the sales tax; to exempt or preferentially assess machinery for purposes of the property tax; and to keep down or reduce business tax rates as well as the top individual tax rate.

To avoid seriously biasing our study against states that have chosen a particular approach to keeping the business tax climate competitive, we will simulate the overall burden of state and local taxes having an initial impact on business: the corporate income tax,[3] the property tax on business realty and personal property, and the sales tax on major business purchases (machinery and equipment, and fuel and electricity). The analysis includes federal corporation income taxes as well. There is another significant advantage to modeling the federal and state income taxes: the results will then automatically measure the value to the firm of the after-tax effects of all state and local incentive programs. To the extent that a local grant program or property tax reduction reduces the firm's deductible costs, the firm's state and federal taxable income will increase and its total state and federal income tax bill will rise, diminishing the net value of the incentive program. Unless income taxes are fully modeled, the value of incentives will be overstated.

Corporate Income Tax

Modeling the complete corporate income tax codes in each state would require a large investment of time involving a host of relatively insignificant differences in law. Papke and Papke (1984) argue that the major differences are due to rates; deductibility of income taxes paid to other states, the federal government, or one's own state; deductibility of property taxes; rules for apportionment of income; depreciation methods; and rules for carrying net operating losses (NOL) backward or forward. Studies using the hypothetical firm method generally account for all of these corporate income tax features except for the NOL carryforward rules. Studies looking at average taxes paid in one year sometimes model firms with losses, but since they do not consider tax burdens in other years, they do not model the NOL carryforward. On the other hand, multiyear models do not include firms with losses because of the logical and practical difficulties in doing so; thus, the NOL provisions, even if modeled, would never apply.[4]

Variations among the selected 24 states with respect to the key features of the income tax are shown later in this book (see Table 4.2). To the Papke list might be added the following: 1) the availability of general credits for other taxes paid, such as sales or property taxes; 2) the treatment of nonbusiness income (how it is allocated, whether it is subject to apportionment); 3) whether the property factor in the apportionment formula is measured by acquisition cost or book value; 4) whether the sales factor includes nonbusiness receipts; and 5) the availability of investment tax credits or jobs tax credits. All of these features are included in our model.

There seems to be agreement that there is little point in modeling the very minor differences in the measurement of the payroll factor or in modeling the differences in the treatment of subcategories of nonbusiness income, such as rents, royalties, interest on federal bonds, interest on state and local bonds, dividends from subsidiaries, and capital gains. We would argue that since the focus of the research is on the location of facilities for the generation of sales of products—business income—the treatment of such items is not relevant. There is a practical argument as well: data at this level of detail are not generally available, and the simulation of the myriad differences in state law would greatly complicate model building. There are two simplifying assumptions that can then be made: 1) the hypothetical firms have no nonbusiness income or 2) the hypothetical firms have aggregate nonbusiness income as given by the statistical data sources, but it is entirely in the form of interest on corporate bonds, which is treated uniformly by the states. The latter approach allows one to model rules for the allocation or apportionment of nonbusiness income without getting into the details of what counts as nonbusiness income and what does not. Also generally ignored (by creating firms that have no such income or asset category) are the treatment of foreign business income, foreign nonbusiness income, foreign tax credits, extraordinary items such as write-offs for plant closures, goodwill, and recapture of federal investment tax credits, or the adding back of federal job incentive credits.

The Sales Tax

Most studies consider only the sales tax on purchases of fuel and electricity and of machinery and equipment. These are the two major categories of expenditure by manufacturers that are sometimes taxed and sometimes exempted by the states. The exemptions are most often targeted exclusively at manufacturing machinery and at fuel and electricity used directly in the manufacturing process, which suggests that at least part of the motivation for the exemption was an economic development one.

Hunt (1985) estimated expenditures on other business purchases that are subject to sales tax (at least in some states): office equipment, furniture, nonmanufacturing supplies, building materials for repair and for new construction, and pollution abatement equipment. Of the total expenditures on these items plus fuel and electricity and manufacturing machinery, the latter two categories represented 74 percent, averaged across Hunt's seven manufacturing industries. Thus the studies that model sales taxes only on fuel and electricity and on machinery and equipment are omitting about 26 percent of the total sales tax. Pollution abatement equipment represented just 2 percent of the total; even though some states tax it and some exempt it, the omission of sales taxation of pollution equipment from a model can have only a trivial effect on overall state tax differentials. Office equipment, furniture and fixtures, and office supplies are almost universally subject to the full sales tax rate; failure to include such expenses in the model thus creates differences only because of variations in tax rates. Our model includes expenditures on machinery and equipment, furniture and fixtures, computers, and fuel and electricity; it does not include expenditure detail for office supplies, construction materials, or pollution control equipment, so the results do not reflect the minor differences caused by state variation in taxing these latter items.

We have chosen not to separately identify, in the results, the effects of state sales tax treatment of purchases of various kinds of machinery and equipment or purchases of fuel and electricity. Each state's sales tax is part of the model; to the extent that the state applies the sales tax fully to purchases of manufacturing machinery, computers, furniture and fixtures, transportation equipment, or other personal property, that will be reflected in a higher acquisition cost for those assets and hence larger depreciation deductions and larger financing requirements. To the extent that the state taxes or exempts purchases of electricity or fuel, or exempts the portion used directly in the manufacturing process, the firm's operating costs will be more or less each year.[5] Some would argue that sales tax exemptions for personal property or utilities used by manufacturers are not tax expenditures, but are better viewed as attempts to make the actual tax base conform to the ideal: a tax on final consumption, not on intermediate goods. For practical modeling reasons as well, sales tax effects are not separately identified in the results but are included in the measure of the state's overall "base" tax system.

The Property Tax

There are three aspects of the property tax system that are modeled. First, state policy will generally determine whether local property taxes apply to business inventories and to personal property in general, whether categories of personal property such as manufacturing machinery and equipment are exempt, and whether different classes of property must be assessed at different ratios to market value. States also generally establish rules or guidelines for local assessors in determining the market value of personal property; typically, the state will publish depreciation schedules by industry and/or type of property. These state guidelines are used by the model to value personal property; book value is assumed for real property, using straight-line depreciation over the life of the building.

Second, local policy will determine the effective general tax rate on business realty and personalty. Third, local policy will determine whether certain new investments in realty or machinery and equipment are fully or partly exempt from property taxes and for how many years, within state-defined limits on such local abatements. The effects of the first two are part of the local "base" tax system; the effects of abatements are identified separately as an explicit local economic development incentive.

Our list of tax features that are modeled, and the implied list of features that are not, can be further justified by considering evidence of what firms think of as state policy incentives, or what state development officials consider relevant when comparing the competitive positions of states. The *Directory of Incentives for Business Investment and Development in the United States*, compiled by the National Association of State Development Agencies (1991), includes the specific economic development tax expenditures that have been cited and also includes information on overall business taxes: the corporate income tax, the sales tax on machinery and equipment and fuel and utilities, and the property tax on machinery and equipment and inventories. It has, in other words, all of Shannon's "sore thumbs" except for individual income taxes. The lists of incentives published annually in the foremost two U.S. location periodicals, *Area Development* and *Site Selection and Industrial Development*, are very similar. It should be noted that none of these directories of incentives includes any broader measures of financing policy, general job training or education expenditures, or infrastructure spending.

NON-TAX INCENTIVES

Hypothetical firm models have not included non-tax incentives since these are mostly negotiated, whereas tax incentives are usually automatic and applied uniformly. Thus, in order to simulate the impact of non-tax incentives on investment, the model must be able to generate a set of incentives that a plant would likely receive from a state or city and then apply those incentives to an investment. This is a very different sort of problem than is found in modeling tax systems. There are four major steps involved in integrating discretionary non-tax incentives into a hypothetical firm model:

- Develop an "administrative history" for each incentive program, such as incentive dollars awarded per jobs created or incentive dollars awarded per associated total investment. These ratios can then be utilized to develop likely amounts that a firm would receive from a particular incentive program.

- Apply the various explicit program rules. Common rules include a maximum amount a firm may receive from an incentive program or a stipulated minimum equity contribution.

- Assemble the best package of incentives available from a unit of government. The model should be able to mirror the way in which economic development officials assemble their incentives into competitive packages.

- Calculate the present value of a firm's return on investment without any discretionary incentives and then again with a particular package of discretionary incentives. The difference between these two amounts measures the after-tax worth of a state's or city's discretionary incentives to a firm.

Competitive non-tax incentive programs fall into three broad categories: general-purpose capital-financing programs, employment training subsidies, and infrastructure subsidies. We now focus on each of these in turn.

General-Purpose Financing Programs

State or local programs providing grants, loans, loan guarantees, or loan subsidies directly or indirectly (through linked-deposit programs) to private businesses in order to finance working capital or the acquisition of land, plant, or equipment are competitive development incentives. The principal or sole purpose of these programs is the attraction of business capital and the creation of jobs. Essentially all of these programs aim to lower the costs of doing business by reducing the cost of capital. Usually the funds are provided by the government or by a quasi-public authority. One could argue that there are other state policies that can improve the terms of business financing and hence foster development. State banking regulatory policies, for example, may well have been reformed in recent years partly in an effort to stimulate the flow of capital to business investment generally. This study focuses on the more narrowly defined set of programs providing direct public financing (or financing subsidies) to particular businesses.[6]

Customized Job Training and Wage Subsidies

State and local job training programs (often run through community colleges) that are customized to the training needs of particular firms opening new facilities or expanding operations fall within our definition of a non-tax incentive. This category includes programs whereby the state pays a portion of the "training wages" for new employees who are trained on the job by the firm, as well as programs providing training per se. Through these programs, the state subsidizes firms' labor costs. Job training programs are usually grants to the firm, but they may also take the form of loans or loan guarantees.

Training programs meant for general skill development and educational purposes, such as those available to laid-off and unemployed workers, are excluded from our model. We consider customized training programs only—those that specifically provide for the training (or

subsidy) of workers at a particular firm. Many such customized programs provide for on-the-job training. Here, the recipient firm, not an
outside educational institution, is paid to train workers for the positions
being created or retained. There is some evidence that on-the-job training often serves as a wage subsidy: funds for on-the-job training continue longer than the individual worker is being trained in the plant,
often much longer. Public funds thus effectively reduce the costs of hiring a worker; they serve to subsidize wages. Since so many state and
local training programs that fit our research criteria allow on-the-job
training, we decided not to distinguish between job training programs
and wage subsidy programs.

Vocational education, or education in general, is a traditional function of state and local government that predates the competition for
jobs and that would continue to be supported even in the absence of a
competitive environment. One could argue that the support for education would be different were it not for competition. Perhaps more funds
have been directed in recent years to education in general and to vocational training in particular because of the concern with economic
growth. There is, in fact, anecdotal evidence to support this. The southern states, for example, have raised taxes to bring their educational systems nearer to the national standard, in recognition that their economic
future is at stake (Shannon 1991). However, it is impossible to identify
the magnitude of public expenditure on education and training that is
attributable to competition, or to make any presumption about its value
to a particular business, or even to be sure that the net effects on education funding of expenditure and tax competition in particular states
have been positive.

Our model does not include any of the federal training programs,
such as Jobs Training Partnership Act (JTPA) funds, Job Opportunities
and Basic Skills (JOBS) training, Trade Adjustment Assistance (TAA),
or the Targeted Jobs Tax Credit (TJTC). These are programs that are
available reasonably uniformly across the states. We model only state
and locally financed and directed training and subsidy programs.
Unfortunately, the situation is complicated by the fact that many state
training programs are organized in concert with JTPA and other federal
funds. Where this is the case, we model (insofar as it is possible) only
the state-capitalized portion of training.

Infrastructure Subsidies

State-funded infrastructure improvements, tied to new investment by a particular firm that is relocating or expanding operations, and part of a program whose primary purpose is job creation, clearly fall within the definition of a competitive economic development incentive. Most states operate at least one infrastructure grant, loan, or loan guarantee. In almost all instances, the instrument is in the form of a direct grant, usually for the building of a section of an access road or a bridge to the new plant. In many cases, the responsible local unit of government applies, on behalf of the firm, to the state Department of Transportation (DOT). Usually, the state DOT, not the state economic development agency, runs the infrastructure program. Many bigger cities have similar programs, but these will often allow expenditures for other site assembly expenses.

It is common for states and cities to use federal Community Development Block Grant (CDBG) funds for infrastructure provision, and many states and cities advertise the CDBG as an infrastructure incentive. We exclude CDBG-based infrastructure subsidies, since the CDBG is essentially a national program with a reasonably standard set of rules applying across all states.

Some cities reported to us that, although they did not have a separate set-aside fund dedicated to providing infrastructure to new and expanding firms, they often used general revenues for this purpose, but on an ad hoc basis. For example, if a road to a plant needed to be upgraded, then a portion of city street maintenance funds would be used for this purpose. In a few instances, state road programs were also ad hoc. Illinois, as an illustration, no longer has a dedicated pot of money to be used for building access roads;[7] nevertheless, general road funds may be used for economic development purposes.

Our research covers only state and local infrastructure grants, loans, and loan guarantees that existed in 1992 as dedicated, separate incentives. We found it impossible to assemble the data necessary to model ad hoc infrastructure incentives, or, for that matter, any ad hoc incentives. Modeling incentives from general revenues would have required a massive historical data collection effort. It is our experience that such data do not exist for the most part; where they do exist, they are not compiled, and time constraints on city officials make it unlikely that they would provide the information. Moreover, the statistical modeling of ad hoc incentives would likely introduce a significant new source of error into our more general simulation of state and local incentives.

From the point of view of our major research questions, the omission of ad hoc incentives is not a major limitation. We aim at measuring the *explicit* economic development incentive effort of state and local governments. Over and above the complex empirical issues of data collection and modeling involved in measuring non-explicit programs, we do not believe there is a good theoretical case for including incentives that may exist only for a single firm's investment. Moreover, to the extent that incentives do influence a firm's locational and investment decisions, explicit incentives will be of much greater importance than implied ad hoc incentives.[8]

As with job training programs, ambiguity arises in defining incentives when one considers the whole range of infrastructure spending by state and local governments, most of which provides transportation or utility-type services used directly by the private sector. It may be that the level of infrastructure spending as a whole is greater than it would have been in the absence of state and local competition for jobs. Again, the magnitude of this effect is very difficult to ascertain; furthermore, much of the infrastructure spending in the past two decades has had primarily a health or environmental purpose. We focus on the portion of infrastructure spending providing special benefits to particular firms and with funding coming from a special program with an economic development purpose.

Other Incentive Programs Not Included

Inevitably, some programs were not included in the model. In many cases, this was because the program was too small or its use was too infrequent. However, many programs were deliberately ignored: in particular, those funded by the federal government in such a way that there is little local control of spending.

The federal government has a long and complex relationship with local economic development efforts. The contours of this relationship were solidified during the Depression and Roosevelt's New Deal and greatly expanded after World War II. In essence, the federal government would pay for programs—for example, Urban Renewal, Urban

Development Action Grants, CDBGs, or the interest exemption for industrial revenue bonds—but the money or benefits would be dispersed by state and local governments. To the extent that these programs have been used as major instruments of state and local economic development policy, the federal government has been subsidizing and encouraging locational competition in the United States.

Currently, CDBGs are commonly used for economic development purposes, in particular, for local infrastructure development. Over the past decade, they have also capitalized local economic development revolving loan funds (RLFs). In addition, many other federal programs may be used for economic development purposes: federal funding for highways and road improvements, the Federal Aviation Authority's subsidization of the building and upgrading of commercial airports, the Economic Development Administration (EDA) Title IX program also capitalizing RLFs, and the JTPA funds for technical training and skills enhancement. There are numerous additional programs that target rural areas, distressed areas, small firms, and disadvantaged population groups through, respectively, Farmers Home Administration business loans, various Small Business Administration capital programs, and Minority Business Administration and Bureau of Indian Affairs loan, loan guarantee, subcontracting, and business education programs.

All such programs serve to reduce the costs of doing business. Other things being equal, the use of any of these programs might confer significant economic development advantages on a locality. However, with one exception, our study does not take into account any of these federal programs affecting local economic development potential. The focus of our study is on the use of resources by states and localities to enhance their position in the competition for investment and jobs. We exclude IRBs, for example, because they require no local commitment of resources and because their availability is nearly universal, so that their use confers no competitive advantage.[9] For similar reasons, most of the other federal programs previously cited are excluded. We do, however, include RLFs capitalized with federal funds, usually with the state's CDBG allocation or with a locality's CDBG entitlement. Even though the funds are federal, RLFs are not a uniformly available program. The states and localities have considerable discretion in use of the funds, so that the decision to capitalize an RLF means that those CDBG monies are not available for other purposes, such as housing rehabilitation or infrastructure improvements. In that sense, the resources do represent a state or local commitment, and variation in their use can result in a pattern of competitive advantage.

Finally, there are a number of other quasi-governmental organizations that are often involved in the building of a particular incentive package offer. These include local power companies, chambers of commerce, bankers and real estate developers, small business investment companies (SBICs), and even community development corporations. Particularly in smaller communities or with smaller investments in larger communities, all or some of these groups may help package local incentives or even offer their own incentives, such as RLFs, so that a local deal may "happen." No attempt to quantify this involvement in the state and local economic development effort exists. On the basis of our experience with economic development officials, we believe the involvement is widespread and that it may be effective in influencing the location decisions of firms, at least compared to many other state and local incentives. Nevertheless, we do not include quasi-governmental incentives in our model. In the first instance, they do not indicate anything of the state or municipal government's commitment to economic development activity, and it is this commitment that is the focus of our study. In the second, it is plausible to argue that the involvement of quasi-governmental organizations is based on self-interest (increasing local demand for energy, enhancing commercial real estate values, expanding the local market for financial services) in a way in which the involvement of state and city government is not. The presumed link between the level of local distress and the intensity of the incentive offer is thus much less clear with quasi-governmental organizations.

THE HYPOTHETICAL FIRM METHOD: AN INTRODUCTION

Our method for measuring the value of each locality's standing offer is based on the process by which firms make investment decisions. According to traditional location theory, a particular firm in a specified industry, with given production technology and needs for various kinds of assets, labor, and other inputs, will evaluate alternative sites for new investment on the basis of the profitability of the marginal investment in each location under consideration. Our measure of this effect is the present value of the increase in a firm's after-tax cash flow over a 20-year period it could expect to derive from an investment in a new plant in a particular state and city, given that state and city's tax and incentive regime.

The present study uses the hypothetical firm method to measure the value of competitive incentives to typical manufacturing firms. The implementation of this method in what we call the Tax and Incentive Model (TAIM) begins with the construction of financial statements for firms representative of various industries and firm sizes. TAIM then measures the net returns to each firm, after state, local, and federal taxes, on a new plant investment. For the state-level analysis, the new plant is located in one of 24 states, the 24 that account for the most manufacturing employment in the United States (Map 2.1). (Together, the 24 states accounted for about 86 percent of total manufacturing employment in 1990.) In the city-level analysis, the plant is located in one of 112 cities of 10,000 population or more (also shown in Map 2.1), randomly selected within these 24 states. The model then measures the increase in return on investment that occurs as a result of the state or local "standing offer": the set of tax incentives, infrastructure incentives, job training programs, and general loan and grant programs available to new businesses. The value of this incentive package to the firm is subsequently compared to the unemployment rate or rate of job growth in the state or city.

Thus, the value to the firm of a locality's incentive package is the amount the package adds to the profitability of a new investment in that locality. The effect of the standing offer on a firm's return on investment depends on the characteristics of the firm. We constructed 16 hypothetical firms, having the characteristics of a typical large and a typical small firm in each of 8 manufacturing industries. Sectoral differentiation is necessary because the responsiveness to taxes and incentives is not uniform across industries due to differences in the relative importance of certain kinds of assets or differences in the ratios of jobs to assets. In general, we chose sectors that are growing and that are, at least potentially, geographically mobile. New plant construction was assumed for each firm, with plant sizes based on employment and asset data for typical large and small manufacturing establishments.

Map 2.1 Geographic Dispersion of States and Cities Included in the Analysis

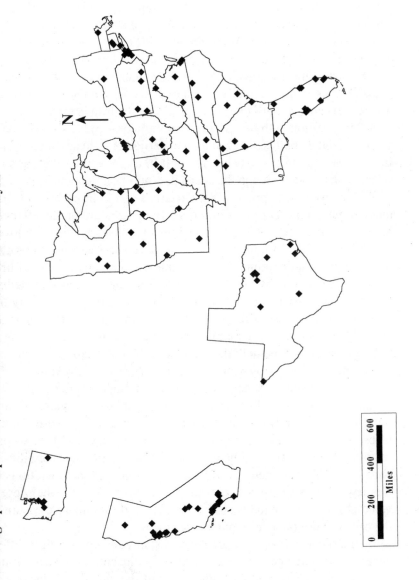

Balance sheets and income statements were developed for each firm based on published data from annual reports, federal tax statistics, and the Census of Manufactures. In each case, we specified a new manufacturing facility (including total plant, equipment, and working capital needed, employment, sales, etc.); the balance sheet and income statement for the new plant mirrored the attributes of the parent firm. (The characteristics of the firms are shown in Table 3.1.)

For each of the 16 firms, two alternative location assumptions were made: 1) that the firm initially has operations only in the state in question and expands at the same site; and 2) that the firm is initially a multistate corporation with facilities spread throughout the 24 states in our sample and then builds a new plant in a particular state among the 24.[10] In all cases, the firm is assumed to sell in a national market, and its sales are distributed among the states in proportion to population.

This analytical approach is a variation of the hypothetical firm method, which has appeared infrequently in literature on the effect of business incentives. The hypothetical firm method has been employed primarily to study differences in state tax systems.[11] Because of its data requirements and computational complexity, most hypothetical firm work has been done by, or for, state governments. To our knowledge, we are the first to use this approach to measure comprehensively the effects of non-tax incentives, such as state grants, loans, and loan guarantees. We have also made a number of significant refinements to the best practice of the method; these are described in detail in Chapter 3.

The model begins by simulating the firm's costs, revenues, and changes in its balance sheet over a 20-year period, producing a stream of annual cash flows. The simulations are performed twice: the first with the firm operating in a "steady state" for 20 years with no new investment and with constant sales and operating costs, and the second with the firm constructing the new plant in one of the states or cities in our study. The incremental cash flow attributable to the operations of the new plant is the measure of project returns. We take the present value of this incremental cash flow as our single summary measure of the firm's return on its new plant investment.

Differences in project returns across states and cities reflect differences in the state and local tax structure and incentive package. Simulations were performed with and without the various categories of incentives included in the analysis. The first run included only the basic tax structure: state (and local) corporate income and net worth taxes, state (and local) sales taxes on machinery and equipment and on fuel and electricity, and state (and local) property taxes on real and personal business property. A second run added tax incentives: state corporate income tax credits for investment or job creation, and local property tax abatements. Subsequent runs added non-tax incentives such as loans, grants, and loan guarantees. The difference between returns with tax incentives and returns with only basic taxes measures the value to the firm of the tax incentives offered. The difference between project returns with all incentives included and returns with just tax incentives measures the after-tax value of the entire non-tax incentive package.

EXTENSIONS TO THE HYPOTHETICAL FIRM METHOD TO INCLUDE NON-TAX INCENTIVES

The modeling of non-tax incentives involves some important modifications. As indicated earlier, states have laws and administrative rules that govern the way in which non-tax incentives are dispersed. In order to be eligible for an incentive, a firm must meet certain criteria. Moreover, the amount of non-tax incentives provided to a firm will depend both on the sort of investment the firm intends to make and on negotiations between program officials and the firm. We call the historical outcome of these negotiations the program's "administrative history."

Once TAIM has created the operating ratios and balance sheets for a new investment (as described in the previous section), this information must then be made available to a rule-based system (or "expert system" or "knowledge base") that determines the non-tax incentives for which the investment is eligible and calculates a likely amount for each incentive based on historical ratios for that type of offering. Each state and local program has its own expert system that attempts to model both the explicit administrative rules and the administrative history of each program. An example of an explicit administrative rule would be "Program X will award no more than $2,000 in grants per job created or retained." An example of a portion of administrative history would be "In most instances, program Y imposes a rate on loans 2 percentage points below the private rate for that asset class." However, most states and cities offer a menu of non-tax incentives. Thus states and cities have rules (or at least precedent) about the ways in which incentive packages may be assembled. As a result, for each state and city there must be another expert system to control the assembly individual incentives into incentive packages.

Once the incentive package has been established, the non-tax section of TAIM distributes incentives to appropriate asset categories (land, plant, machinery, infrastructure, working capital). Finally, for incentives in the form of loans, loan guarantees, and linked deposits, future interest and principal payments must be generated in accordance with program rules. The firm's income and tax statements are then recalculated by the hypothetical firm section of TAIM using new data on public financing.

SELECTION OF THE STATE AND CITY SAMPLES

Using the 1990 Annual Survey of Manufactures (U.S. Bureau of the Census 1992a), we identified the 24 states with the greatest manufacturing employment.[12] The 24 states chosen accounted for 86 percent of all manufacturing jobs in the United States. The study was limited to these states; this reduced the task of state-level data collection by about 50 percent (compared with a study of all 50 states) while losing little in generality, since we included the vast majority of states that can be considered serious players in the game for more industrial employment. A list of the states, with population and employment data, can be found in Appendix A, Table A.1.

We then used a geographic information systems (GIS) database based on the 1990 Census to identify all cities and places in these 24 states with a population of over 10,000 and with some manufacturing presence. We excluded locations that were not either incorporated places with active government units or consolidated cities. This resulted in a set of 1,960 cities. We stratified this set of cities by population size in order to avoid drawing mostly small cities into the sample. We also established a threshold ratio of manufacturing employment to population; cities below this threshold were excluded from the sample on the grounds that they represented purely residential communities, which were not in the competition for manufacturing jobs.

Four population classes were created: 10,000–24,999, 25,000–99,999, 100,000–499,999, and 500,000 or more. We included in our sample all 21 cities with a population of 500,000 or more. We listed the cities within each of the other three size classes randomly; the sample of cities in those classes was then drawn by proceeding down the list, excluding any that fell below the manufacturing employment threshold, until we had a sufficient number of cities of that size. The number of cities in each size class in our original sample and the number for which complete data were obtained are shown in Table 2.1. The final city sample (with state and city characteristics) is listed in Appendix Table A.2.

Data on state taxes and tax incentives were obtained largely from the Commerce Clearing House *Multistate Corporate Income Tax Guide* and from copies of corporate income tax forms and instructions for each state. State non-tax programs were initially identified from published sources, including the *Directory of Incentives*, published by the National Association of State Development Agencies (1991), and 1992 incentive checklists published in *Site Selection* and *Area Development*, and brochures published by state departments of economic development.[13] Appropriate state agencies were then contacted by letter and by phone, with numerous follow-up calls, mailed survey forms, and letters, to verify the existence of the incentive programs during 1992 and

Table 2.1 Sample of Cities

		Number of cities		
Size class	Population	Sampled	Data complete	Percentage complete
1	500,000 or more	21	12	57
2	100,000 to 499,999	87	41	47
3	25,000 to 99,999	98	38	39
4	10,000 to 24,999	57	21	37
	Totals	263	112	43

to secure details on program eligibility, operation, and performance. Local property tax rates and property tax abatement schedules and information on the details of local non-tax incentive programs were obtained from community chambers of commerce, development agencies, and city and county officials, with a similar combination of telephone and mail surveys and follow-up inquiries. State sources were sometimes helpful in providing the details on enterprise zone incentives and local property tax rates throughout the state.

NOTES

1. This is similar to Kieschnick's (1981) distinction between automatic and discretionary incentives.

2. Haug's (1984) work on incentives in the Scottish electronics industry seems to agree with this. We know of no direct comparison of automatic and discretionary economic development incentives in the United States.

3. Since some states integrate a net worth tax with the income tax, we also consider all state taxes based on assets, net worth, stockholders' equity, or similar measures, and any investment or jobs credits associated with such taxes.

4. If one is modeling a firm over a long period of time, obviously it makes no sense for the firm to continue in business losing money every year. To incorporate losses in some years but profits in others would be possible, but it is difficult to do so in a nonarbitrary fashion, it would complicate the calculations enormously, and the number of possible scenarios would multiply.

5. Other features of the sales tax are not included in the model, such as the taxation of construction materials or of repair parts or services. Data on expenditures for such items by industry are not available, to our knowledge. Almost all states exempt purchases of raw materials or intermediate goods actually incorporated into the final product, so the absence of sales taxation of these items is not a competitive issue.

6. The choice was also subject to certain program size constraints. For state incentives, grant programs had to have awarded $100,000 in funds during fiscal year 1992, loan and loan guarantee programs had to have awarded at least $500,000. For city incentives, programs had to have awarded at least $100,000, and program rules should have allowed individual awards of $50,000 or more. The size constraints were used to exclude small, seldom-used programs and programs aimed only at microbusinesses.

7. Previously, Illinois did have such an incentive as part of the broader package of funds available through the *Build Illinois* program.

8. As far as we are aware, there has been no academic work done on this issue.

9. The existence of federally imposed state-by-state caps on the annual volume of private activity bonds, of which IRBs are one variety, may limit this universality to a degree, but this would be difficult to assess by state.

10. We do not specify particular locations in these states but represent them by assuming that the firm is initially situated entirely in a mythical "median state," which has a state and local tax system representing the median of our 24 states.

11. See, for example, Papke and Papke (1986), L. Papke (1987, 1991), Hunt (1985), Hunt and O'Leary (1989), and Laughlin (1993). Earlier work is discussed in Kieschnick (1981). A complete discussion of this literature is provided in Chapter 3.

12. There is one minor exception: we substituted the 25th state (Iowa) for the 24th state (Mississippi) due to the ease of data collection in the former and severe difficulties in obtaining data in the early stages of the project for the latter. Iowa accounted for 1.22 percent of the jobs, Mississippi 1.24 percent.

13. Bradshaw, Nishikawa, and Blakely (1992) was useful for some states.

3 The Hypothetical Firm Method Extended

The Tax and Incentive Model (TAIM) described briefly in Chapter 2 is an extension of what has been called the hypothetical firm (or representative firm) method, previously used primarily in studies comparing tax burdens across states or cities. We developed a model of the state and local tax systems in the 24 states and 112 cities in our study and extended the model to incorporate tax incentives and a range of non-tax incentive programs as well. This chapter describes our implementation of the hypothetical firm method in detail. We critique alternative methods of measuring incentive competition, describe criticisms of the hypothetical firm method, explain how we dealt with the problems identified, and spell out the assumptions and procedures built into the model. We also specify how non-tax incentive programs such as job training subsidies and loan guarantees are incorporated into the model. This chapter is intended for those interested in the technical methodological issues; those who are primarily interested in the results of the study can safely skip to Chapter 4.

The majority of previous studies of interstate differences in business taxation have relied upon aggregate summary measures, such as statewide taxes on business per capita, per $1,000 of personal income, or per $100 of estimated business profits. A handful of studies have used the hypothetical firm approach, in which financial statements for an average manufacturing corporation are constructed and the firm's tax burdens in a number of different states are then calculated. Most studies of either kind have not included tax incentives. Discretionary programs—such as capital grants, low-interest loans, loan guarantees, or subsidized job training—have generally been measured simply by counting the programs.

There are serious problems with the summary measures of tax burden and with the counting of programs or measurement of total program expenditure. The best yardstick for measuring tax effects, as well as the whole range of financial incentives, is the hypothetical firm approach. While this approach is not without problems, most of these can be resolved or minimized. To understand the advantages of the hypothetical firm method, it is useful to review the major alternatives. We will then describe the implementation of the hypothetical firm method in the present study and the refinements we have made to the method.

ALTERNATIVE APPROACHES

Aggregate Tax Measures

Researchers attempting to assess the effects of state and local taxes on business investment have generally relied upon some aggregate measure of state tax levels, such as the total state (or state and local) taxes per capita or per $1,000 of personal income or the effective business tax rates, defined as total state business tax collections divided by business income or business assets (see Bartik 1991b, for a comprehensive review of such studies). Many have confined the measure to taxes with an initial impact on business, on the grounds that personal taxes have a more tenuous relationship to location decisions. Business taxes would generally include the corporate income tax, local property taxes on commercial and industrial real estate and personal property (inventories and machinery and equipment), and perhaps sales taxes on inputs purchased by businesses (primarily machinery and equipment, and fuel and electricity); workers' compensation taxes and unemployment insurance taxes have rarely been included.

There are serious problems with such measures. First, the level of aggregation is excessive; if the research question focuses on investment decisions by firms in certain sectors (usually manufacturing), one needs to assess at the very least the average state tax burden on those kinds of firms. Aggregate measures reflect state differences in the taxation of all business sectors—including such diverse enterprises as insurance companies, banks, restaurants, electric utilities, hospitals, construction companies, janitorial services, and railroads—and will not indicate even the average actual burden for any particular industry. State statistics on corporate income tax and sales tax receipts are rarely broken out by industrial sector, and property tax collections can be separated at best into industrial and commercial categories.

Second, aggregate measures show average, not marginal, tax burdens. The industrial location decision, if it is affected by taxes at all, is affected by the change in a firm's tax burden as a result of a change in investment—i.e., the effective marginal tax rate on new investment. Few location decisions entail the uprooting of an entire corporation from one place to another. Marginal tax rates can be significantly altered by such factors as accelerated depreciation, investment tax credits, and temporary property tax abatements. States and localities concerned with the incentive effects of taxes have probably focused their attention more on measures to reduce the marginal rates on new investment rather than on reductions in the overall average rate of tax. L. Papke (1987) compared taxes in 20 states using two alternative measures: Wheaton's (1983) average effective tax rate for manufacturing in general, and the marginal tax rate on new investment for particular manufacturing industries. The Spearman rank-order correlation between the two indices was only 0.29.

Program Counting

Studies attempting to explain the pattern of incentive adoption—why some places offer more than others—have generally relied on program counting. A variety of problems render this measure almost meaningless. In a survey of state and local economic development officials in 24 states, the authors have found 1) programs on the books, and in the incentive directories, that were never funded; 2) states that consolidated several programs into one program without changing the actual incentives available, and vice versa; 3) states with several programs providing essentially the same thing, such as loans, but in slightly different circumstances; 4) similar sounding programs of very dissimilar magnitude because of differences in program constraints or ceilings; 5) multiple programs in one state providing less of value to a business, taken altogether, than a single large program in another state; and 6) multiple programs that were independent and additive in one state, but mutually exclusive in another. While program counting may be appropriate when researching how programs of a particular type are adopted (innovation diffusion studies, for example), the number of incentive programs offered is clearly useless as a proxy for the actual value of the incentive package to a potential new business.

Program or Tax Expenditures

One is tempted to use total state expenditures on economic development programs or tax incentives as a comprehensive measure of the state's generosity. Such expenditures would best be expressed as a rate—probably expenditures per $1,000 of new business investment—in order to make comparisons among states of widely varying size and level of business activity. The denominator should be the total volume of investment potentially eligible for those incentives included in the numerator. However, the aggregation problem here is just as severe as with the summary measures of business tax burden, particularly when the numerator includes a variety of programs with differing eligibility criteria. The rate calculated may bear little relation to the actual incentive value to firms in any particular industry.

Another problem with this approach is that expenditure data are difficult to assemble in a consistent fashion. It is very hard to determine, from state budgets, the actual outlay on any particular incentive program, exclusive of administrative costs. Data on tax incentives are available only for those states that regularly conduct tax expenditure studies.[1] The expenditure approach also precludes consideration of the state's overall tax system or of the incentive value net of taxes.

THE HYPOTHETICAL FIRM METHOD

The hypothetical firm method can be designed to avoid all of the preceding problems: it can be highly disaggregated, it can model marginal rather than average effects, it measures the actual value of incentives or taxes to the firm (instead of simply the existence of a program), and it does not rely on the availability of state tax expenditure studies or detailed program budgets. It can be used to measure overall tax burdens, the value of particular tax incentives, and, with some modification, the effects of any economic development programs that provide direct financial benefits to the firm.

The method works as follows. A model of a hypothetical firm is constructed. The core of the model is an income statement and a balance sheet representative of an average firm in an industry. The financial statements are based on published data such as the *Census of Manufactures* or Internal Revenue Service (IRS) corporate income tax return summaries. The tax liabilities of the firm, to the federal government and to any states in which it is taxable, are calculated as a "subroutine" to the financial statements by applying the appropriate tax laws to the firm, given its individual asset composition and profit level. One can then observe how a particular tax regime changes the firm's net income or cash flow.

In a comparative tax burden study, that might be the end of the story. For purposes of analyzing economic development incentives, however, the next step would be to model the opening of a new plant in state X; appropriate changes would be made to the firm's asset and liability accounts and to its income statement. One could then simulate all of the tax incentives and economic development programs offered by state X for which the firm would qualify. For example, below-market interest rates on public loans used to finance the new plant would reduce annual interest expense, while subsidized job training would reduce first-year labor costs. The interaction between incentives and the state and federal income taxes is automatically taken into account. The hypothetical firm model thus becomes the yardstick for comparisons among states (or localities); it measures the after-tax value to the firm of all the economic development programs and taxes that one chooses to include in the model, taken in combination.

This approach is not new. It has been used primarily to study differences in state tax systems; in most cases, the studies were commissioned by a particular state. Among the earliest of such studies were those conducted by Williams (1967), the Wisconsin Department of Revenue (1973), and Price, Waterhouse & Co. for the State of Missouri in 1978. More recently, state tax comparisons have been undertaken by Papke and Papke (1984)[2] for Indiana, Hunt (1985) for Michigan, Brooks et al. (1986) for Massachusetts, Laughlin (1993) for Indiana, Brooks (1993) for Massachusetts, and KPMG Peat Marwick for New York (1994). The Wisconsin study has been updated several times, most recently in 1990 and 1995. A few econometric studies of the influence of taxes on business investment have used the hypothetical firm approach to measure tax burdens: Steinnes (1984), L. Papke (1987, 1991), and Tannenwald and Kendrick (1995). We believe our model to be the first to include comprehensive simulation of non-tax incentives.

The use of hypothetical corporations to measure the relative size of tax and non-tax incentives is not without problems. Kieschnick (1981, pp. 38–41) has identified a number of these issues, three of which are of particular theoretical importance: 1) the burden of taxes is assumed to rest entirely with the corporation, while theories of tax incidence tell us that significant shifting may occur; 2) the focus on tax effects ignores the expenditure or benefit side of state and local government; and 3) the use of hypothetical firms assumes that the firm operates in all locations using the same relative proportions of factors such as labor and machinery, but a firm may, for example, use a more labor-intensive technology in a low-wage state. With regard to issue 3, it is conceivable that a firm will not only change its location as a result of tax and other incentives, but will also change its asset composition, using relatively less of the factors that are more heavily taxed in a particular place.

These criticisms apply with equal force to alternative methods, but it is worthwhile to consider whether they in fact indicate serious problems. Insofar as the issue of tax incidence is concerned, the entities modeled are usually intended to represent multilocational firms selling in national or international markets under reasonably competitive conditions (the hypothetical firm method is difficult to adapt to modeling new entrepreneurial firms, although Brooks et al. [1986] attempted to do so). As such, multilocation firms will have very limited ability to pass tax burdens forward to consumers (which would render taxes irrelevant to the location decision). With regard to the argument that they may pass taxes back onto immobile factors, land and labor, the response is, indeed, they may. That, in fact, is precisely the point of studies of relative tax burden. The ability to pass taxes backward does not imply that the firm bears no burden, so that taxes are irrelevant to the location decision, but quite the opposite: it is by inducing firms to change location that the taxes are passed back to local immobile factors. If taxes in high-tax states are borne by labor, it is because firms avoid locating there, creating surplus labor and driving down wages.

As for the expenditure issue, the purpose of the hypothetical firm method is limited: it is to model the effects of taxes and of incentive programs that raise or lower the costs of doing business. There is nothing in the method itself that prevents incorporating estimates of the effects of state expenditure (for example, on highways) on firm costs. It is simply that such estimates are extremely difficult to make and therefore are usually omitted from the analysis; as a result, one must use the model's outcomes in full knowledge of what they portray and what they do not. In an econometric model of business investment or location, the tax estimates from a hypothetical firm approach could be used as the tax variable in the equation; other variables could be included as proxies for service levels, as in fact some studies have done (for example, L. Papke 1987, 1991; Tannenwald and Kendrick 1995).

The factor proportions problem appears to be the most serious one. All tax or incentive studies that we are aware of have assumed constant proportions across localities—that is, proportions that do not vary even though some locations may substantially reduce the cost of capital, while others reduce primarily the cost of labor. The changing of factor proportions in response to variations in factor prices or incentives would require current, industry-specific empirical estimates of factor price elasticities and presents formidable problems for modeling.

It is not possible to say whether the constant proportions assumption produces results that overstate or understate tax differences. For example, suppose states A and B impose identical property taxes on capital (plant and equipment). State A is a low-wage state, while state B is a high-wage state, so that the firm choosing to locate in state B would employ a higher proportion of capital (and lower proportion of the high-cost labor) than if it located in state A and therefore would pay higher property taxes in B. By forcing constant proportions of capital and labor, the model fails to capture this tax difference. On the other hand, suppose factor costs were identical in the two states, but that state B imposes a much higher property tax rate. The firm choosing B could reduce this tax burden by substituting labor for capital. In this case, the use of constant proportions results in *overstating* the difference in tax burdens between A and B.

However, factor price differences appear to be most important to location decisions only at the first spatial decision stage: the choice of a broad region or of a state in which to locate (McMillan 1965; Kieschnick 1981; Schmenner 1982; Wardrep 1985). Taxes and incentives are generally thought to be influential at the next level in the location decision process, i.e., the choice of a particular site within the region. Factor prices will probably vary less within a region or labor market than across regions.

As for the second part of the problem, is there reason to believe that tax-induced changes in factor proportions are significant in magnitude? This is a problem for interpretation of the results of hypothetical firm studies only if 1) there is significant variation among the states in the size of capital and labor incentives, and 2) the firm's behavioral response to this differential would be so substantial that the actual value of the incentive package would be significantly affected. Among the 24 states in this study, incentives are for the most part directed at capital rather than labor. Only 3 of the 24 offer a jobs tax credit that is generally available (as opposed to a credit only for firms located in enterprise zones or the like). In these three states (Missouri, Iowa, and South Carolina), the jobs credit reduces total wage costs over the first 10 years of a new investment by less than 1 percent. This is hardly enough to induce a noticeable shift towards more labor-intensive production techniques.

Four states offer a statewide investment tax credit, ranging from 0.5 percent to 1.0 percent of the investment in plant and equipment; again, this is hardly enough to induce firms to alter factor proportions. New York has a very substantial combined tax credit related both to investment and jobs created; for a large firm, the credit (which extends over several years) could be worth about 8 percent of the firm's investment. However, the incentive is tied to both capital and labor, so the effect on factor proportions is probably nil. A state loan program that reduced the interest rate on machinery and equipment loans by 1 percentage point would, over a 20-year period, produce savings (in present value terms) equal to at most about 1 percent of the investment in property, plant, and equipment. Our investigation of incentives in these states, then, leads us to conclude that the factor proportions effects of tax and other incentives are probably small or even non-existent.

A similar problem of modeling behavioral responses arises with respect to the firm's assumed method of financing new investment. Taxes can affect the firm's optimal capital structure, the proportions of debt and equity. Development incentives in the form of below-market-rate loans or loan guarantees lower the relative price of debt financing and may lead the firm to employ more debt and less equity. Grants represent free equity and may be used to reduce borrowing rather than simply to substitute for other forms of equity (issuing additional shares). Nonetheless, all of the studies assume constant proportions of debt and equity financing across states (although this may be allowed to vary across industries).

The additional problems identified by Kieschnick (1981) and others are not inherent in the hypothetical firm method but are simply limitations of some of the studies employing that approach. In the next several sections of this chapter, we address these and further problems, in the context of the crucial decisions and assumptions that we made in developing a satisfactory hypothetical firm model to measure tax and incentive differences.

WHICH INDUSTRIES AND FIRM SIZES?

There is substantial variation across industries on a number of dimensions that can significantly affect the firm's tax liability and the value of incentives. Industries also differ in the importance of the role they play in the interstate competition for jobs. For these reasons, it is not very satisfactory to construct only one or two firms to represent the entire manufacturing sector, as in some of the early studies (e.g., Price, Waterhouse & Co., 1978). The questions are how many industries, at what level of disaggregation, and which particular ones?

We constructed financial statements typical of firms in selected industries with the commercial Compustat database, which is widely used in business research. It is a micro database (each observation being a single firm) of corporations, with detailed annual financial data. Our selection process began with an examination of the employment growth between 1980 and 1990 of each of the 125 three-digit Standard Industrial Classification (SIC) manufacturing industries. From the fastest-growing 32 such industries (those which added at least 9,000 jobs), we eliminated a few (guided missiles, aircraft, meat products, plywood) on the grounds that their plant location choices were too constrained. The Compustat database did not contain a large enough sample of firms from each of the remaining industries to produce reliable averages for financial ratios in every case; as a result, some three-digit industries among this group of 32 were combined, and others had to be omitted. Industries were also eliminated if the average firm in that industry in the Compustat database had negative earnings in 1992. Since we simulated firms in a "steady state" over a 20-year period, we needed an average positive rate of return for that industry. It would not make sense to simulate a firm remaining in operation for 20 years while losing money every year. In the end, we settled on 8 industries (encompassing 12 of the high-growth three-digit industries), which exhibit a high degree of variability on most of the preceding dimensions.

The three-digit SIC code level, which contains 125 manufacturing industries, is probably the most appropriate level of aggregation. Use of two-digit industries would yield greater coverage or representativeness[3] but would conceal substantial variability within the industry. Four-digit industries are more homogeneous, but there are many hundreds of such classifications, making summarization of results very difficult. The three-digit level represents a compromise. The three recent state studies that examine average tax burdens for a single-location firm for a single year use two-digit industries (Hunt 1985; Wisconsin Department of Revenue 1990; Laughlin 1993). The recent studies applying the more sophisticated approach—marginal tax rates for multilocation firms over a period of years—use firms defined at the two- or three-digit level (the various Papke studies and Brooks 1993). All of the studies reviewed focus exclusively on manufacturing with the exception of Hunt (1985), in which one business services firm is included, and KPMG Peat Marwick (1994), which includes three nonmanufacturing sectors: communications, depository institutions, and security and commodity brokers.

In narrowing the selection to a manageable number of firms, we tried to create a set of industries that exhibits substantial variation in the characteristics that affect tax liability and eligibility for incentives. The most important of these characteristics are 1) asset composition, since states vary in terms of the types of assets included in the sales and property tax bases and since incentive programs are targeted at certain classes of assets; 2) capital intensity, which affects the relative importance of investment and employment incentives; 3) the ratio of sales to total assets, which affects the relative importance of income and property taxes; 4) the average wage, which can alter the value of employment incentives; 5) the importance of energy costs, which may or may not be subject to sales tax; 6) the average employment or asset size of a firm or establishment, which may be a factor is program eligibility; and 7) profitability, which affects the relative importance of income and property taxes.

The variability on these dimensions for the firms in our study is shown in Table 3.1. The 16 firms represent 8 industries, with a small and a large firm in each industry. The financial characteristics are based on aggregations of firm-level data in the commercial Compustat database for 1992. As Hunt (1985, p. 20) has pointed out, "the industry identification of these firms should not be over-emphasized." Looking at Table 3.1, one could think of study results for firm number 14 as a measure of the tax and incentive differences relevant to the location of a typical auto plant. It is probably preferable, however, to think of the results as applying to the typical large, capital-intensive, low-profit firm, regardless of industry, for it is those kinds of features, by and large, that will account for the differences in taxes and incentives.

Variation in firm size is at least as important as variation in industry. This is because tax codes and incentive programs are rife with discontinuous functions, such as eligibility criteria requiring a minimum amount of new investment, a minimum number of new jobs, or a minimum percentage increase in employment or assets; annual ceilings on tax credits; and requirements that taxes be calculated two ways with the firm paying whichever is larger, or whichever is smaller. One reason for simulating many firms of widely varying characteristics and sizes is to be able to illustrate the effects of these various thresholds and ceilings. If the firms are chosen at the two-digit level, and with only one average firm size, it is likely that these effects will be concealed. The average firm may always or never qualify for a particular incentive, for example, so to use that firm to represent all potential firms results in overstating or understating the importance of that incentive. There are also ceilings on the dollar amount of certain incentives, with the result that the relative value to large firms is much smaller than to small firms.

Table 3.1 Characteristics of the 16 Hypothetical Firms, by Industry, SIC Code, and Size

Characteristic	Furniture & fixtures SIC 25		Drugs SIC 283		Soap, cleaners, toiletries SIC 284	
	Small #1	Large #2	Small #3	Large #4	Small #5	Large #6
Firm total assets ($ millions)	10	500	500	4,000	500	4,000
New plant assets ($ millions)	5	40	50	470	20	110
New plant employees	67	625	362	2,056	148	960
PP&E (net): % of total assets	24	27	26	35	26	29
M&E (gr): % of PP&E (gr)	67	69	50	61	70	65
PP&E per employee ($)	13,127	16,385	39,330	75,733	35,892	35,913
Average annual wage ($)	20,376	20,376	39,096	30,096	30,512	30,512
Energy expense: % of COGS	1.7	1.8	1.7	3.0	1.7	1.5
LT debt/(equity + LT debt), %	36	33	19	14	30	30
Operating margin (EBIT/sales), %	3.8	8.4	17.5	23.4	9.5	9.1
Sales/assets	2.11	1.74	1.09	1.03	1.88	1.95
Earning power (EBIT/assets), %	8.0	14.6	19.1	24.2	17.9	17.8
Overall return on equity, %	17.5	14.1	16.2	28.7	16.7	17.3

SOURCES: All data except wages and energy costs are based on averages for firms in that SIC group and asset size class from the Compustat database for 1992. Wages and energy costs are from the 1987 *Census of Manufactures* (U.S. Bureau of the Census 1990), which shows average wage by SIC code but not by firm asset size within SIC grouping.
DEFINITIONS:
    PP&E (net) = property, plant and equipment, net of depreciation.
    M&E (gr) = machinery and equipment, gross (at acquisition cost).
    PP&E (gr) = property, plant and equipment, gross (at acquisition cost).
    LT debt = long-term debt.
    COGS = cost of goods sold.
    Operating margin = net operating income (earnings before interest and taxes [EBIT]) divided by net sales.
    Sales/assets = net sales divided by assets (current assets plus net property, plant, and equiment).
    Earning power = product of above two ratios, or earnings before interest and taxes divided by assets. This is the best measure of the return to be expected on new plant investment, because it excludes extraordinary items and income from investments, both of which are included in the firm's return on equity.
    Return on equity = net income divided by stockholders' equity.

Table 3.1 (continued)

Miscellaneous plastic products SIC 308		Industrial machinery SIC 35 less 357		Electronic components SIC 367		Motor vehicles and parts SIC 371		Instruments SIC 382+384	
Small #7	Large #8	Small #9	Large #10	Small #11	Large #12	Small #13	Large #14	Small #15	Large #16
10	300	300	4,000	200	2,000	1,000	20,000	35	1,000
5	70	10	250	20	200	120	600	10	180
53	572	84	2,007	223	1,652	1,386	4,589	103	1,438
35	36	26	25	27	35	31	30	14	25
72	73	74	74	74	72	75	75	65	66
24,739	41,755	26,805	30,795	19,687	34,440	26,489	41,781	12,388	31,000
20,204	23,204	29,761	29,761	29,798	29,798	36,569	36,569	32,069	32,069
3.7	3.8	1.9	1.7	2.3	2.4	1.0	0.9	1.7	1.6
26	46	27	31	17	20	34	41	22	27
6.1	9.2	7.6	6.8	10.1	10.9	6.2	4.1	10.0	12.6
1.75	1.60	1.39	1.50	1.32	1.14	1.81	1.80	1.44	1.24
10.7	14.8	10.6	10.3	13.2	12.3	11.1	7.4	14.4	15.6
11.3	16.3	9.0	8.8	13.6	12.3	11.8	8.0	14.7	14.8

Firm (and plant) size is sufficiently important that it should be an additional dimension, or the hypothetical firms should vary substantially in size across industries. This is not always done, however. Papke and Papke (1984) modeled three asset sizes for each industry—$25–$49 million, $50–$99 million, and $100–$249 million—and assumed the same percentage of expansion for all firms. Brooks (1993) assumed that all firms had $100 million in assets and expanded by 10 percent. In the Wisconsin and Indiana studies, the six firms varied in size but were all small, with assets ranging from $9 million to $18 million. Hunt (1985) used eight firms ranging in asset size from $1 million to $759 million, in the only study that varied size substantially and that used sizes appropriate to the industry.

These assumptions can be compared to the asset sizes for the 16 firms in Table 3.1. The total asset size of the large firm in each industry is approximately the 75th percentile in the distribution of firms by total assets in that industry. The small firm represents approximately the

25th percentile; that is, 25 percent of the firms in that industry have lower total assets. These distributions come from the Internal Revenue Service *Corporation Source Book 1990*. The substantial industry variation in firm size is apparent; a firm that is large for the plastics industry, for example, would be quite small in the automobile sector. The total asset sizes represented at the 75th percentile are also much larger, in many cases, than the sizes assumed in previous studies; in six of the eight industries, the typical large firm has in excess of $1 billion in assets. Of the 16 firms, 12 have assets greater than the largest asset class assumed by Papke and Papke (1984) and greater than the $100 million assumed by Brooks (1993).

Previous studies that modeled an expansion decision, rather than the average tax burden on a static, single-location firm, had to assume an asset size for the new establishment as well (the six Papke studies and Brooks 1993). All assumed that the new establishment assets were a certain percentage of the firm's total assets before expansion, a percentage that did not vary by industry. This turns out to be an important assumption, in part because the size of a new plant relative to the total firm can affect the value of certain tax incentives. This is because corporate tax credits are usually not refundable and so cannot exceed tax liability. In some states, the ceiling is the firm's total corporate income tax liability in that state, while in other states the ceiling is the income tax liability attributed to the new plant only.

Plant or establishment sizes typical of an industry can be constructed in a fashion similar to the firm size distributions, using establishment data from the 1987 *Census of Manufactures*. These data show distributions of establishments by employment size. For each of the eight industries, we estimated the establishment employment size at the 25th and 75th percentiles. Using industry average ratios of assets to employment, we then inferred establishment total asset size. We assumed that large firms build large plants, and small firms build small plants. This seems to be a reasonably harmless assumption, but one we cannot confirm empirically. Again, substantial industry variability is exhibited, both in terms of typical small or large plant sizes (varying from $5 million to $600 million) and in the ratio of plant size to firm size (which varies from about 3 percent to 50 percent). We assumed, as has been done with all previous "marginal investment" studies, that the operating characteristics of the parent firm are mirrored in the new plant: the same ratio of sales to assets, the same asset composition, average wage, and assets per employee.

The critical importance of industry, firm size, and plant size assumptions is illustrated in Table 3.2. The 24 states in our study were ranked according to net returns on investment in a new plant in that state by an out-of-state firm, after state and local taxes and tax incentives. (Local taxes were computed for a representative city in each state; a more complete discussion of these results is deferred to chapter 4.) We show the rankings for eight of these states and for five of the hypothetical firms. States A and D were consistently near the top of the rankings regardless of firm, while states B and C were consistently near the bottom of the rankings. (This was true for all 16 firms, not just for the five illustrated in Table 3.2.) On the other hand, states W, X, Y, and Z changed rank drastically depending on the firm, from near the top to near the bottom of the 24 states.

Table 3.2 How Firm Characteristics Affect Rankings of Investment Returns for Selected Multistate Firms

State	Firm #2: Furniture ($40)[a]	#4: Drugs ($470)	#7: Plastics ($5)	#14: Autos ($600)	#16: Instruments ($180)
States with least variation					
A	5	4	3	3	3
B	23	23	23	21	24
C	21	19	20	20	20
D	1	1	2	1	2
States with most variation					
W	7	3	9	17	5
X	13	17	22	5	14
Y	12	24	6	9	22
Z	2	21	8	12	11

NOTE: See Chapter 4 for an explanation of the representative city modeling. Rank is based on the firm's return on investment in a new plant in a representative city in each state after state, local, and federal income, sales, and property taxes and after state and local tax incentives, including enterprise zone incentives. Highest return among the 24 states is ranked 1. In this and subsequent tables, "Furniture" is short for "furniture and fixtures," "Soaps" for "soaps, cleaners, and toiletries," "Plastics" for "miscellaneous plastic products," and "Autos" for "motor vehicles and parts."
a. Plant size in millions.

The hypothetical firm method leads to a *set* of interstate comparisons: for each hypothetical firm, one can rank the states according to the after-tax return on investment in a new plant of the assumed size in that firm's industry. Is it possible then to construct a single summary measure, to compute an overall average tax rate or incentive package value for a state or an average ranking over all firms? Probably not. If a limited number of firms have been selected, then they are unlikely to be representative of all manufacturing firms (or all footloose ones), and certainly not in equal proportions. There is no way around this problem, short of conducting a massive number of simulations based on a stratified sample of the actual universe of corporations (itself impossible due to the absence of a comprehensive micro database) and weighting each firm.[4]

FIRM, PLANT, AND HEADQUARTERS LOCATION

Some studies using the hypothetical firm approach to compare state business tax burdens treat each firm as if it consisted of a single plant, or at least a single location. This may make sense for comparative tax studies, but it is not appropriate for the measurement of development incentives, which are provided for *new* investment. An entity with the financial characteristics and asset size of the average mature firm in the industry cannot be treated as if it were a brand new establishment. The sensible approach is to assume an ongoing profitable business that invests in a new branch plant.

The question immediately arises, does it matter where the parent firm and the new plant are located? Suppose one is examining 24 sites, one in each of our 24 states. If one assumes that the parent firm, before building the new plant, has facilities at only one location but allows the new plant to be at another, then there are 24 times 24 or 576 possible combinations of firm and plant location: the parent firm in each of the 24 states, paired with each of the 24 possible locations for the new plant. In reality, of course, things are much more complicated than this, with existing firms already having facilities in many states rather than in just one.

All of this matters, of course, because tax burdens can differ dramatically depending on where a firm's sales, property, and payroll are located; these factors determine what proportion of income is taxed in each state. States vary significantly in how they apportion and tax income of multistate firms. How does one render the simulation process manageable while doing justice to the importance of location of multiplant firms? The problem becomes quite intractable if one includes multiple localities within each state so as to capture actual local tax and incentive policies.

Our solution was to simplify the computations and the interpretation of results by modeling an additional hypothetical state intended to represent all of the other locations for the initial parent firm. This mythical state was given a tax system with rates, tax base, and other features representing the median among the 24 actual states in the study. The median sales tax rate among these states is 5 percent (21 of the 24 states have rates between 4 percent and 6 percent), and the median sales tax base would fully exempt manufacturing machinery and equipment (19 of 24 states) and fuel and utilities used directly in manufacturing (15 of the 24 states). The median corporate income tax would follow federal depreciation rules, allow no deductions for federal or state income taxes, apportion income on the basis of a three-factor formula with double-weighted sales, would not require the throwback of sales to states in which the firm has no tax nexus, and would apply a flat rate of 7 percent (only 3 of the 24 have a progressive rate structure) with no credits. We did not need to model investment incentives in the median state (such as jobs credits or property tax abatement) because the new plant would always be located in one of the 24 actual states or 112 actual cities. For the city level analysis, we assumed a "median city" location for the parent firm in the median state, with a property tax rate of 2.4 percent and a local sales tax of 1 percent.

By constructing the mythical median state, we can produce a single ranking of the 24 states for each hypothetical firm. In each instance, the parent firm is located and taxed in the median state, while the new plant is located in each of the 24 actual states in turn, generating tax liabilities in that state as well. The firm's return on the new plant becomes the measure of competitiveness for new investment by out-of-state firms. (For comparisons of the return on investment in an expansion within the home state by a firm that is currently located solely in that home state, the median state is not necessary.)

Is the median-state simplification valid? The median-state approach provides one ranking of the 24 states for each firm. Generating the 576 pairwise comparisons, on the other hand, would yield 24 rankings, one for each initial firm location, which could then be averaged for some overall assessment of competitiveness. Whether the median-state ranking would diverge significantly from the average of the 24 separate rankings is difficult to say. However, if most firms in fact already have facilities in many states, the median-state method may be a satisfactory approximation. Simple pairwise comparisons will illuminate and emphasize state differences that may not be particularly relevant, if those differences tend to be swamped by the average policy in other states.

The importance of looking at differences in headquarters assumptions is illustrated in Table 3.3. The 112 cities in our study were ranked by returns on new investment in each city after federal, state, and local taxes, and after economic development incentives, under two sets of assumptions: 1) the investing firm is initially located out of state (entirely in the mythical median state) or 2) the firm is initially located entirely within the state in question and remains a single-location firm. For places with certain kinds of tax systems, the location assumption is clearly critical, while for others it makes little difference.[5] Some locations clearly favor multistate firms, others clearly favor domestic single-location firms, and still others sometimes favor one, sometimes the other. Certain cities maintain a similar ranking regardless of location assumption, but the general rule is for rankings to differ substantially.

HOW ARE THE FIRM'S SALES DISTRIBUTED AMONG STATES?

Assumptions regarding the destination of the hypothetical firm's sales are critical because of the way in which states apportion business income for purposes of taxation. Most states use a three-factor apportionment formula, where the three factors are payroll, property, and sales. The payroll factor, for example, is the ratio of the firm's payroll

Table 3.3 Selected Cities Ranked by Returns on Investment for Multistate and Single-Location Firms

City	#2: Furniture		#4: Drugs		#7: Plastics		#13: Autos	
	Multi-state	Single-location	Multi-state	Single-location	Multi-state	Single-location	Multi-state	Single-location
Cities ranked higher for single-location firms								
A	95	2	83	3	95	2	73	2
B	106	29	80	20	99	24	101	21
C	98	34	51	24	96	23	100	26
Cities ranked higher for multistate firms								
D	2	65	4	52	10	37	12	64
E	8	21	5	8	21	36	25	25
F	14	35	2	25	34	64	10	64
Cities with no clear location bias								
G	49	45	47	48	58	49	49	44
H	54	61	111	63	5	62	45	61

NOTE: Among the eight cities in this table, there are no two cities in the same state. Cities are ranked according to returns on new plant investment after federal, state, and local taxes and after state and local economic development incentives. The highest return among the 112 cities is ranked 1.

located within the state to the firm's payroll everywhere. The sales factor is the ratio of the firm's sales with a destination within the state to the firm's sales everywhere. A weighted average of the three factors produces the apportionment factor; when multiplied by the firm's taxable income derived from operations everywhere, the result is income taxable by the state in question. The weight applied to the sales factor varies from 33 percent in a number of states (i.e., equal weight given to the three factors) to 50 percent in many states (double-weighted sales) and 100 percent in a few states (single-factor apportionment).

The sales factor is complicated by throwback rules. In several states, shipments from facilities in that state to states in which the firm has no tax nexus, or to the federal government, are thrown back to that state, i.e., counted as part of the numerator in the sales factor. Sales destined for a state where the firm is taxable (and where those sales will be reflected in that state's apportionment formula) are never thrown back.

In constructing a hypothetical firm simulation, arbitrary assumptions must be made with respect to the proportion of firm sales destined for 1) the state in which the new plant is located, 2) the state(s) in which the original firm is located, 3) other states in which the firm is taxable, and 4) other states where the firm has no tax nexus. These assumptions significantly affect the apparent relative competitiveness of states. If a large share of sales is assumed to go to category 4, states such as Wisconsin and Massachusetts that require throwback of all such sales and that double-weight sales in the apportionment formula are at a disadvantage. On the other hand, assuming all sales are to states where the firm is taxable increases the firm's tax liability to those states; this, in turn, puts a premium on the deductibility of other states' income taxes (allowed in only a few states) and eliminates throwback effects entirely.

The design of the model may constrain the sales assumptions that one can make. If the model permits each firm to be located and taxed in only one or two states, as most models do, one must assume that sales are quite unevenly distributed (with all or most sales going to just those one or two states) or one must assume that most sales are to the other 48 or 49 states and that the firm has no tax nexus (not even a sales office) in any of those states.[6] The first assumption is not consistent with the supposition that one is modeling relatively footloose firms competing in national markets. The second assumption is unrealistic.

Tannenwald and Kendrick (1995) report that throwback sales are in fact insignificant for most Massachusetts manufacturers; they assert that firms tend to have a tax nexus (even if it is only a sales office) in states where they do substantial business. Data from Wisconsin corporate income tax returns indicate that, among apportioning corporations, about 16 percent of total sales are thrown back in the aggregate.[7]

The creation of a median state to represent all other states in which the firm has facilities provides a solution to the sales allocation dilemma. This mythical state can be given a population representing a large share of the total U.S. population, and sales can then be allocated between the particular actual state, the mythical median state, and the remaining (non-taxing) states in proportion to population. This has the effect of attributing only a small share of sales to non-taxing states (we assume 20 percent) without forcing the remainder to occur in the actual state; most of the remainder will be destined instead for the median state, where the firm is taxed. This should provide more accurate comparisons of throwback versus nonthrowback states, as well as of states allowing the deduction for other state's income taxes versus states that do not. It is also consistent with the national markets assumption; the actual state is allocated sales only in proportion to its share of national population.

INTERSTATE OR INTERLOCAL COMPETITION?

Since location choices are made among actual sites, with particular local taxes and incentives, studies of location competition should take local public policies into account. This raises the question of how local tax variables are to be included in an analysis of interstate competition. Two approaches have been used: 1) a statewide average property tax rate is employed, generally without consideration of any abatements, or 2) particular localities are modeled rather than the state as a whole, so the actual tax regime in that community governs the local tax component. The first approach raises questions of accuracy, while the second brings up questions of representativeness. We apply both approaches in this study; a discussion of the estimates of average property tax rates is contained in the notes to Appendix Table A.3.

A similar, but more difficult, question arises with respect to state-provided tax incentives. Of the many states that offer investment or jobs tax credits, only a few do so on a uniform basis throughout the state. The others offer the credits only in specified areas such as enterprise zones or counties with above-average unemployment rates or offer the credits on more favorable terms in such places. The targeted areas may be limited to a small number of neighborhood enterprise zones, or they may include a majority of the counties in the state. If one is comparing state tax regimes, how is geographic variation in such incentives to be incorporated? There are four alternatives: 1) include only incentives available generally throughout the state; 2) model the most generous incentive package the state offers, regardless of how limited the availability in geographic terms; 3) attempt to calculate an average over the entire state, taking into account the prevalence or coverage of the targeted incentives; or 4) calculate an average for some arbitrary subset of locations, such as the three largest cities. The best approach is probably the first. States can then be compared on the basis of their lowest offer (or highest effective tax rate), which will also be the typical offer, unless targeted incentives are quite widespread.

The concept of a statewide average incentive offer, or property tax rate, is problematic.[8] How are the different locations with different tax and incentive rates to be weighted in the computation of the average—by their shares of land area, population, industrial property value, manufacturing employment, number of unemployed, manufacturing value added, or tax collections, to mention some of the possibilities? How are we to know whether any of these will reflect the future distribution of plant locations within the state? Narrowly targeted incentives are best studied not by looking at states as the unit of analysis but by looking at localities.

Complicating matters further, however, is variation in taxes and incentives within a particular city. This can occur for two reasons: the city includes multiple taxing jurisdictions (such as school districts or improvement districts that have issued bonds for local infrastructure), or the city contains an enterprise zone with special state and local incentives. In the first case, we have obtained the local tax rate for the area of the city most likely to be the site for new industry; if this cannot be determined, we have computed a citywide average tax rate. Substantial variation in rates within cities occurs only in a few states.

As for the treatment of enterprise zones, we have chosen to use the tax rates and incentives that prevail within the zone to represent the entire city for purposes of computing the tax on income from new investment. In some cases, the zone is the whole county, so this approach is strictly correct. In other instances, the decision is equivalent to assuming that the majority of new industrial expansion in a city with an enterprise zone will occur within that zone. This is justified to the extent that the zone location compared with nonzone locations would bring with it similar costs for labor (the labor market presumably being broader than the city in most cases) and for transportation and utilities, but would provide significant additional tax benefits.

For multistate firms, the initial production facilities are located entirely in a single median city (with a median local tax system) in the median state. The new plant is located in a particular city in the sample state (except for the state-level analyses, where local taxes and incentives are not included). If the city contains an enterprise zone, we assume that the new plant is located in that zone.

For single-state firms, the location assumption possibilities become more complex. For simplicity, we assume that the new plant represents an expansion of an existing facility at the same site. Thus, if a city has an enterprise zone, the existing firm's production facilities as well as the new plant are located in that zone. The alternative would have been to model an existing firm at some hypothetical average city in the state, with only the new plant being located in the sample city (and in the enterprise zone, if any). This assumption makes a difference only in a state that provides investment or jobs tax credits that can be applied solely to the tax attributable to facilities within enterprise zones (whether new facilities or not). In most cases, such credits can be applied against the firm's total state tax liability from all facilities wherever located, or only to the firm's state tax liability attributable to the new plant, so the assumption regarding the location of the existing firm has no bearing.

In many instances, jobs tax credits are available only for certain categories of employees rather than for all those employed at the new plant. Most often, the criteria relate to the employee's location of residence and previous employment status. Appendix Table B.3 shows our assumptions regarding the percentage of new plant employees residing within the city as a whole and within the enterprise zone itself, and the percentage who were unemployed at the time of hiring or who were unemployed at least 90 days prior to hiring. Since some states apply both criteria, we also show how these two assumptions combine.

MEASURING EFFECTS OVER TIME

Kieschnick criticized the hypothetical firm method for ignoring the life cycle of firms. The method is indeed limited in this regard; it is not practicable to simulate in a nonarbitrary fashion a new firm over the first 20 years of its life cycle. The method is thus not suitable for measuring tax effects on new businesses or incentive programs aimed at stimulating entrepreneurship or new business formation.

A multiyear analysis is nonetheless essential. Taxes and incentives affect the profitability of new investment not just in the initial investment year, but for many years thereafter. Credits sometimes must be used in the first year but in other instances can be carried forward for up to 20 years. Property tax abatements often provide the largest benefit the first year but frequently continue at some level for 10 years or more. Favorable loan terms are felt over the life of the loan. It is very difficult to accurately capture these effects over time with a one-year analysis that includes, for example, the present value of future property tax abatements. Such an approach ignores the interaction year by year between incentives and state and federal taxes. Furthermore, location decisions are surely made on the basis of a longer time horizon. A 20-year span is probably sufficient to capture all of the significant differences in state policy, although some studies have carried the analysis to 60 years (Papke and Papke 1986; Brooks et al. 1986; Brooks 1993).

When the hypothetical firm method is used to analyze the competitive effects of taxes or incentives, the question being posed, implicitly, is this: For a given firm contemplating an investment in a new plant of a specified size, which location for that new plant produces the greatest profit? The answer is found by simulating the firm's revenues and costs over some time period, producing a stream of annual cash flow figures. If two simulations are performed—with and without the new plant—then the difference measures *project* returns: the increase in the firm's cash flow attributable to the investment in the new plant.

How is this flow of project returns over time to be reduced to a single measure of profitability? There are two logical contenders: the net present value (NPV) of project returns and the internal rate of return (IRR) on the investment in the new plant. In capital budgeting terms, the decision is between a set of mutually exclusive projects of equal size: the same investment is contemplated in each location, but only one location will be selected. By which measure should these projects (each one representing a state or site) be ranked?

The capital budgeting literature has generally come down in favor of the NPV as the best criterion for ranking projects (see for example, Stevens 1979 or Brigham 1985) because of three problems with the IRR. First, the IRR can produce the wrong rankings when there are differences in project size, although that is not an issue here. Second, the IRR method can produce multiple solutions whenever there is a non-normal income stream (one containing a negative flow in at least one future year); such streams can readily exist with the hypothetical firm method if substantial replacement investment occurs within the time horizon. Since machinery and equipment is the major asset category, generally with an economic life of less than 20 years, substantial replacement investment will have to be modeled. The third problem is the reinvestment rate assumption. The IRR calculation is based on the implicit assumption that project returns will be reinvested at the project's IRR. For example, the firm choosing a $10 million plant in state A will reinvest the returns from that plant in a series of similar projects in the same state, each producing the same rate of return. This further requires the assumption that similar investments are available each year in small increments, so that all net income can be immediately reinvested. The NPV rule, on the other hand, is based on the assumption that project returns will be reinvested at the firm's discount rate, which should be equal to the firm's cost of capital. The returns from project A, in other words, substitute for retained earnings, debt, and new shares of stock in the financing of other firm projects, saving the business the cost of raising capital. The NPV assumption is more defensible than the IRR reinvestment assumption.

The AFTAX model, employed by J. and L. Papke and in the Massachusetts study (Brooks 1993), uses the IRR as the measure of project profitability and differences in after-tax rates of return as measures of the tax implications of one location versus another. They argue that this avoids making an arbitrary assumption regarding the discount rate. Use of the IRR, however, requires an arbitrary assumption itself regarding the reinvestment of project returns. Furthermore, there is something to be said for the heuristic value of results expressed in NPV terms. Public discussion of the competitive effects of taxes and incentives is invariably carried on in relation to the dollar value to the firm of a particular incentive or package, and NPV provides a way of expressing the value of a tax program or incentive in just those terms: How much it is worth to a firm in today's dollars to receive certain benefits over the next 20 years?

We conclude that the competitive effects of taxes and incentives are best analyzed by simulating capital budgeting decisions by hypothetical firms. The textbook solution to a capital budgeting problem begins with an estimate of the stream of cash flows produced by the planned project. It is the incremental cash flow that is relevant: the difference between cash flows with the project and cash flows without the project. Cash flows are measured by net income after taxes, with noncash expenses added back (depreciation deductions and deferred taxes). The result is the annual incremental cash flow from operations. The acquisition cost of new property and plant and equipment and the additional net working capital required by the project are deducted from the first-year cash flow. The cost of replacement equipment is deducted in the appropriate years. The project is assumed to have a finite life; salvage value (assumed equal to book value) becomes an additional source of cash at the end of the project, as does the return of net working capital. Finally, debt financing flows are added, with the proceeds of bond issues being a source of cash and the repayment of principal a use of cash. The end result is the stream of net cash flows available to equity investors. This stream is discounted at the firm's assumed cost of equity to arrive at the NPV of project cash flows. A detailed description of the operation of the model and of the assumptions employed is contained in Appendix B.

Almost all hypothetical firm studies have assumed zero inflation; that is, the financial projections are in real terms. At first glance, this assumption seems harmless. A firm's cost of capital will reflect inflation premiums incorporated into current nominal interest rates and required rates of return on equity. Suppose the inflation premium were 5 percent. If all project revenues and costs were inflated at 5 percent per year over 20 years, and the resulting cash flow discounted at the current nominal cost of capital, the result would be the same as if one had discounted real (uninflated) cash flows at the real discount rate. In the absence of good reasons to assume different rates of inflation for each project component, or different rates for each year, one may as well leave the analysis in real terms. This would be true enough if it were not for taxes; deductions are allowed for depreciation and interest expenses, and these expenses will not rise each year with inflation (although they will jump up as assets are replaced at inflated cost). The higher the inflation rate, the longer the replacement period, and the larger the replacement cost relative to income, the greater the will be divergence between tax calculations based on nominal flows and those based on uninflated flows.

The zero inflation assumption could bias comparisons across states to the extent that depreciation rules or the timing of incentives differ. Almost all states allow federal Modified Accelerated Cost Recovery System (MACRS) depreciation, with California and New Jersey being among the notable exceptions that require a less accelerated form of depreciation. By ignoring inflation we disregard the lesser real value of the depreciation rules of California and New Jersey as compared to those of other states. Similarly, consider state A, which provides incentives up front in the form of grants, and state B, which provides incentives spread over 10 years in the form of below-market rate loans. Inflation has no effect on the value of A's grants but reduces the real value of B's annual interest cost reductions unless the interest subsidy is increased during periods of high inflation.

How substantial is the bias produced by assuming no inflation? Brooks et al. (1986) tested the effects of a 5 percent inflation rate over the entire 60-year period of their analysis, which calculated after-tax rates of return on new investment at 16 sites in 11 states. Ten of the states allowed federal Accelerated Cost Recovery System (ACRS) depreciation at that time; one (New York) required pre-ACRS depreciation, resulting in quite different allowances in the first few years. The analysis also provided a test of the significance of incentive timing differences: investment tax credits (ITCs) were offered at various rates by 4 of the 11 states. (Unlike other tax features that apply uniformly from year to year, an ITC usually provides all its benefits in the year an asset is acquired.) Despite these differences among states, the researchers found that "the actual rankings of the sixteen sites are virtually identical to those calculated assuming zero inflation" (p. 65).

DISAGGREGATING THE RESULTS

The basic result produced by the simulation model is the present value of net income over 20 years attributable to investment in a new plant at a particular location, given the taxes and the package of incentives available at that location. The overall value of the incentive package represents the maximum benefits obtainable by a firm if it were able to take advantage of all of the programs available in the state, given the state's income and sales tax structure. In order to identify how different components of the tax and non-tax program package contribute to the total incentive value, we also calculate the value of components of that package. This is done by performing the simulations in six ways. For state-level comparisons, with state taxes and incentives only, the simulations are as follows:

- Level 1 = present value of net cash flow attributable to investment in the new plant over 20 years, taking into account the state's basic tax system (including corporate income taxes and sales taxes on machinery and equipment and on fuels and utilities, but not including economic development incentive credits).

- Level 2 = level 1 plus the effects of state economic development entitlements (income tax investment and jobs credits).

- Level 3 = level 2 plus the effects of state infrastructure subsidy programs.

- Level 4 = level 2 plus the effects of state job training and wage subsidy programs.

- Level 5 = level 2 plus the effects of state general purpose financing programs (grants, loans, and loan guarantees).

- Level 6 = level 2 plus the effects of all state incentive programs included separately in levels 3 through 5.

The increment in net income attributable to the state's economic development entitlements (income tax investment and jobs credits), compared with net income under the state's basic tax system, is calculated in level 2. This represents the value of the tax credits to the firm. Levels 3 through 5 are not additive; each assumes the existence of the state's tax system, including development credits, but no other non-tax programs. This is because there are overall constraints on the use of incentives, as well as individual program constraints. An infrastructure program might award a firm $500,000, for example, and a general capital grant might award it $300,000 to be applied to infrastructure, if each program operated independently. However, if the firm's total infrastructure needs are only $600,000, it will receive only $600,000 in total from the two programs, not $800,000. Thus, amounts from levels 3, 4, and 5 cannot be added together to arrive at the total (level 6), nor is there a nonarbitrary way of disaggregating the level-6 total to identify the contribution that each type of program made. In the preceding example, how would one decide how much of the $600,000 for infrastructure came from a specific infrastructure program and how much from the general grant program? The purpose of simulation levels 3, 4, and 5, then, is simply to allow comparisons among states for different kinds of programs.

Localities are compared in similar fashion. Local sales, corporate income, and property taxes are included in the calculation of project income at level 1, including the effects of deductibility of local property taxes from state and federal income taxes. Local property tax abatements for new investment are added in level 2, as are state or local tax incentives automatically available in enterprise zones or similar, targeted areas (where applicable). Level 2 project income minus level 1 project income now measures the value to the firm of the combined state and local tax incentive package. Discretionary locally funded loan, grant, or job training programs are included in levels 3 through 5, as with the state analyses. Level 6 net income minus level 1 net income then produces the value of the combined state and local incentive package for that locality.

SIMULATING THE WORTH OF NON-TAX INCENTIVES

Hypothetical firm models have not included non-tax state and local incentives such as grants, loans, loan guarantees and subsidies, and linked deposits. In order to model discretionary incentives, a hypothetical firm model must be able to generate a set of incentives that a firm would likely receive from a state or city and then apply those incentives to an investment. As we noted in Chapter 2, this is a very different sort of problem from that of modeling tax systems. Discretionary incentives are negotiated; tax incentives are automatic and applied uniformly. There are four major steps involved in integrating discretionary incentives into a hypothetical firm model.

The first step is to develop historical "administrative" ratios for all non-tax incentives offered by each state or city. The most important ratios are incentive dollars awarded per jobs created or retained and incentive dollars awarded per associated total investment, although others are also used in TAIM. These ratios can then be employed to develop likely amounts that a firm would receive from a particular incentive program. Once incentive amounts have been generated, the various program rules must then be applied (step 2). Common rules include a maximum amount a firm may receive from an incentive program, from all incentive programs (in other words, a stipulated limit on total government-sponsored funding of a project), a minimum equity contribution, or a stipulated minimum number of jobs created. Most incentive programs have further rules governing the way in which an incentive may be spent (on land, plant, infrastructure, machinery, or working capital); whether it is extended only to firms headquartered in the state; whether it is offered only to small firms; and whether it is available, or available on more favorable terms, only in targeted regions of the state. Essentially, an expert system must be built so that these and other rules can be applied to the incentive amount generated in the first step. For example, if an incentive program requires an equity stake equal to or greater than the incentive amount awarded, the expert system should be able to vary the amount awarded in step 1 so that this program rule is not broken.

Next, since states and cities usually offer multiple incentives, the expert system should be able to assemble the best package of incentives available from a unit of government (step 3). In other words, it should not only be able to apply the administrative rules guiding the delivery of a particular program, but it should be able to mirror the way in which economic development officials assemble their incentives into competitive packages. Here the expert system must be able to apply the explicit and implicit rules that govern how packages are assembled (for example, a state may have more than one general capital grant program but may nevertheless require that a firm be awarded funds from only one of these), and within these rules it should be able to create an optimum package (the one that maximizes after-tax returns) for the firm being simulated.

In order to simplify modeling, awarded discretionary incentives can be divided into two broad classes: grants (including capital, training, and infrastructure grants, tax increment financing bonds, and other instruments providing cash payments to the firm or the equivalent of such cash payments) and loans (any discretionary debt instrument). Grants and loans can then be applied to the appropriate (and allowable) asset classes. Again, the application of incentives to the various asset classes should be such that returns on investment are maximized and naturally should not result in a situation where any incentive program rules are broken. In the case of debt instruments, payback schedules including appropriate rates, fees, and terms for each asset class need to be developed and applied to the firm's balance sheets.

The present value of a firm's return on investment may be calculated without any discretionary incentives and then again with a particular package of discretionary incentives (step 4). The difference between these two amounts provides the measure of the after-tax worth of a state's or city's discretionary or non-tax incentives to a firm.

Our simulations always assume that an incentive, be it general-use, training-based, or for infrastructure, is used to replace private investment expenditures the firm would otherwise have made, provided such a replacement does not result in any breach of the administrative rules governing the award of the incentive. Thus, an infrastructure grant of $0.5 million replaces $0.5 million in equity expenditures the firm would have made on infrastructure. Similarly, a $0.5 million loan or loan guarantee replaces $0.5 million of private debt the firm would have otherwise raised. However, if the $0.5 million grant results in the firm reducing its equity stake below that allowed by program administrative rules, then the incentive award is decreased to the point where the rules are no longer broken.[9] The worth of a grant, then, is the extent to which its use raises the firm's rate of return on investment. The worth of a public loan or loan guarantee is the extent to which the more favorable rates, terms, or fees of the public loan or loan guarantee, relative to a private loan, raise the rate of return on a firm's investment.[10] Assumptions concerning the impact of discretionary incentives on the size of the investment amount and on factor proportions are consistent with the assumptions previously described for the tax part of the hypothetical firm model. In other words, the firm chooses a standard, fixed plant and technology and a capital financing plan before selecting a location and before knowing the terms of any public component of that financing.

Practically, TAIM assigns state and local discretionary incentives to each firm modeled and then replaces private debt and equity expenditures with these amounts. Incentives are assigned using a series of expert systems that, in the first place, model both the "administrative rules" and the "administrative history" of each non-tax program and in the second, model the way in which incentives are combined to create "incentive packages." TAIM then recalculates a firm's income and tax statements using the new data on public financing. The general method is summarized in Figure 3.1. The remainder of this chapter is concerned with the major assumptions involved in implementing this method. A computational description of the method is found in Appendix C.

Figure 3.1 TAIM Extended to Include Non-Tax Incentives

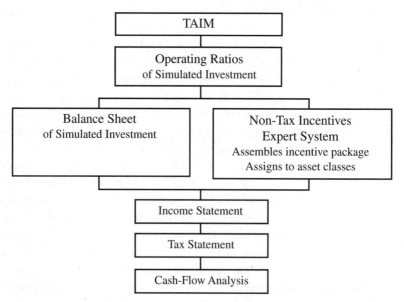

Infrastructure Incentives

Our measurement of infrastructure incentives is based on five broad principles.

Principle 1: In our model, the amount a firm receives from an infrastructure incentive program (or from a package of such incentives) is never more than the firm's simulated expenditure on infrastructure for its new plant.

Principle 2: We treat all infrastructure and all related incentives as homogeneous.

Thus, for example, we do not distinguish between incentives providing funds for roads and incentives providing funds for sewerage mains. All infrastructure programs are treated as if they could apply to any and all categories of infrastructure expenditure. The reason for this is that there are no reliable data on the ways in which firms make detailed expenditures on different categories of infrastructure. In theory, this assumption could lead to significant errors. As an illustration, imagine a state-level infrastructure grant program that provides funds for road building and improvement. Suppose that our model simulated that a firm would be spending $10 million on infrastructure for its new plant and that the firm would be eligible for $1 million from a road fund program. It is quite conceivable that, while the firm might have a total infrastructure expenditure of $10 million, it might spend only $0.25 million on roads. If this were the case, our model would award the firm $0.75 million too much.

Unfortunately, there is no easy way around this problem since, as we indicated earlier, there are no data providing sufficient detail for better modeling of infrastructure expenditure categories. How big a concern is this? Given the lack of data, it is impossible to provide a definitive answer; nevertheless, we are inclined to believe that the problem is minor. In practice, most infrastructure incentives are very small relative to the amount being invested in a new plant's infrastructure. Thus, the probability is reasonably small that our model will, because of the homogeneity assumption, award too much.

Principle 3: We assume that the use of an infrastructure incentive does not result in any substitution.

Consider the following example. A firm is about to invest in a new plant and believes it will have to upgrade the roadway connecting it to the city's existing street system. The firm would prefer a four-lane connection but for cost reasons decides to build a two-lane roadway. However, the provision of a state road incentive reduces the cost of road building just enough that the firm decides now to build the preferred four-lane roadway.

We discussed the more general version of this problem earlier in this chapter. There we were concerned that, while economic theory suggests capital subsidies result in the substitution of capital for labor, our model assumes the elasticity of substitution is zero. The model assumes that a firm employs a technology with fixed factor proportions and so does not respond to changes in relative input costs. We reiterate our justification for this assumption here, but now in the context of non-tax incentives.

First, no hypothetical firm model has comprehensively simulated the substitution effects of incentives because of the practical data and technical difficulties presented by such a research project. Although there have been empirical estimations of production functions showing the elasticity of factor proportions with respect to relative factor prices, there has been no work on the impact of incentives on factor proportions. In the much more specific infrastructure case at hand, there is absolutely no literature to guide our simulation of the situation. In fact, in order to accomplish such modeling within a hypothetical firm framework, an enormous amount of detailed data would be required on the various infrastructure-related and other costs experienced by the firm and on the amount by which incentives could reasonably be expected to reduce these costs. This information is unavailable. Modeling without such data is likely to introduce further error into our simulations.

Second, our research purpose is not to model investment decisions across space but to measure the standing offer. The standing offer is a standardized assessment of the worth of an incentive to a typical firm in a particular sector. The investment (and the composition of investment) of the firm is a given within the model (by the size and structure of typical plants within a sector), not as an outcome of the model. In other words, we measure the worth of various state and city incentive packages for identical amounts and compositions of investment. Thus, we ignore substitution.

Principle 4: We assume publicly funded infrastructure is no more expensive to produce than privately funded infrastructure.

It is possible that infrastructure supplied through incentives is more costly than infrastructure supplied without incentives. For example, many road programs have rules specifying maintenance and public usage, both of which are likely to increase the long-term costs of infrastructure provision and maintenance. If this is the case, then each dollar of public incentive money will only replace some fraction of each private dollar of investment in infrastructure. In situations such as this, our simulation will over-estimate the financial worth of an incentive to a firm. We return to this issue later in this chapter.

Principle 5: As we indicated in the discussion of substitution, we assume that the provision of a public subsidy does not change the size of the firm's investment. In theory, the profit-maximizing firm will add capital up to the point where the expected marginal income equals the marginal cost. Suppose that a firm receives a $1 million infrastructure grant (for simplicity's sake, assume also that the incentive may only be used on capital improvements). The opportunity costs of adding that $1 million of infrastructure will drop to zero; so, all other things being equal, the firm will add $1 million to its capital investment (provided that this does not result in the rate of return becoming negative). Incentives, inasmuch as they lower the cost of investment, encourage more investment. The reason we do not model the impact of incentives on the investment decision is that we are measuring the standing offer for a typical investment; we are not modeling the optimal investment.[11]

Wage Subsidy and Worker Training Incentives

The problems with modeling wage subsidy programs and worker training programs are much the same as those with infrastructure. It is unclear whether public funds replace private training expenditure on a one-for-one basis, or whether public training is less cost-effective than private training. It is also true that most public funds have associated conditions, which may mean that the cost of providing training is more expensive using public funds. For example, the program may require that workers be trained at designated community colleges, which may be less efficient at providing training than a private firm. Moreover, training funds, insofar as they function as a subsidy for labor, may promote some substitution. Generally, such monies may encourage firms to train workers more than they otherwise would have. Since there are no useful data on these issues, we have ignored them in the model. The worth of training and wage subsidies is measured in the same way as that of infrastructure subsidies. A public grant, loan, loan guarantee, or loan subsidy is valued as the amount by which its use raises a firm's 20-year after-tax cash flow.

General-Use Grants, Loans, Loan Guarantees, and Related Debt Instruments

General-use grants, loans, loan guarantees, and related instruments (such as linked-deposits and interest subsidies) may be applied to a wider list of asset classes than infrastructure or training incentives. Most often, general-use incentives may be used for all asset classes. The most frequent exception to this pattern is the limitation that public funds should not be used for working capital. Presumably, the funds applying this restriction do so with the goal of protecting the security of public investment. There are also a few funds that exclude other asset classes: plant and land, machinery, or infrastructure.

On the whole, we treat public grants as replacements for the private equity stake in an investment and public debt instruments as replacements for private-sector debt, provided that such replacements do not result in breaching program administrative rules. Some of the problems associated with the directed programs that have been discussed should not be as apparent with general-use incentives. In particular, while it is always the case that general-use incentives have rules governing the ways public monies may be spent, they usually do not have rules governing the mechanisms of spending. Unlike training programs, which often specify in great detail how training should be provided, or infrastructure programs, which specify how roads are to be built and maintained, general-use programs tend not to prescribe a particular spending mechanism. As a result, the efficiency problems are likely to be less obvious (although some may still exist).

However, as indicated earlier, the substitution problem remains. General-use grants, loans, and loan guarantees tend to cheapen the cost of capital and, thus, from a theoretical and possibly practical perspective, are likely to result in the substitution of capital for labor. We also ignore the impact of general-use subsidies on the size of the investment. A further problem pertains to the structure of public debt. Very often the public general-use debt instruments of a firm are subordinated. The result is that private debt is more secure and thus presumably costs less (at least in the case of smaller firms). We collected information on subordination but found no reasonable way to model reductions in private debt interest rates. TAIM thus ignores the rate effect that the subordination of public debt may have. On the whole, the worth of general-use grants, loans, loan guarantees and related debt instruments is treated the same as that of infrastructure and training subsidies: their worth is the increment they provide to firm income.

Generating Incentive Amounts and Incentive Terms

As simulated by our model, the amount a firm may receive from a particular incentive program is determined by applying the explicit rules of the program and by multiplying the average fiscal year (FY) 1992 incentive amount per job or per dollar of total investment by the number of new jobs or dollars of investment by the hypothetical firm.[12] The incentive ratios are based on data provided by state or local officials. From a practical standpoint, all of the rules applied by program officials (rules deriving from the state code or city ordnance, general-use departmental rules, specific program guidelines, and the informal input of program administrators) could not be simulated. This would have required creating a detailed "expert system" or "knowledge base" for each program in each city and state. Setting up such "expert systems" would have necessitated an enormous amount of historical information on each incentive. Program administrators, in our experience, would be unwilling to provide such detailed material, for the rather simple reason that most work with severe time and labor constraints.

We developed simplified "expert systems" for each state program. Here we applied a streamlined set of rules for every program:

- The maximum amount available from a program;
- The maximum amount per job created or retained, and per dollar of investment;
- Leverage ratios required and equity contribution required;
- Limitations on the size of a given program's contribution to a project and on a project's particular asset expenditures;
- Restrictions on the size of all public financing of a project;
- Other basic limitations—to firms of a particular size (however size is construed), to firms in particular sectors, and to firms headquartered in and out of state;
- Any other limiting rule that seemed crucial to the operation of the program.

The actual amount of the incentive simulated for a firm was determined by applying the preceding rules to the average of the historical ratios of public funds per job created or retained and public funds per dollar of investment size. In some cases, the size of an incentive award is based on a schedule, which we used to generate the actual incentive amount. Where a schedule-based program had to meet some other administrative criteria of the type that have been described, those criteria were applied to the award.

City programs could not be modeled in this way. The data we have on city grant, loan, and loan guarantee programs are not detailed enough to permit the creation of even the limited "expert systems" that have been discussed. Instead, we applied the historical ratios of public funds per job created or retained and public funds per dollar of investment size and then applied the relevant size limits (such as maximum incentive amount or maximum amount per job), finally adding the city incentives to the state incentives.

Many states and a few cities have incentive programs with some substantive overlap. For example, Ohio has two general-use capital programs, one of which is directed towards smaller firms. In fact, this pattern—a state having different programs for different sizes of firm—is reasonably common. However, in many cases, it is possible that a particular investment project may be eligible to receive incentives from more than one state incentive program of the same type. Based on our discussions with state officials, in cases such as these, states would be inclined to offer only a single discretionary incentive. Thus, the model must not only simulate a likely amount from each incentive program, it must also be able to create a package of likely incentives.

For general-use incentives, the following rules have been applied. If two programs in a state have a broadly similar purpose, they are treated as mutually exclusive. If a state offers more than one incentive in a broad category, our model simulates the amount for which a firm is eligible from each of these incentives and then chooses one for the firm. The one chosen is always that which, within the program rules, is worth more to the firm. This is interpreted to mean the one that most reduces the costs of debt to the firm. Practically, the present value of the flow of interest and principal payments on each public sector loan is compared to such payments on a private sector loan (these comparisons are made within individual asset classes and then summed over all asset classes).[13] TAIM is programmed to choose the public sector loan maximizing that difference between public and private loans.[14] In a few cases, this method results in large swings in the debt structure of the firm. As an illustration, very generous incentive loan programs with terms considerably shorter than those available for the same asset class in the private sector result in the firm retiring too much debt too early (the firm accepts a large and generous loan and pays it off quickly). The outcome is a sudden decline in debt at the end of the term of the public loan. This can result in a generous public loan actually lowering project returns.[15] To solve this problem, TAIM has an algorithm that refinances excessive early principal payments using the private debt market, thus maintaining a reasonably constant debt structure.

These same rules have been applied to the city incentive simulation. However, state and city incentives were treated as additive. If a state and a city within that state each has a separately capitalized general-use grant, and a firm is eligible for both, then the firm will receive both. The exception to the latter rule is that some city Community Development Block Grant (CDBG)-capitalized revolving loan funds effectively replace similar state-level CDBG loan programs and have been treated accordingly.[16]

Where there was more than one incentive within a particular category, but where each incentive program in such a category was aimed at a different substantive purpose, then the various incentives have been treated as inclusive or additive. For example, within the category of infrastructure incentives, a state may have a fund to provide roads and a fund to aid site assembly. Both of these programs will be included in the final package because they are aimed at achieving specific but non-overlapping goals. Pennsylvania has a very complex set of non-tax incentives. Within the broad category of general-use incentives, it has a loan program directed at subsidizing the purchase of machinery and another directed at the purchase of land. On top of these, it has a number of other general-use programs for a wide range of asset expenditures. In this case, the machinery-directed fund and the land-directed fund were treated as additive, but the programs whose activities overlapped are treated as exclusive. A firm may only receive incentives from one of these. We believe the application of this rule simplifies our comparison of non-tax incentives across states and agrees with the way that states and cities package incentives to firms.

There is one important complication to this scheme. Tax increment financing instruments (TIFs) pose special problems. TIFs are discretionary instruments financed out of future increments to property taxes (and sometimes payroll taxes).[17] Essentially, property taxes on real improvements are used to retire notes issued for those improvements. TIFs and property tax abatements work at cross purposes; because an abatement relieves the property owner of the need to pay taxes on improvements, it also removes the mechanism to retire TIF debt (at least for a period of several years), thus making such debt financially difficult, if not impossible. However, one can imagine a situation where the optimal financial solution for a firm would be TIF debt raised on *a portion* of property improvements, with taxes on the remaining improvements subject to abatement. This would be most likely in situations where the firm would prefer TIFs over abatements and could not (for one reason or another) make full use of TIF funds raised on all property improvements. Since this sort of situation is extremely unusual and would severely complicate our model, we treat property tax abatements and TIFs as mutually exclusive. Abatements are on the whole more generous than TIFs, so our model only assigns TIFs if abatements are not available in a community (the exception being payroll tax-retired training TIFs). Since the TIF is, in effect, a lump-sum payment made to the firm, which the firm does not pay back (essentially the city, county, school, and other districts pay it back for the firm out of diverted property taxes), we treat TIFs as grants. As is true for grants, the TIF is used to replace private equity investment and is applied to allowed asset classes.

Distributing Incentives across Asset Classes

Once TAIM has generated an incentive package from a state or city, it distributes the package to the appropriate asset classes. As indicated, infrastructure incentives are always applied to infrastructure, and wage subsidy and worker training incentives are always applied to working capital. In all instances, the distribution of these directed incentives occurs before the distribution of general-use incentives. In the case of general-use incentives, three broad principles apply: 1) funds are distributed only to those asset classes allowed under program rules; 2) the funds distributed to an asset class may be no greater than the expenditure the firm would have made on that asset class had the incentives not been available; and 3) insofar as this is possible under program rules, general-use funds are distributed first to plant and land, then to infrastructure, then to machinery, and finally to working capital. The reason for this order is quite simple. Public money is used, wherever possible, on assets that do not depreciate, or that depreciate more slowly, allowing private money to be spent on assets which depreciate more quickly. Because longer-lived assets are generally financed with longer-term debt, and because in normal times interest rates are higher the longer the term, this rule has the effect of substituting low-cost public money for the most costly private funds first. This arrangement maximizes the after-tax income impact of an incentive.

Awarding Grants, Loans, and Loan Guarantees

In the case of grants (and TIFs), once the various awards have been distributed to land and plant, infrastructure, machinery, and finally working capital, the model assumes that the recipient firm is able to make full use of all funds going to each asset class in the initial year of establishing the new plant. TAIM assumes that public grants are first used to replace private equity. In the case of loans, the situation is more complex. TAIM assumes that public debt is first used to replace private debt. The full loan award must be distributed across appropriate asset classes. Once this has been done, loan repayment schedules must be developed. This requires that appropriate interest rates, terms, and fees be applied to the loan for each asset class. A few programs had schedules that specified rates, terms, and fees by asset class or by size of the loan. Indeed, in a very few cases, the marginal interest rate increased by the size of the total loan amount. For those state programs that did not specify a schedule or a term and rate specific to individual asset classes, we use the lowest reported interest rate in FY 1992 and longest reported term (and where applicable, lowest fees) available in FY 1992, and we apply these to loans made to all asset classes. Thus, if a firm were eligible for a $1 million loan from a program that in 1992 had a low rate of 7 percent and a term of 10 years, and if $700,000 of that $1 million went to plant and land and $100,000 went to each of infrastructure, machinery and working capital, the 7 percent rate and 10-year term would be applied to each of these four amounts. One result is that, in highly unusual situations, public loans may still be outstanding on assets that no longer have value. As an illustration, most categories of machinery have a book value of zero after 10 years.

The only reasonable alterative to this method of applying the best rate and term to the entire loan is to restrict the term on a public loan for a particular asset class to no longer than the term available on a private sector loan for that class (or to the private sector term plus some chosen time period meant to account for the relative generosity of public loans). This latter strategy is highly arbitrary and is too restrictive. Our method seldom causes mistakes: most programs fund such a small proportion of the total investment that almost all public funds are applied to asset categories with the full 20-year life.

For our purposes, loan guarantee programs only serve to reduce risk on private sector loans by guaranteeing to a financial institution that a firm's loan will be repaid. Guarantees thus tend to have the effect of reducing interest rates on private sector loans. Our model treats a loan guarantee program as a public loan incentive; in other words, the model replaces a firm's private sector loan with a public sector loan at the now lower interest rate. Obviously, the loans secured by public guarantees are always private sector loans. However, from the point of view of the recipient firm, the guaranteed private sector loan functions as a public loan. Most guarantee programs keep records of the impact of the public guarantee in reducing interest rates. These reductions are then applied to our data on average rates for private loans. If a guarantee resulted in an average rate reduction of 1.5 percent, and if our historical data on private loans to finance working capital showed that the average rate for a loan of that size was 12 percent over three years, then a rate of 10.5 percent on a 3-year term to the loan would be applied by our model. Thus, one important difference between our treatment of public loans and guaranteed loans is that for the guarantee we always maintain the usual private sector term for that type of firm and that asset class, unless a different term is explicitly specified by the guarantee program. It is common for states to charge extra fees on loan guarantees (the fees usually help capitalize the guarantee fund). In our model, these fees are added to the interest payment for the first year, except where fees are explicitly multiyear. The private interest rate and loan term assumptions are described in Appendix B, Table B.2. In those cases where program officials were unaware of the impact of the guarantee on rates, we applied a standard rate reduction of 2 percent. This figure was near the middle of the range of the interest rate reductions reported in our surveys.

A very few states provide a "loan subsidy" incentive. Although this instrument is related to the loan guarantee, it operates in a different manner. For example, in Michigan, one program makes interest payments, for a limited period of time, on private sector loans negotiated by a firm. Effectively, the firm receives two subsidies. On the one hand, it receives a series of small grants—the interest paid by the state. On the other, because there is an implied guarantee that the state will make the required payments, the private sector interest rate is likely to be reduced. Our model treats "loan subsidies" as public loans but decreases the loan repayment schedule appropriately (the annual interest payment being reduced by the amount of the annual subsidy). Interest rates are reduced by the standard 2 percent used in loan guarantee programs with terms usual for specific assets classes in the private sector.

"Linked-deposit" programs also closely resemble loan guarantees. States or cities keep funds in specific financial institutions on the understanding that the institutions will make below-market rate loans to qualified firms. Thus, the "linked deposit" reduces the interest rate charged to the firm. We treat linked deposits as loan guarantees: private sector terms and fees are retained, and interest rates are decreased by an appropriate amount. The linked deposit loan is treated as though it were a public sector loan.

Adding State and City Incentives

For the complete simulation of a state and local tax and incentive regime, we first calculate a firm's local (and in a few cases, state) property taxes, then state non-tax incentives, then city non-tax incentives and TIFs, and finally add other local taxes, state taxes, and state and local tax incentives. One result is that if a state and a city within a state both offer a similar type of incentive, the state's incentive will be applied to the firm first. To illustrate, if a state and city both have a general-use loan program, the firm will have the state program applied to it first. This method is employed in order to simplify some of the more complex computational issues associated with the design of the model. This method would only miscalculate the best potential package available from a state and city in that state where the city and state loan programs were both large enough to cover most of the debt requirements of the firm and where the rate and term of the city loan were more favorable than the rate and term of the state loan.[18] In the state and local loan programs covered in this research, these conditions are never both true.

LIMITATIONS OF THE ANALYSIS I: THE ADMINISTRATION OF INCENTIVES ALTERS THEIR WORTH

There is tremendous variability in the way a given category of incentive is implemented at the state or local level. Insofar as the particular financial arrangements allowed by a certain discretionary incentive are clear and explicit, their impact on business operating costs may be calculated. Our general method for these calculations was presented above. However, before progressing any further, we need to discuss some of the broader empirical issues that the variability in program administration poses for modeling the worth of non-tax business incentives to private firms. We focus on a single crucial issue that clearly illustrates the impact of program administration on incentive worth: clawbacks.

Non-tax incentive programs usually come with a range of financial and nonfinancial rules and regulations. Commonly imposed nonfinancial performance requirements include the following:

- The recipient firm will create or retain a specified number of jobs.

- The jobs created will pay above some stated level, such as 75 percent of the county median manufacturing wage.

- The jobs created will not result in job cutbacks elsewhere in the state or city.

These performance requirements often have associated sanctions to encourage compliance from recipient firms. Such sanctions might include the cancellation of a subsidy agreement or the recovery of all or part of the incentive costs (Ledebur and Woodward 1990). These sorts of sanctions are generically referred to as program *clawbacks*. In most cases, the clawback operates in the following manner: a firm is given an incentive for relocation or expansion on the written understanding that it will either create or retain a certain number of jobs or make some compensating payment to the state. Not only do many major incentive programs impose clawbacks on recipient firms, they administer the clawbacks in quite different ways. We will discuss only two issues here: 1) defining performance and 2) monitoring performance.

Although much loved by politicians, job "creation" and "retention" are notoriously ambiguous concepts. The theoretical issue lies in the "counterfactual" problem faced by all attempts to measure the effectiveness of policy. Should all and any jobs created by a firm be counted as new jobs, or only those jobs that would not exist "but for" policy intervention?[19] How do we know what jobs would not exist "but for" policy? A similar set of issues arises over the meaning of job retention. There is also a range of more practical difficulties relating to job creation and retention. For full-time equivalents, how long need a job exist to count as new or retained? How long should a firm be given to create a specified job level, and, once that level has been achieved, how long need it last? Should a low-paying job count as much as a high-paying one? Programs that have job creation and retention requirements must attempt to answer these definitional questions. Peters (1993) found that major Midwestern loan and grant programs gave quite varied answers to these questions. In one incentive program, recipient firms were given two years to create jobs, in another program, three. Some programs required that the jobs, once created, should continue to exist for the life of the loan, while other programs left the period undefined.

Moreover, the actual monitoring of firm employment performance varied, with rigorous evaluation by field officers in some programs but not in others. Also, not all incentive programs reflected a willingness to impose clawback penalties on underperforming firms. In some cases, program directors felt the rigorous application of clawback penalties was rendered impossible by the need to maintain an understanding attitude towards the risks of business. One program director reported that he was concerned about the impact of rigorous enforcement on the state's perceived business climate.

It is clear that the day-to-day administration of incentives, particularly discretionary non-tax incentives, has direct financial consequences for a firm. Consider this example.[20] A firm, in the final round of its location search, is evaluating two industrial sites in two states. Site A offers a direct cash grant of $1 million from the first state's incentive program X; site B also offers a direct cash grant (of similar magnitude) from the second state's program Y. Each program has a stipulated maximum job/cost ratio of at least one new job for each $10,000 of incentives received. Thus, both incentives require the creation of 100 jobs. Both X and Y define job creation in the same way and have similar clawback requirements. However, Y's clawback regime is much more rigorously enforced, having a historical record of imposing clawback penalties in a higher proportion of cases than does X. From the point of view of the firm, the two incentive programs offer identical initial financial benefits and require identical performance. However, in the medium to longer term, accepting an incentive from Y is a much more risky proposition than accepting an incentive from X. If the firm does not meet its job creation performance requirements, the probability is that an incentive from Y will offer less financial benefit than an incentive from X.

This example could be made much more involved. Suppose that while X is less rigorous in imposing clawbacks, its definition of job creation is much stricter than Y's: X allows one year for job creation, Y two. A more difficult question then is, how the firm reacts to the admin-istrative complexities that are part and parcel of many, if not most, non-tax incentive offers. Theoretically, the firm could put a price on the risk associated with the more rigorous clawback regime, using well-known financial techniques. The costs associated with earlier rather than later job creation could also be calculated, but in reality it is unlikely that they ever are. The calculations would rely on too many unknowns (both about the future economic climate and the behavior of program administrators) to be of much practical use in making location deci-sions.

Although we have no scholarly evidence, we have yet to hear from program directors that potential firms were interested in their clawback rates. Certainly the survey-based location literature, contradictory as it is on the issue of whether incentives in general influence location deci-sions, is completely silent on how executives deal with more practical incentive matters, such as the specifics of job creation and clawback requirements, in their investment behavior.[21] Our model also ignores these issues. It should nevertheless be clear that the real value of an incentive, particularly a discretionary incentive, is mediated by the way the incentive is administered.[22] Firms may or may not deal with these issues in a quantitatively sophisticated way. Our models assume (and we believe) that they do not. On the other hand, it is quite possible that even if firms do not evaluate quantitatively the risks and associated potential costs of a particular administrative regime, investment and location decisions may still be influenced by the regime. For instance, rigorous clawback enforcement might be associated with a stormy local business climate and thus raise doubts about the real worth of an incentive package to a firm. In summary, business incentives have a range of associated administrative rules and conditions that have potential financial consequences for recipient firms. Whether firms take these rules and conditions into account when making location decisions, is unknown. TAIM ignores them.

This raises a much more general point. Colgan (1995) in a recent review of the impact of the General Agreement on Tariffs and Trade (GATT) on state and local business incentives, indicates that the agree-ment stipulates that incentives should be measured in a manner not too different from ours, except that we focus on the after-tax impact on cash flow, not on the before-tax comparison to sales. This latter point aside, the two methods are concerned essentially with differences in the cost of debt (and equity) between public and private financing. These differences are the basis for the calculation of the subsidy amount. However, a number of European negotiators to GATT claimed that this sort of measurement of public loans and loan guarantees fundamentally overstates their worth. Their argument was complex but is directly related to the issues surrounding clawbacks (and the worth of incentives) that we have discussed. Essentially, the Europeans argued that public loans and loan guarantees do cheapen the cost of debt for a firm, but that the administrative conditions associated with public loans (such as job creation and minimum wages) also impose significant and simultaneous costs on the firm. On the whole, the size of the debt subsidy is likely to be close to these performance costs. If this is the case, firms should on the whole be indifferent to public or private debt. For clarity, we will call this the "subsidy indifference" argument.

If the subsidy indifference argument is correct, then the method we have used to measure the worth of subsidies is entirely mistaken. Indeed, if firms are essentially indifferent to public or private debt, then the simulation of discretionary incentives is probably unnecessary. The only job for public policy is to make sure that the subsidies given are as close as possible in worth to the conditions applied.

However, the subsidy indifference argument is not correct. First, the argument did not prevail in the latest GATT agreement; rather, the method we have described did. Moreover, we know of no American city or state that has explicitly maintained that the conditions it imposes on subsidies are equal to, or even related to, the explicit financial worth of the subsidy. In fact, states and cities specifically advertise their incentives as reducing the costs of doing business. Also, businesses seek out incentives (Owen 1990), implying that firms are not indifferent to their use. It seems wholly inconceivable to us that states and localities are duping businesses into receiving debt instruments that only look as though they provide some public subsidy but actually impose costs equal to that subsidy, and that the businesses have failed to catch on. Nevertheless, we believe that public subsidies have conditions that probably do impose some costs on the firm. On balance, given that businesses actively search for subsidies, we assume that the costs are a small proportion of the subsidy itself. We know of no research that has looked at this issue in any empirical detail, and thus our model entirely discounts the costs implied by subsidy conditions. We believe that while our model probably overstates the worth of incentives, the overstatement is slight and applies across all states.

LIMITATION OF THE ANALYSIS II: COMPLETENESS OF THE NON-TAX PORTION OF TAIM

One central concern in a hypothetical firm simulation as large and complex as this is that something will have been omitted. In the case of taxes this is, of course, most unlikely. The tax code is part of local, state, and federal law. The concern is really about the completeness of and soundness of information on non-tax incentives. Unfortunately, a casual perusal of the most complete directories of state incentives (those published in *Area Development*, *Site Selection*, and by the National Association of State Development Agencies [NASDA]) shows discrepancies. Partly, this is a matter of the definition of an economic development incentive; partly this is due to difficulty in getting the correct information. It should be emphasized that none of these publications provides the detailed financial data necessary for our simulation: their discrepancies are over such "brute" facts as whether a program actually exists or not. Thus, our data, being much more detailed, may actually exaggerate this problem. Given the time, care, and effort we put into the collection of data, we believe that this is not the case; nevertheless, it would be foolhardy to claim complete accuracy even at the state level.

At the city level, the situation is much worse. There exist no reasonably reliable directories to guide the gathering of information. Moreover, many cities do not have a single department or agency that coordinates economic development. One result is that it is much less clear at the city level that our information is complete. However, there is a positive mitigating factor at the local level. It appears that the biggest and most important incentives that cities provide are abatements; we believe that our information on abatements is quite reliable, more so than our information on city grants, loans, and loan guarantees. On the whole, we found it difficult and time-consuming to obtain data on city grants, loans, and loan guarantees.

Still, some incentive programs are missing. Most federally and privately capitalized programs have been excluded, and mall and very infrequently used city and state programs have been ignored.[23] We have also left out what we call ad hoc programs—those not part of a state's or city's standard standing offer, but made with a particular investment in mind. Our justification for these exclusions is provided in Chapter 2. In addition, we have ignored some programs that could not be modeled without introducing significant bias into our results. City infrastructure programs have been left out, not because these are unimportant, but because modeling them would distort our results. Only a few cities have properly established economic development infrastructure set-asides. Nevertheless, almost all cities in our sample reported that they would provide some sort of help with infrastructure to a new investment. This assistance would not come from an established program but from a range of other ad hoc sources, such as general revenues and works department resources. At this stage, we do not believe it is feasible to model this type of help. Ignoring such aid while continuing to model formally established city infrastructure programs would inappropriately privilege the standing offer of some cities. As a result, we decided to disregard all local infrastructure programs. Similar problems arose with "payment in lieu of property taxes" incentives; these too, were ignored.

LIMITATIONS OF THE ANALYSIS III: TARGETING GEOGRAPHY

Many states and some cities have developed very complex targeting geographies for their various programs. Sometimes, small geographic regions in a state will be chosen for incentives (enterprise zones are an example); sometimes the value of an incentive available throughout the state will be increased in specified areas. There is tremendous variation in the areas targeted. In Washington, one incentive program is directed at almost the entire state but Seattle. In some Pennsylvania programs, counties are used as the targeting unit, while in Georgia individual census tracts (about 4,000 people each) are targeted. Moreover, states often have levels of targeting. A state may have a loan program that provides up to $1 million to a firm, at the prime rate plus 2 percentage points throughout the state, at prime in targeted areas, and at prime minus 2 percentage points in the most targeted areas. There is one further, very important complication in targeting geography. In Iowa, as in many other states, the terms of the state's major capital incentive program, the Community Economic Betterment Account (CEBA), do not necessarily change in targeted areas, but the likelihood of a firm receiving a loan is increased if the firm locates in a high-unemployment county. TAIM takes into account broad state targeting and targeting within enterprise and similar zones. At this stage TAIM does not cover any fine-grained state targeting (to the tract level, for example), nor does it take into account award probabilities such as those associated with the CEBA program in Iowa.[24]

CONCLUSIONS

The hypothetical firm method, properly implemented, provides the best measures of the burden of business taxes or the value of investment incentives across different sites. Most of the criticisms of the method are either misplaced or can be nullified by the appropriate use of assumptions and model structure. Studies measuring the average tax burden on a single-location firm for one year do not provide useful indicators of competitiveness either for purposes of making state policy or for purposes of conducting econometric analyses of the effects of or determinants of state policy. While the few recent studies assessing the marginal tax effects—rates of return on new investment by multilocation firms—do provide correct measures for the most part, they have not always dealt satisfactorily with the sales destination problem. Constructing a "median state" provides a simple way of modeling the destination of sales, with shares to taxing and non-taxing states that reflect actual sales patterns of manufacturing firms.

Aggregation remains an unresolved problem. Results of previous hypothetical firm studies, confirmed here, demonstrate convincingly that comparisons of sites are firm-specific, or at least vary substantially across industries. The value of incentive packages varies significantly by the characteristics of the firms modeled, so that it becomes crucial to model a variety of firms, to model firm and plant sizes that are relevant, and to avoid aggregating results inappropriately.

Modeling the tax system and incentive programs for many states and cities requires making numerous assumptions. We have discussed the major critical assumptions regarding the hypothetical firm method and the special and thorny problems peculiar to the modeling of discretionary incentives. A more detailed discussion of the operation of TAIM and the assumptions that underlie it is contained in Appendixes B and C.

NOTES

1. According to Ladd (1995), 17 states produce fairly comprehensive tax expenditure studies on a regular basis, and another 13 produce partial or intermittent studies.

2. A more recent study by J. Papke using the AFTAX model (so named because it measures the after-tax rate of return) is Papke (1995).

3. Researchers in Wisconsin, for example, by modeling six firms at the two-digit level, were able to say that the six industries represented in the study accounted for 60 percent of manufacturing employment in the state (Wisconsin Department of Revenue 1990). On the other hand, in the Massachusetts study (Brooks 1993), the five three-digit industries represented 20 percent of the state's manufacturing employment.

4. One can, of course, average a state's ranking across the different firms, recognizing that such an average ranking does not actually represent the competitive position of the state for an average manufacturing firm.

5. For example, Alabama's tax system favors domestic (Alabama-headquartered) over foreign (out-of-state) corporations in two ways: 1) the percentage of federal income taxes deductible is equal to income from Alabama operations divided by total firm income, which is 100 percent for our single-state firm headquartered in Alabama, but a small fraction for most multistate firms; and 2) domestic corporations are allowed a credit for income taxes paid to other states. Other factors that favor single-state or multi-location firms include the weight given to sales in apportionment, throwback sales, and the ability of single-state firms to fully utilize income tax credits (against a much higher state tax liability since most income is apportioned to that state), whereas multistate firms get the same credit (since it is based on the same plant investment or new jobs) but can apply it only against the small share of income apportioned to that state, the rest being apportioned to the taxing states.

6. The early AFTAX model described by Papke and Papke (1984) handled initial locations in up to three different states. The Wisconsin, Indiana, and Michigan studies assumed a single location for the firm.

7. Telephone conversation, Peter Fisher with Joe Malloy of the Wisconsin Department of Revenue, 1993.

8. If one divides state total property taxes paid on industrial property by state total assessed value of industrial property, the result is an average tax rate weighted by tax collections and industrial property value. A simple average of tax rates, on the other hand, weights the largest city and the smallest rural community equally.

9. This is accomplished by integrating a "knowledge base" (i.e., a set of computer-coded rules) with the financial model of each incentive and each package of incentives. The technical details of this are discussed in Peters and Fisher (1995).

10. However, we do not look at a related issue—the extent to which loan guarantees encourage "additional" or "additive" investment.

11. There are other reasons for not modeling the impact of incentives on investment decisions. First, we acknowledge that with most big investments, the state and city incentive package will be "negotiated" and an incentive "deal" will be struck; however, there is evidence that the investment decision of the firm will be influenced by incentives the firm believes, prior to the deal being struck, it will receive, or—at least—has a good chance of receiving (Owen 1990). The point is not that the firm fixes its capital plans before it seeks public funds, although it may, but that the firm will take into account "likely" subsidies when developing its original capital plans. Our own practical knowledge of how deals are struck supports this idea: the firm brings an investment plan to economic development officials, and based on that plan, the officials provide a package of incentives. From a theoretical standpoint this means that a firm will not always maximize its profits, since, in order to do so, the firm should continue adding to its capital stock until the marginal efficiency of investment equals the interest rate, adjusted for taxes and subsidies. In practice, this requirement may never be met. Work on the site selection process suggests that, because of data complexity, and thus cost, location decisions are made sequentially at various spatial scales. A firm will first choose a broad geographic region, then possibly a state within the region, a metropolitan area, and finally a site (see Blair and Premus 1987). Since lowest tax regions do not necessarily have the lowest tax industrial sites (and similar arguments can be made concerning inputs), firms may not end up maximizing their profits. This is well understood in the location literature. "A feasibility analysis must normally show that the proposed plan will earn a high enough [not maximum] rate of return to justify construction costs" (Blair and Premus 1987, p. 75).

The British literature on the impact of incentives on investment decisions, although somewhat dated, appears to support the argument made in the previous paragraph. Most of the British literature concerns the way investment decisions were influenced by Regional Development Grants (RDGs; entirely automatic regional subsidies available to all firms meeting certain basic requirements—equivalent to tax incentives in the United States) and Regional Selective Assistance (RSH; negotiated discretionary regional grants—equivalent to discretionary incentives in the United States). Most of the evidence suggests that the automatic subsidy was more likely than the discretionary subsidy to be incorporated into the investment decision, precisely because the former was automatic and the amount of the subsidy was given by a simple formula; "the discretionary element of aid generates uncertainty which reduces the effectiveness of the grant . . . The main reason for the non-inclusion of [the discretionary] RSA [as opposed to the automatic RDG] was uncertainty over both whether an award would be made and also the size of the award" (Swales 1989). For a review of this literature, see Begg and McDowall (1987); see also Allen et al. (1986). There have been contrary findings (McGreevy and Thomson 1983).

We interpret these findings as supporting two of our claims. First, discretionary incentives are probably less likely to affect investment decisions than are taxes and tax incentives. Second, ad hoc or special discretionary incentives of the sort discussed earlier in this chapter will probably have much less influence over the industrial location or the investment decision than will ordinary discretionary incentives.

12. Where fiscal year 1992 was not available, we used calendar year 1992. For those states with biennial budgets, we divided the data by two.

13. This same method is used with linked-deposits and loan guarantees.

14. TAIM does not optimize the choice of loan program on the basis of after-tax cash flow, but on the basis of direct loan costs to the firm. See Rasmussen, Bendick, and Ledebur (1984) for jus-

tification. We adopt this method for practical reasons. Optimizing on the basis of increments to project returns would slow TAIM considerably. In almost all cases, optimizing on direct loan costs rather than on increments to project returns has no impact on our results.

15. The reason for this is that such loans cause changes to the debt structure and thus to the income and tax structure of the firm. TAIM optimizes incentive program choice on the basis of loan costs, not after-tax income. Even if TAIM optimized awards on the basis of income, the debt-structure problem would remain, although it would probably be less visible. The text describes our solution to this problem.

16. City-level CDBG-capitalized revolving loan funds (RLFs) are usually available in so-called "entitlement" cities, meaning that they have direct access to federal CDBG funds. State-level CDBG-capitalized RLFs are directed towards "non-entitlement" cities and are not available in "entitlement" cities. There are, however, non-entitlement cities that have used CDBG funds received through state government to set up local RLFs.

17. Since we are concerned with manufacturing, sales tax TIFs are not included.

18. More precisely, the model would only miscalculate the best package where prior use of the "inferior" state debt instrument precluded full use (on any or all asset classes) of the "superior" city instrument.

19. Howland (1990) provides a very useful discussion of these issues in a program evaluation context.

20. The administrative rules in this illustration are based on rules culled from our sample of state programs.

21. Schmenner's (1982) survey work on locational incentives found that a very large proportion of firms were unaware of incentives for which they were eligible. If this is the case, it is unsurprising that there should be even less knowledge of the details of incentive administration. The situation in Europe may be somewhat different, with greater awareness of clawback regimes; see, for example, Bachtler (1990).

22. This is not a problem for general use programs only: similar problems arise for other types of incentives. Many states sponsor customized labor training programs that allow on-the-job training provided at the plant site. A common problem with on-the-job training is that its supposed beneficiaries, the firm's workers, do not gain much in the way of skills enhancement. In other words, the job training scheme acts as a disguised wage subsidy. Some states rigorously enforce their job training schemes to ensure that skills are provided to workers, while other states have much less stringent enforcement.

23. These are described in Chapter 2, note 6.

24. At this stage, TAIM merely has small databases on broad state targeting. However, it is highly impractical to deal with tract and other small-area targeting using this system. Clearly, there are thousands of tracts in most states, making the creation and maintenance of traditional databases much too labor-intensive. Moreover, in many American states, counties are so small that even the management of county-level information poses problems (Iowa, a state of fewer than 4 million, has 99 counties). An extension to TAIM deals with targeting geography by putting it directly into a GIS. TAIM then queries the GIS to discern the level of incentive for which a firm is eligible in the substate region.

4 Tax Systems and Incentive Programs in States and Cities

Are the variations in economic development incentives across states and cities large enough to make a difference? This has been a point of contention between critics and supporters of competitive economic development policy for many years. Critics have often pointed out that the value of tax breaks and incentive programs to firms is diminished by the income tax effects and that taxes, in particular, are a very small part of business costs. Thus, incentives are unlikely to affect most location decisions. Economic development practitioners have generally operated under the opposite assumption—that every program is effective for every location decision. The evidence from econometric studies of tax effects on economic growth, and from previous studies of tax differences using the hypothetical firm method, appears to support a middle position: differences in rates of return due to taxes are significant enough to influence location decisions at the margin and hence to affect rates of growth, even if the majority of location decisions are unaffected.

Previous empirical studies, however, have not incorporated the full range of tax incentives and so have not measured accurately actual after-tax rates of return on *new* investment. Furthermore, non-tax incentives have not been incorporated at all. This raises several questions that can now be addressed by the present study. Do tax and other incentives widen or narrow the differences among places in rates of return on new investment? Are differences "large" or "small" using various standards of comparison? Are non-tax incentives greater in value than tax incentives? Are the variations in returns among cities due more to the differences in state taxes and programs or to differences in local taxes and incentives? How important are enterprise zones and similar programs in changing the relative positions of cities in the competition for jobs? Is there a type of state/local industrial policy implied by the sectoral differences in rates of return? We explore these and other questions in this chapter. We do not address the larger issue of whether the tax and incentive variations measured by TAIM can explain the variation in state or local rates of growth; this must await subsequent research.

We begin by describing the tax systems and tax incentive programs in our selected states and cities, and we then explore the implications of making arbitrary distinctions between basic features of the tax system on the one hand and "tax incentives" on the other. We then consider the importance of states versus cities in establishing the tax parameters and incentive programs that affect rates of return. Next, we describe the range of non-tax incentive programs available in the states and cities in our study. We subsequently present the model results in terms of the spatial variation in taxes and incentives, and we investigate the issue of incentive size.

VARIATION IN TAXES AND TAX INCENTIVES

There was wide variation in 1992 among the 24 states in our study with respect to the relative importance of income, net worth, sales, or property taxes, and with respect to the definition of the base of each of these taxes and the tax rate to be applied. All 24 states have a local property tax that applies at least to business realty and a sales tax that applies to some business purchases. All but two have a corporate income tax; Michigan instead has a form of value-added tax called the single business tax, and Washington taxes businesses based on their gross receipts.[1] Both of these taxes are included in our analysis. Four of the income-tax states actually have a combined income-net worth tax, whereby the firm must calculate a tax liability based on income and a tax liability based on net worth, stockholders' equity, intangible property, or some other definition of wealth. The firm then pays whichever is greater, the income-base tax or the wealth-base tax. Another eight states have a separate wealth tax that is always additive with the income tax.

Sales Taxes

State sales tax rates vary from 4 percent in five states to a high of 6.5 percent in Washington and Illinois (see Table 4.1). These taxes apply to

Table 4.1 State Sales Taxes on Business Purchases as of 1992 (%)

State	General rate	Manufacturing machinery and equipment	Electricity and natural gas
Alabama	4.00	1.50	4.00
California	6.00	6.00	Exempt
Connecticut	6.00	Exempt	Exempt
Florida	6.00	Exempt	7.00
Georgia	4.00	Exempt	4.00
Illinois	6.50	Exempt	5.00 [a]
Indiana	5.00	Exempt	Exempt if used directly in manufacturing
Iowa	5.00	Exempt	Exempt if used directly in manufacturing
Kentucky	6.00	Exempt	6.00 [b]
Massachusetts	5.00	Exempt	Exempt if used directly in manufacturing
Michigan	4.00	Exempt	Exempt if used directly in manufacturing
Minnesota	6.00	Exempt	Exempt if used directly in manufacturing
Missouri	4.60	Exempt	4.60
New Jersey	6.00	Exempt	Exempt
New York	4.00	Exempt	Exempt if used directly in manufacturing
North Carolina	4.00	1.00	3.00 [a]
Ohio	5.00	Exempt	Exempt
Pennsylvania	6.00	Exempt	Exempt if used directly in manufacturing
South Carolina	5.00	Exempt	Exempt
Tennessee	6.00	Exempt	Lower rate (1.50) if used directly in manufacturing.
Texas	6.25	6.25	Exempt

(continued)

Table 4.1 (continued)

State	General rate	Manufacturing machinery and equipment	Electricity and natural gas
Virginia	4.50	Exempt	Natural gas exempt; electricity exempt if used directly in manufacturing
Washington	6.50	6.50	Exempt
Wisconsin	5.00	Exempt	5.00
Median state	5.00	Exempt	Exempt if used directly in manufacturing

SOURCE: Commerce Clearing House, *State Tax Guide*; American Bar Association 1993; Federation of Tax Administrators, 1991.

NOTE: In all of these states, other items of capital equipment (non-manufacturing machinery, furniture and fixtures, computers) are taxed at the general sales tax rate except that computers are exempt in Iowa. In several states, sales tax exemptions beyond those shown here apply in enterprise zones; see Table 4.4.

a. Rates are lower than general sales tax rate for the state.

b. In Kentucky, expenses for energy and energy-producing fuels used in manufacturing are exempt to the extent that such expenses exceed 3% of the cost of production.

purchases of furniture and fixtures, computers, and other non-manufacturing machinery and equipment by manufacturers in all 24 states.[2] However, manufacturing machinery and equipment have been excluded from the sales tax base in all but 5 of the 24 states, and only 6 states tax electricity and natural gas used by manufacturing firms at the full rate. Three tax fuel and electricity at a lower rate, eight exempt the portion of fuel and electricity used directly in the manufacturing process,[3] and another seven exempt fuel and electricity altogether. The exemptions for manufacturing machinery and equipment, as well as the exemptions or preferential rates for fuel and electricity used directly in manufacturing, could be viewed as tax incentives. They are targeted at the manufacturing sector, as are the majority of economic development incentives.

Corporate Income Taxes and Credits

State corporate income taxes are imposed in 22 of the 24 states in our study. The remaining two levy a value-added tax (Michigan) or a gross receipts tax (Washington) instead. Among the 22 income tax states, tax rates range from 4.5 percent in Texas to 12.25 percent in Pennsylvania (Table 4.2). These are flat rates applied to all taxable income; only 3 of the 24 states have a progressive rate structure, and among these 3 the highest top-bracket rate was 12.0 percent in Iowa. More significant than rate differences are variations in the definition of taxable income and in the credits permitted. In most states, the corporation's determination of taxable income starts with federal taxable income or with something practically equivalent to it. Federal taxable income is net of deductions for federal depreciation, state and local taxes on income, and property taxes, as well as other normal business expenses. Three of the 24 states then permit deduction of all or part of federal income taxes in arriving at state taxable income. Most states require the firm to add back in to federal taxable income the deductions for state income taxes. However, six states permit the deduction of corporate income taxes paid to other states (which in our model means the deduction of median state income taxes), and two states do not require the firm to add back their own state income taxes, in effect allowing the deduction of their own state income taxes. All but Indiana allow deduction of property taxes; California and New Jersey require use of depreciation schedules less accelerated than current federal law.

Once the taxable income of the corporation as a whole has been determined, the portion of that income taxable in the particular state must be calculated, assuming that the firm has operations in other states as well. This is done according to the state's rules for the allocation and apportionment of income. Generally, nonbusiness income is allocated (assigned) entirely to one state or another. Rental income is allocated entirely to the state in which the rental property is located, while dividends are usually allocated to the headquarters state.

Business income derived from the sale of the manufacturer's goods is apportioned. All but two of the income tax states use a three-factor apportionment formula: payroll, property, and sales. Each factor is a percentage: the firm's payroll paid out in the taxing state divided by its total payroll everywhere, property located in the state divided by prop-

Table 4.2 State Corporate Income and Net Worth Taxes as of 1992

| | Deductions from Income | | | Apportionment of Income | | | | | | |
| | Income taxes | | Other deductions | Payroll (%) | Property (%) | Sales (%) | Throwback sales | Income tax rate (%) | General credits against income tax | Net worth tax |
	Federal	Other state								
Alabama	Yes*	See credits		33.3	33.3	33.3	Yes	5.00	Other state income taxes*	Separate
California	No	No	Pre-1981 depreciation	33.3	33.3	33.3*	Yes	9.30		No
Connecticut	No	No		25.0	25.0*	50.0*	No	11.50		Integrated
Florida	No	No		25.0	25.0	50.0	No	5.50		No
Georgia	No	No	GA income taxes ded.	33.3	33.3	33.3	No	6.00		Integrated
Illinois	No	Yes		25.0	25.0	50.0	Yes	7.30*	Investment credit	Separate
Indiana	No	No	Property taxes not ded.	33.3	33.3	33.3	Yes	7.75*		No
Iowa	Yes (50%)	Yes				100.0	No	12.00*	New jobs credit	No
Kentucky	No	No		25.0	25.0	50.0	No	8.25*		Separate
Massachusetts	No	No		25.0	25.0	50.0	Yes	9.50	Investment credit	Separate

State									
Michigan*	No	No	Capital acquisition cost	30.0	30.0	40.0	Yes	2.35		No
Minnesota	No	No		15.0	15.0	70.0	No	9.80		No
Missouri	Yes (100%)	No		33.3*	33.3*	33.3*	Yes	5.00	Investment & jobs credits	Separate
New Jersey	No	Yes	Pre-1981 depreciation	33.3	33.3*	33.3*	No	9.00		No
New York	No	No		25.0	25.0*	50.0	No	9.00	Investment credit	Integrated
North Carolina	No	No		25.0	25.0	50.0	No	7.75	Inventory property tax*	Separate
Ohio	No	Yes	OH income taxes ded.	25.0	25.0	50.0	No	9.12*		No
Pennsylvania	No	No		33.3	33.3	33.3	No	12.25	New jobs credit	Separate
South Carolina	No	No		33.3	33.3	33.3	No	5.00	New jobs credit	Separate
Tennessee	No	Yes		33.3	33.3	33.3	No	6.00	Investment credit	Separate
Texas	No	Yes				100.0*	Yes	4.50		Integrated
Virginia	No	No		33.3	33.3	33.3	No	6.00		No
Washington*	No	No				100.0	No	0.484*		No

(continued)

Table 4.2 (continued)

	Deductions from Income			Apportionment of Income					General credits against income tax	Net worth tax
	Income taxes		Other deductions	Payroll (%)	Property (%)	Sales (%)	Throwback sales	Income tax rate (%)		
	Federal	Other state								
Wisconsin	No	No	No	25.0	25.0	50.0	Yes (50%)	7.90	Sales tax on fuel and electricity*	No
Median state	No	No	No	25.0	25.0	50.0	No	7.00	None	No

SOURCE: Commerce Clearing House, *Multistate Corporate Income Tax Guide*; state corporate income tax forms and instructions.

NOTE: * indicates an explanation is included in these notes. All states but two have corporate income taxes: MI single-business tax is a value-added tax, WA has only a gross receipts tax. Except as noted, all states allowed depreciation on assets acquired in 1992 or later essentially similar to current Federal MACRS depreciation, did not allow deduction of their own state income taxes, and did allow a deduction for property taxes. In AL, a percentage (income from AL operations divided by total federal income) of federal income taxes are deductible. Apportionment percentages are the weights applied to the firm's in-state share of payroll, property, and sales. MO allows firms to substitute single-factor 100% sales formula. Definitions of payroll vary only slightly among the states; property is defined as acquisition cost in most states, but CT, NJ, and NY use book value. Nonbusiness income is included in the sales factor only in CA, CT, NJ, and TX. Non-business income is generally allocated entirely to the state where earned; i.e, the location of the property. We assume dividends are allocated to headquarters state. However, nonbusiness income is apportioned in CT, MA, MN, and NJ, is not part of tax base in WA, and is allocated by a separate formula in NY and TN. Rates in all but six states are flat rates applied to all taxable income; for the three states with a progressive rate structure (IA, KY, and OH), the rate shown is the top bracket rate. In IL, IN, and OH, the rates shown are a combination of two tax rates (in effect, combining a regular and supplemental tax.) In WA, the rate is applied to gross receipts. General credits are those generally available to any corporation; credits available only in enterprise zones or the like are described in a later table. AL allows domestic (AL) corporations a credit for income taxes paid to other states. NC credit is for 40% of local property taxes on inventory of finished goods. WI allows credit for the sales tax on fuel and electricity used directly in manufacturing. Net worth taxes include all taxes on capital, stockholders' equity, or assets; they either operate as a separate tax or are integrated, in which case the firm usually pays whichever is larger, the income tax or the net worth tax.

erty owned everywhere, and sales destined for that state divided by total sales. The apportionment percentage is a weighted average of these three factor percentages. Ten states use equal weights; 11 weight sales more heavily, including 9 that double-weight sales (so that the payroll and property factors are weighted 25 percent each, sales 50 percent). Two states use single-factor apportionment, 100 percent based on sales, while another allows this as an option. The popularity of the apportionment formulas weighting sales more heavily is undoubtedly due to the advantage this provides to the exporting firm. It creates a tax incentive to locate a manufacturer's plant (and hence payroll) in that state when the majority of the goods will be sold in national or international markets.

Another important feature of the apportionment rules has to do with sales to states in which the firm has no tax nexus. Offices for the solicitation of sales are generally sufficient to establish a tax nexus that makes the firm taxable in that state; production facilities need not be located there. Nine of the 24 states require that sales to states in which the firm is not subject to state income tax (or to the federal government) be "thrown back" to the state in question, raising the sales factor and hence taxable income.[4]

Once taxable income has been determined—the sum of nonbusiness income allocated to the state and business income apportioned to the state—tax liability is found by multiplying the flat rate by taxable income or by applying a progressive rate table to taxable income. Credits may then be deducted to arrive at the final tax liability. We have modeled the significant credits generally available to manufacturing firms, and the investment or new jobs credits permitted statewide or in places such as enterprise zones. Investment credits are usually a fixed percentage of the acquisition cost of new property, plant, and equipment, sometimes subject to a minimum amount of new investment or a minimum number of associated new jobs. Jobs credits are either a percentage of the wages paid to new employees or a fixed dollar amount per new job. Only 8 of the 24 states have investment or jobs credits that apply statewide.

Property Taxes

The property tax is primarily a local tax, although 3 of our 24 states impose a small state property tax. The states play a significant role by defining the property tax base, by sometimes imposing ceilings on property tax rates, and by permitting or not permitting localities to provide abatements of local property taxes on new industrial property. The wide variation among states in the size of a manufacturer's local property tax bill, compared to its state income and sales tax expense, is also directly related to variation in the division of responsibilities between the state and local governments for funding certain kinds of programs, particularly the state share of education, health, and welfare programs.

Of the 24 states, 6 exclude all personal property from the property tax base; at the other extreme, 2 tax all classes of personal property fully (at the same assessment ratio as real property). The remaining 16 exempt some portion of personal property or require that it be assessed at a lower rate than real (Table 4.3). For these states that do tax personal property, exemptions for manufacturer's inventories or for manufacturing machinery and equipment could be viewed as tax expenditures or development incentives. Twelve of the 16 exempt inventories, and the other 4 tax only a portion of inventories or assess them at a lower percentage. Of the 18 states that tax personal property, however, only 2 (Kentucky and Wisconsin) exempt manufacturing machinery and equipment; another 4 tax this category at a lower rate than real property (Iowa, Ohio, and Tennessee) or provide a temporary exemption (Connecticut). Seven of the 18 personal property states exempt transportation equipment. Virginia is an oddity in that manufacturing machinery and equipment and transportation equipment are taxed, while other kinds of personal property are exempt.

Targeted Tax Incentives

Geographically targeted tax incentives have become nearly universal; 20 of the 24 states have enabling legislation for the creation of enterprise zones or development zones (generally areas smaller than a city, created at the option of the city), and 3 states have designated selected counties as distressed areas eligible for state development incentives (Table 4.4). Eligibility as an enterprise zone or distressed area is usually determined primarily on the basis of the local unemployment rate and some measure of income or poverty.

Of the 22 states with enterprise zone laws and/or distressed counties, 21 provide state income tax incentives and 7 offer sales tax incentives to firms locating in the zone or designated county. Ohio is the only state that allows enterprise zones but provides no associated state incentives, relying solely on local tax abatements to stimulate development. Four states provide investment tax credits (ITCs) only in enterprise zones; another four have statewide ITCs but provide more generous versions in zones. Fourteen states provide new jobs tax credits only in enterprise zones, while two provide more generous versions of statewide jobs credits in zones. Three states, in lieu of investment or jobs credits, simply exempt all or 50 percent of the income attributable to zone operations from state income tax. Four states provide such income exemptions in addition to credits. Tax incentives targeted to areas of high unemployment are now nearly universal, are usually much more generous than the statewide versions, and have all been established since 1981 (U.S. Department of Housing and Urban Development 1992).

BASIC TAX SYSTEMS VERSUS TAX INCENTIVES

Of the various features of the state tax systems described, only those with clear and explicit economic development purpose are separated in our analysis: the statewide investment and jobs credits and all the enterprise zone tax incentives. Other elements, including heavier weighting of sales in apportionment formulas and exemption of manufacturing machinery or fuel and electricity from the sales tax, are part of the state's "basic tax system." To provide an understanding of the relative importance of the major aspects of income, sales, and property taxes, some of which may indeed have been liberalized in response to state economic development concerns, Table 4.5 illustrates, for selected hypothetical firms, the value of each tax feature.

The first step in producing Table 4.5 was to generate after-tax returns from a new investment in a fictional high-tax state. This state is a "worst case": it has the highest (7.25 percent) combined state/local

Table 4.3 Property Tax Base, Effective Property Tax Rates, and Abatements Offered, by State, 1992

| State | State statutory assessment ratios and exemptions (%) | | | | | Effective property tax rates (%) | | | Number of sample cities | | | |
| | Real property | Personal property | | | | State | Local: real prop. | | Total | With EZs | With abatements | |
		Mfg. M&E	Inventories	Trans. equip.	Other M&E		Low	High			Citywide	EZs only
Alabama	20.0	20.0	Exempt	20.0	20.0	0.65	1.16		1	0	1	0
California	100.0	100.0	Exempt	Exempt	100.0	None	1.01	1.25	23	6	NA	NA
Connecticut	70.0	70.0*	Exempt	70.0	70.0	None	1.84	4.75	3	2	2	1
Florida	100.0	100.0	Exempt	Exempt	100.0	None	1.95	2.91	12	5	NA	NA
Georgia	40.0	40.0	40.0*	40.0	40.0	0.025	0.76	2.44	4	1	1	1
Illinois	33.3	Exempt	Exempt	Exempt	Exempt	None	2.44	3.55	5	5	0	5
Indiana	33.3	33.3	Part exempt*	Part exempt*	33.3	None	3.72	4.39	3	2	3	0
Iowa	100.0	30.0*	Part exempt*	Exempt	Exempt*	None	4.23	4.68	2	NA	2	NA
Kentucky	Local var.	Exempt*	Part exempt*	Local var.	Local var.	0.184*	0.97		1	0	NA	0
Massachusetts	100.0	Exempt	Exempt	Exempt	Exempt	None	2.51		1	NA	NA	NA
Michigan	50.0	50.0	Exempt	Exempt	50.0	None	2.31	3.90	5	NA	3	NA
Minnesota	100.0	Exempt	Exempt	Exempt	Exempt	None	4.81	5.30	2	NA	NA	NA
Missouri	32.0	33.3	Exempt	33.3	33.3	None	1.68	2.68	3	3	1	2
New Jersey	Local var.	Exempt	Exempt	Exempt	Exempt	1.3*	2.30	3.46	5	2	2	0
New York	Local var.	Exempt	Exempt	Exempt	Exempt	None	1.78	3.66	3	2	2	0
North Carolina	100.0	100.0	Exempt	100.0	100.0	None	1.32	1.40	2	1	NA	0
Ohio	35.0	26.0	26.0	Exempt	26.0	None	1.45	2.31	3	1	1	1
Pennsylvania	Local var.	Exempt	Exempt	Exempt	Exempt	None	1.92	6.56	5	2	3	0

South Carolina	10.5	Exempt	10.5	10.5	None	2.93	3.03	2	0	2	0
Tennessee	40.0	25.0	30.0	30.0	None	1.15	2.33	3	0	NA	0
Texas	100.0	100.0	100.0	100.0	None	1.84	3.13	10	9	10	0
Virginia	100.0	Exempt	100.0	Exempt	None	0.50	1.45	5	1	NA	0
Washington	100.0	Exempt	Exempt	100.0	None	1.21	1.83	5	0	NA	0
Wisconsin	100.0	Exempt	Exempt	100.0	None	2.87	4.23	4	2	NA	0
Median state	100.0	Exempt	Exempt	100.0	None	2.40		1	0	0	0

SOURCE: Prentice-Hall, *All States Tax Guide*; Commerce Clearing House, *State Tax Guide*; state statutes; authors' survey data.

NOTE: "M&E" refers to machinery and equipment. "Effective property tax rates" are taxes as a percentage of market value; local rates shown are the lowest and highest among the cities in our sample. "EZs" refers to enterprise zones or similar distressed areas with tax incentives. "Local var." means that the assessment ratio is not mandated by state law; it varies by locality. "NA" means not applicable, either because the state does not have an active enterprise zone program or because state law does not permit localities to provide property tax abatements.

*Asterisked items by state:

Connecticut: Manufacturing M&E is exempt for the first four years after it is acquired.

Georgia: Localities may choose to exempt inventories.

Iowa: Manufacturing M&E and computers are assessed at 30% of acquisition cost.

Indiana: Inventories are valued at 65% of cost, then assessed at 33.3%; inventories of finished goods destined for out of state are exempt; vehicles are exempt unless licensed for over 8 tons.

Kentucky: State tax rate shown applies to real property; lower rates apply to manufacturing M&E and inventories of raw materials and goods in process, which are exempt from local tax. Inventories of finished goods are subject to local tax.

New Jersey: State tax applied in 1993 to 50% of acquisition cost of personal property (excluding inventories and vehicles) in use as of October 1992 but was repealed for subsequent years.

Table 4.4 State Tax Incentives Available Statewide and in Enterprise Zones for Distressed Areas, 1992

State	Targeted program	Number of zones	Income tax credits		EZ income exemption	Sales tax exemptions and credits			Other tax incentives
			Investment	Jobs		Mfg. M&E	Fuel & elect.	All pers. prop.	
Alabama	EZs	12	EZs only	EZs only	Yes	None	None	None	
California	EZs & program areas	34	None	EZs only		EZs only (credit)	Statewide	None	Business expense deduction
Connecticut	EZs	11	None	None	50.0%	Statewide	Statewide	None	
Florida	EZs	30	None	EZs only*		Statewide	EZs: elect.*	EZs: 97%	Credit for EZ property taxes
Georgia	EZs	3	None	None		Statewide	None	None	
Georgia	Less developed counties	80	None	EZs only		Statewide	None	None	
Iowa	None		None	Statewide		Statewide	Statewide	None	
Illinois	EZs	90	EZ > SW	EZs only		Statewide	EZs only	None	
Indiana	EZs	15	None	EZs only	100.0%	Statewide	Statewide	None	
Kentucky	EZs	10	None	EZs only		Statewide	Statewide*	None	
Massachusetts	None		Statewide	None		Statewide	Statewide	None	
Michigan*	EZs	1	None	None	100.0%	Statewide	Statewide	EZs only	

							Credit for prop. tax/interest*	Job training credits
Minnesota*	EZs	5	None	EZs only		Statewide	Statewide	None
Missouri	EZs	50	EZ > SW	EZ > SW	50.0%*	Statewide	None	None
North Carolina	Distressed counties	33	None	EZs only		None	None	None
New Jersey	Urban EZs	10	EZs only	EZs only		Statewide	Statewide	EZs only
New York	Economic devel. zones	19	EZ > SW	EZs only		Statewide	Statewide	None
Ohio	EZs	227	None	None		Statewide	Statewide	None
Pennsylvania	EZs	45	EZs only	Statewide		Statewide	Statewide	None
South Carolina	EZs	3	None	EZ > SW		Statewide	Statewide	None
Tennessee	EZs	2	EZ > SW	None		Statewide	None	None
Texas	EZs	103	None	EZs only*	50.0%	*	Statewide	None
Virginia	EZs	18	None	None	100.0%	EZs only*	Statewide	EZs only*
Washington	Distressed areas (counties)	22	None	EZs only		None	Statewide	None
Wisconsin	Development zones	12	EZs only	EZs only		Statewide	Statewide (credit)	None

(continued)

124

Table 4.4 (continued)

SOURCE: U.S. Department of Housing and Urban Development 1992; authors' survey data; state enterprise zone reports; Commerce Clearing House, *Multistate Corporate Income Tax Guide*; state corporate income tax forms and instructions.

NOTE: Income tax credits are credits against the corporate income and/or net worth tax and are generally either a percentage of the value of enterprise zone investment or a jobs credit equal to a percentage of wages or a dollar amount per job. "EZ > SW" means that the credit available in enterprise zones is more generous than one available statewide. The "EZ income exemption" column indicates the percentage of taxable income attributable to operations in an enterprise zone that is exempt from state income tax. Sales tax preferences are exemptions unless noted as (credit), indicating an income tax credit. "M&E" refers to machinery and equipment. "EZs" refers to enterprise zones or similar distressed areas.

*Asterisked items, by state:

Florida: Jobs credit applies only to employees earning $1,500 per month or less; exemption from sales tax on electricity is available only if the municipality votes to exempt EZ firms from at least 50 percent of local public service tax.

Kentucky: Energy sales tax exemption only to extent that energy costs exceed 3 percent of production costs.

Michigan: EZ was allowed in only one city; purchases of machinery and equipment for use in an EZ are exempt from sales tax for the first 10 years.

Minnesota: As of 1992, "competitive zones" had been phased out; five small "border city" zones remained in cities bordering the Dakotas; credit is allowed for EZ property taxes and interest on EZ facility debt.

Missouri: EZ income exemption is for 10 years.

Texas: Jobs credit is called a refund for sales taxes paid on manufacturing M&E, but the credit is equal to $2,200 per job. We treat the sales tax paid as a ceiling on the jobs credit.

Virginia: All purchases are exempt from sales tax for the first 5 years that the firm is located in an EZ.

Table 4.5 Value to the Firm of Selected Features of State and Local Taxes: % Reduction in Tax Burden

Tax features	Firm #2: Furniture $40[a]	#4: Drugs $470	#5: Soaps $20	#7: Plastics $5	#14: Auto $600	#16: Instruments $180	Median state tax parameters
Sales tax: exemptions							
Manufact. machinery & equipment (M&E)	11.7	9.7	11.0	13.5	17.0	9.4	Exempt
Fuel & electricity: direct manufacturing use	3.4	1.2	2.2	6.6	2.5	1.9	Exempt
Median sales tax	15.5	11.3	13.6	20.8	20.1	11.9	6.0
State corporate income tax							
Federal depreciation allowed	0.0	0.1	0.1	0.2	0.0	0.1	Yes
Federal income taxes deductible	9.7	16.2	13.8	4.7	4.2	11.2	No
Other state income taxes deductible	2.2	3.5	3.1	0.9	1.0	2.4	No
Apportionment: double-weighted sales	2.9	6.0	2.1	2.4	0.3	4.8	Yes
Apportionment: throwback sales eliminated	1.5	3.0	1.1	1.2	0.2	2.5	Yes
Apportionment: both features	5.2	10.5	3.8	4.2	0.5	8.5	Yes
Median flat tax rate	5.6	9.5	7.8	3.0	2.2	6.8	8.0
Median corporate income tax system	9.8	17.9	10.8	6.4	2.6	13.7	*
Local property taxes							
Inventory exemption	16.5	8.6	15.3	16.0	13.9	17.5	Yes

(continued)

Table 4.5 (continued)

Tax features	Firm #2: Furniture $40[a]	#4: Drugs $470	#5: Soaps $20	#7: Plastics $5	#14: Auto $600	#16: Instruments $180	Median state tax parameters
Manufact. M&E exemption	22.8	16.4	20.0	26.4	34.8	17.7	No
Average personal property valuation	5.0	3.3	4.1	5.9	7.3	4.1	Yes
Median property tax rate	11.3	8.3	10.0	12.1	13.8	10.5	2.4
Median property tax system	28.6	18.0	25.7	30.1	31.0	28.0	*
Tax incentives							
Typical investment tax credit	5.0	4.7	4.7	5.1	6.2	4.5	None
Typical jobs tax credit	17.5	3.3	14.0	17.3	5.0	8.2	None
Both tax credits	20.7	7.0	17.4	20.3	8.7	11.5	None
Typical property tax abatement	32.0	20.3	28.9	36.5	33.2	23.4	None

NOTE: This table shows the percentage reduction in state and local taxes (i.e., the present value over 20 years of taxes attributable to a new plant) as a result of adopting each modification to a baseline tax system. The plant is located in a hypothetical city and state (population 6 million) where the baseline tax system includes a 6.0 percent state plus 1.25 percent local sales tax rate that applies to machinery and equipment and to fuel and utilities; pre-1981 depreciation; no deductions for federal or state income taxes; equal-weighted three-factor apportionment with throwback of sales from non-taxing states; and a flat 10 percent income tax rate. The 3 percent property tax rate applies to all real and personal property and employs a very slow depreciation schedule for the valuation of personal property. This represents the "worst" features of the 24 state tax systems and is approximately California's state tax system (with the addition of personal property tax system (with the addition of a tax on inventories and a higher tax rate). Changes are taken one at a time. The investment tax credit is 2 percent of plant and equipment; the jobs tax credit is $1,000 per new job. Both are nonrefundable, one-time credits but can be carried forward 10 years. The typical property tax abatement schedule reduced the following percentages of local taxes for years 1 to 10: 100, 100, 100, 90, 75, 60 45, 30, 20, 10.

*The median tax system is defined by the parameters shown in the last column.

a. Headings for columns should be read as "Firm #2, furniture industry, plant size = $40 million."

sales tax rate among our 24 states, with no exemption for manufacturing machinery or fuel and electricity; an income tax law that requires pre-1981 depreciation (which is less accelerated than post-1986 rules); no deductions for federal or other state income taxes; equal-weighted three-factor apportionment with throwback sales; and a flat 10 percent tax rate. (This state's income and sales taxes are identical to California's with two exceptions: California does exempt fuel and electricity from the sales tax, and the income tax rate is only 9.3 percent.) The property tax applies to personal property, including inventories and manufacturing machinery and equipment; the state guidelines for the valuation of personal property are the least favorable among the 24 states (Alabama's), applying the slowest depreciation rates; and the tax rate is a relatively high 3 percent.

We assume that a multistate firm headquartered in our median state builds a new plant in this mythical high-tax state. The project returns after paying state and local taxes in this high-tax state are then compared with returns for the identical investment in the same state but with all tax rates set to zero. The difference is the baseline state and local tax burden on the investment in a new plant.

The model then modifies one feature of the tax system at a time and recalculates net project returns and state/local taxes. Table 4.5 shows the percentage decrease in state/local taxes that results from each tax modification. This allows us to compare the relative value to the firm of different conditions, such as a property tax versus a sales tax exemption. The model also shows the tax reduction resulting from adopting the median version of each tax; the median sales tax, for example, is a 5 percent state plus 1 percent local rate with exemptions for both manufacturing machinery and fuel and electricity. Median taxes are constructed by using, for each feature or rate, the median value among our 24 states, shown in the right-hand column of the table. Results are shown for six multistate firms that portray the diversity of characteristics underlying wide variation in tax burdens.

Somewhat surprisingly, the sales tax exemption for manufacturing machinery is one of the most valuable incentives, in all six cases of more value to the firm than double-weighting sales, and of much more importance than the impact of allowing federal depreciation under the state corporate income tax. Eliminating the throwback sales rule is about half as valuable as double-weighting sales; changing both features of the apportionment rules to the median position saves the firm from about 4 percent to 11 percent of its tax burden, except for firm number 14. The two rules together are worth more than the sum of the individual percentages because the double weighting of sales is more advantageous when the factor does not include throwback sales.

Table 4.5 illustrates the importance of property taxes. Changing even a relatively obscure feature of the property tax system—substituting the average state guidelines or rules for valuation of personal property in order to arrive at full value (before applying assessment ratios) for Alabama's rules—turns out to be of more significance for these firms than depreciation rules or state income tax deductibility under the income tax.

The three most common incentives with explicit economic development purposes, and the only tax incentives that we model separately, are included in Table 4.5 for comparison with the other tax features that are less clearly for economic development and that are part of our "basic tax system." The value of the "typical" investment tax credit (2 percent of plant and equipment) or jobs tax credit ($1,000 per new job) is comparable to the benefit from such tax features as a total exemption of manufacturing machinery and equipment from the sales tax or liberalization of apportionment rules. The typical property tax abatement program, on the other hand, is worth much more, about a fifth to a third of the firm's total state/local tax burden.

It is clear from Table 4.5 that a study of state and local incentive competition must include a complete modeling of the state and local taxes that fall directly on business, as well as of the explicit tax incentives. Two-thirds of the states in our sample have no statewide investment or jobs tax credits, yet tax policy in these states may very well have been driven by economic development concerns over the past two decades as much as in the states with incentives. Those concerns may have resulted in liberalized sales tax exemptions or apportionment rules, or simply in reduced tax rates, rather than in tax credits.

THE IMPORTANCE OF STATE VERSUS LOCAL TAXES AND TAX INCENTIVES

Is variation in taxes and incentives among cities within a state more significant than variations across states? There is reason to believe that the state is more important than the locality. States play a very important role in setting the parameters of local taxation and in providing or limiting the use of tax incentives. The level of local property taxation is affected strongly by state policy regarding the functional responsibilities of the state versus local governments and by the share of local spending on education, mental health, and other programs financed by state grants or shared revenues. States also define the property tax base and assessment rules; set limits on property tax rates on increases in local spending, or on growth in assessments; limit local indebtedness; and establish policies on bond approval. In addition, states determine what nonproperty taxes are available to local governments (such as sales and corporate income taxes) and often set limits on rates for such taxes.

Our sample of cities is too small to determine the extent of variation in returns across cities within each state. We can, however, examine how states vary in terms of the relative importance of state versus local taxes and in the relative magnitude of state versus local tax incentives. We can also analyze the extent to which low state taxes (or large state incentives) compensate for high local taxes (or small local incentives). To accomplish these comparisons, we created 24 "representative cities," one for each state, and gave each city the median or "typical" sales tax rate, property tax rate, and property tax abatement schedule among the cities in that state in our study.

It is important to note the limitations of this analysis; the median is in most states defined by a small group of one to five cities. While the city sample was drawn randomly, the sample for any one state (except California, Florida, and Texas) is too small to produce a reliable estimate of the state median. For property taxes, this was deemed a serious problem. As a result, we relied on other data sources to a large extent in determining average property tax rates for each state. The data sources and rates are described in Appendix A. There is no alternative data source for typical property tax abatement schedules; we were forced to use a schedule typical of the cities in our sample.

Table 4.6 summarizes the results of the representative city analyses for the 5 multistate firms that best illustrate the important firm differences among cities and for the average of all 16 firms. Effective state tax rates measure the reduction in project returns that results when state income, net worth, and sales taxes are introduced into the analysis. Each firm's project returns in a particular state, after state taxes but no local taxes, are compared with project returns if the same firm (headquartered in the median state) had built the new plant instead in a hypothetical state having no taxes.[5] State tax burdens are measured net of the effects of federal deductibility. The effective tax rate is equal to the state tax burden (measured as the reduction in the present value of project cash flow) divided by the present value of income attributable to the new plant before all taxes (federal, state, and local). Similarly, the local tax burden is the further reduction in project returns (after federal and state taxes) caused by introducing local sales, income, and property taxes.

The range of effective tax rates is quite large, both at the state and at the local level. As would be expected, the interstate variation in combined state/local tax rates is less than the variation in either state or local taxes considered separately; states with high state tax rates tend to have below-average local tax rates, and vice versa. This is reflected in the share of local taxes in the combined state-local tax burden, which varies greatly. (The highest local share would be about 60 percent instead of 98 percent were it not for one state with very low corporate income taxes on multistate firms, due to single-factor apportionment with no throwback sales; this state has by far the lowest effective state tax rate, but high property taxes.) The highest combined state-local tax rate is generally about three times the lowest rate.

Differences across states are not reduced by tax incentives. One might expect that state and local tax incentives are larger in places with higher tax rates; that is, the incentives are compensating for high basic taxes. This does not appear to be the case; the variation in combined state-local effective tax rates is about the same with general (non-enterprise zone) tax incentives included as it is with no tax incentives. When enterprise zone incentives are added, the variation in tax rates actually increases. Enterprise zone incentives are not offsetting higher basic

Table 4.6 Effective Tax Rates in a Representative City in Each State (as a Percentage of New Plant Income before Taxes)

Taxes	Effective tax rates (%)			Coefficient of variation*
	Lowest	Mean	Highest	
Basic state taxes				
#2: Furniture	0.2	4.2	9.1	0.41
#5: Soaps	0.0	4.4	11.7	0.50
#7: Plastics	0.5	5.1	9.2	0.38
#14: Autos	0.2	5.3	12.9	0.57
#16: Instruments	0.2	3.4	6.6	0.38
Average: all 16 firms	0.2	4.6	10.5	0.45
Basic local taxes				
#2: Furniture	1.3	3.9	8.3	0.48
#5: Soaps	0.9	2.8	6.0	0.50
#7: Plastics	2.2	7.0	14.5	0.48
#14: Autos	2.6	9.3	19.0	0.49
#16: Instruments	1.0	2.8	6.0	0.49
Average: all 16 firms	1.6	4.9	10.5	0.50
Basic state and local taxes				
#2: Furniture	4.4	8.1	13.1	0.28
#5: Soaps	3.0	7.2	13.4	0.33
#7: Plastics	7.5	12.1	21.2	0.30
#14: Autos	7.0	14.7	26.5	0.39
#16: Instruments	3.1	6.2	9.8	0.25
Average: all 16 firms	5.0	9.5	16.6	0.31
Local taxes as a percentage of state and local taxes				
#2: Furniture	21.4	48.4	96.5	0.38
#5: Soaps	12.7	40.6	98.3	0.47
#7: Plastics	28.9	56.6	93.4	0.30
#14: Autos	31.3	62.6	97.8	0.28

(continued)

Table 4.6 (continued)

Taxes	Effective tax rates			Coefficient of variation*
	Lowest	Mean	Highest	
#16: Instruments	20.2	45.6	95.1	0.40
Average: all 16 firms	21.1	49.3	96.4	0.38
State and local taxes after non-EZ tax incentives				
#2: Furniture	2.8	7.5	11.6	0.27
#5: Soaps	1.7	6.7	13.4	0.34
#7: Plastics	6.1	11.2	17.0	0.25
#14: Autos	6.9	13.2	23.9	0.35
#16: Instruments	2.1	5.8	8.3	0.25
Average: all 16 firms	3.6	8.7	14.7	0.30
State and local taxes after all tax incentives				
#2: Furniture	2.8	6.1	9.6	0.31
#5: Soaps	1.7	5.6	10.2	0.36
#7: Plastics	4.9	9.4	15.9	0.34
#14: Autos	4.1	11.1	23.8	0.47
#16: Instruments	2.1	4.9	7.2	0.29
Average: all 16 firms	3.2	7.3	13.2	0.35

NOTE: Data refer to multistate firms only. The basic tax rate is the difference between the present value of new plant cash flow after all basic taxes and the present value of new plant cash flow in the absence of taxes levied by the state and city in which the new plant is located, divided by the present value of income attributable to the new plant before all federal, state, and local taxes. The state and local tax rate after non-enterprise zone tax incentives is the effective tax rate after investment and jobs tax credits available statewide and after local property tax abatements available city-wide.
*Coefficient of variation = standard deviation/mean.

taxes on average. There are also wide differences in tax rates across firms, reflecting differences in profitability, the proportion of assets subject to the sales tax or property tax, and other factors.

Effective tax incentive rates can be calculated in a similar fashion by dividing the value of the incentive (that is, the present value of the increment in cash flow caused by the incentive) by income before taxes. Incentive rates could be interpreted as negative tax rates. Table 4.7 shows the average and highest incentive rate among the 24 representative cities and the variation in rates across cities.

Where the state provides enterprise zone tax credits, or allows cities to do so, we have given the representative city an enterprise zone. However, even though enterprise zones are fairly numerous in many states, it does not appear that a significant portion of job growth occurs inside enterprise zones in more than a few states. We computed annual average net employment growth between 1980 and 1990 for each of our 24 states. From published data on jobs created in enterprise zones by state and the number of years such zones existed (U.S. Department of Housing and Urban Development 1992), we also calculated average annual jobs created inside enterprise zones. We were then able to calculate the ratio of jobs created in enterprise zones to total state job growth.

The results are suggestive but certainly not definitive. Data are missing from the HUD study for Indiana and North Carolina, and the accuracy of state-reported jobs data is quite doubtful. Illinois, for example, reports having produced about 29,000 jobs in enterprise zones per year over the first nine years of the program, while total state job growth has averaged about 10,000 per year. The two numbers can be reconciled only by assuming an average annual net loss of about 19,000 jobs from areas of Illinois outside enterprise zones, either to Illinois enterprise zones or to other states. Ohio claims that almost 14,000 jobs per year have been created in enterprise zones, or about 27 percent of the average annual job growth in 1980. Apart from Ohio and Illinois, enterprise zone jobs appear to account for 4 percent to 9 percent of annual job growth in six states: Connecticut, Florida, Kentucky, Missouri, New Jersey, and Texas. In the remaining 10 states with data, the percentage was about 2 percent or less, including 5 where it was under 0.5 percent. These figures compare gross job creation in zones with net job growth in the state; the significance of enterprise zones would appear even smaller if the numerator were net zone job creation or the denominator were gross state job creation.

Arguably, the typical city for a particular state should include an enterprise zone only if the majority of likely sites for industrial expansion in that state are located within enterprise zones. This is unlikely to be the case in any state. For this reason, Table 4.7 includes a section showing tax incentive rates among the 24 cities with all enterprise zone incentives eliminated.

There is even wider variation in tax incentive rates, at the state and at the local level, than in basic tax rates. Once again, however, the variation across states is substantially reduced when one combines state and local incentives. States where local tax incentives are limited tend to offer larger state tax breaks, and vice versa. Interestingly, enterprise zone incentives considerably decrease the differences across states. The coefficient of variation for state/local tax incentives without enterprise zones is about 1.6; this is reduced to about 0.75 with the introduction of enterprise zone incentives. This suggests that enterprise zone incentives are largest in the states with the smallest general tax incentives. Overall, state and local tax incentives represent a substantial portion of the state/local tax burden, averaging abut 23 percent but reaching as high as 65 percent in some states for some firms.

NON-TAX INCENTIVE PROGRAMS AND THEIR VALUE TO THE FIRM

As we argued in Chapter 1, a common mistake made by both popular and academic analysts is to assume that the value of an incentive is the nominal amount of a subsidy award. This ignores the impact of taxes on non-tax awards and also has the effect of counting apples (a $1 million grant) with oranges (a $1 million loan). The two central aims of TAIM are to model different incentive awards appropriately and then to capture the effects of federal, state, and local taxes on the private benefits provided by non-tax subsidies.

The impact of taxes on non-tax incentives can be measured in a number of ways. The simplest is provided by running the TAIM model, but replacing actual state and local non-tax incentives with a standard

Table 4.7 Effective Tax Incentive Rates in a Representative City in Each State (as a Percentage of New Plant Income before Taxes)

| Tax incentive | Effective rate (%) | | Coefficient of variation |
	Mean	Rate	
State tax incentives			
#2: Furniture	1.1	5.2	1.04
#5: Soaps	1.0	4.2	1.03
#7: Plastics	1.3	5.1	0.94
#14: Autos	1.2	4.8	1.08
#16: Instruments	0.6	2.4	0.92
Average: all 16 firms	1.0	4.3	1.00
Local tax incentives			
#2: Furniture	0.9	4.2	1.27
#5: Soaps	0.6	2.3	1.23
#7: Plastics	1.4	6.1	1.31
#14: Autos	2.4	9.8	1.26
#16: Instruments	0.7	3.0	1.27
Average: all 16 firms	1.1	4.8	1.26
State and local tax incentives			
#2: Furniture	2.0	5.2	0.72
#5: Soaps	1.6	5.2	0.76
#7: Plastics	2.7	6.8	0.74
#14: Autos	3.6	9.8	0.83
#16: Instruments	1.3	3.4	0.74
Average: all 16 firms	2.2	6.0	0.75
State and local tax incentives: percentage of state/local taxes			
#2: Furniture	24.1	56.7	0.64
#5: Soaps	21.9	59.6	0.68
#7: Plastics	22.1	54.8	0.68
#14: Autos	24.6	65.1	0.77
#16: Instruments	20.8	56.6	0.68
Average: all 16 firms	22.5	58.1	0.69

| | Effective rate (%) | | Coefficient |
Tax incentive	Mean	Rate	of variation
Stateand local tax incentives: no EZ incentives			
#2: Furniture	0.6	3.3	1.50
#5: Soaps	0.5	2.5	1.60
#7: Plastics	0.9	6.1	1.74
#14: Autos	1.5	9.0	1.66
#16: Instruments	0.4	2.3	1.53
Average: all 16 firms	0.7	4.2	1.59

NOTE: Data refers to multistate firms only. Tax incentive rate is the difference between the present value of new plant cash flow after taxes and incentives and the present value of new plant cash flow after basic taxes only, divided by the present value of before-tax income. In all cases, the minimum value is zero.

incentive scenario across all 112 locations. In this case, the standard incentive is a $100,000 grant with no important threshold limits for the 16 firms under consideration. In effect, each investment is given $100,000 in cash. For multistate firms, the cash grant of $100,000 improves 20-year cash flow by $61,318 on average; for single-location firms, the figure is $60,494. In the case of multistate firms the range around the mean is small ($1,896), but for single-location firms it is roughly 10 times that amount ($18,154). On the whole, multistate firms benefit by 60–62 cents per nominal award dollar, single-location firms by 58–73 cents. Where does the rest of each award dollar go? Indirectly, it is recaptured through federal, state, and local income taxes. One obvious result is that a state's or city's subsidy to a firm effectively transfers tax revenues to other taxing jurisdictions, including possibly neighboring or competing states and cities. Thus, non-tax incentives produce the paradoxical result of subsidizing both private investment and other jurisdictions.

There is minor variation in the worth of incentives across sectors. To illustrate, the multistate small furniture and fixtures firm benefits by an average increment to returns of $61,407 ($61,106, single-location) with a range of $1,625 ($8,888, single-location). In the case of the large drugs firm, the benefit average is $61,290 ($60,866, single-location), the range $546 ($8,567, single-location). The relative size of the multistate range compared to the single-location firm range remains constant and large across sectors. The reason for this is that, under the single-location firm assumptions, states are better able to tax the private benefits provided by grants, loans, and so on, because firms have all plant and employment in-state. Thus, differences among state tax regimes show up much more visibly.

Of course, states and cities vary not only in the way their tax regimes limit the benefits of non-tax incentives but also considerably in the menu of non-tax incentives they offer. Table 4.8 summarizes the non-tax state incentives modeled. It is important to emphasize again that all the states had many more non-tax incentives than those listed in the table. Table 4.8 covers only major programs that made awards to more than just a couple of firms in 1992.

Almost all states offer a general customized training incentive, and, of the two that do not, Massachusetts has a variety of other training plans, including customized programs (all of which were occupationally or sectorally too specific to meet our inclusion criteria), and South Carolina has noncustomized programs. In most cases, training is provided in the form of a grant or grant equivalent. In Michigan, however, the state makes interest payments on training loans. In both Iowa and Missouri, one training grant is actually a variety of a tax increment financing instrument. In most cases, infrastructure subsidies are provided not by state departments of economic development but through state departments of transportation. Usually subsidies are in the form of a grant, and most states offer such programs. Few states offer general-use grants; mostly, general-use programs are loans, loan guarantees, linked deposits, or related instruments.

Table 4.8 should not be read as providing an indication of a state's overall development effort. First, the number of programs offered within a class of program says nothing of the state's generosity to business. Pennsylvania, as an example, has four quite distinct general-use programs, but even when combined they are still less generous than some single general-use programs. Second, Table 4.8 makes some states look much less generous than they actually are. This is particularly true of Florida, Massachusetts, and Minnesota. In Florida, the state disburses funds to regional Community Development Corporations, which then award subsidies to clients. Since the state has limited

Table 4.8 State Non-Tax Incentive Programs That Were Simulated

State	General-use grant	General-use loan	General-use loan guarantee[a]	Infrastructure grant	Infrastructure loan	Training grant	Training loan
Alabama		1	1	3		1	
California		1		1		1	
Connecticut		2	1			1	
Florida	1			1		1	
Georgia						1	
Illinois		2				1	
Indiana			1			1	
Iowa	2[b]			1		2[c]	
Kentucky		1		1		2	
Massachusetts		1	1				
Michigan		2		1			1[d]
Minnesota						1	
Missouri		1	2			2[c]	
New Jersey		1	1			1	
New York		2		1		2	
North Carolina				1		1	
Ohio		1	1			1	

Pennsylvania	4			1
South Carolina	1		1	1
Tennessee	1		1	1
Texas	1[e]			1
Virginia	1	1	1	1
Washington			1	1
Wisconsin	2		1	1

a. Including loan subsidies and linked deposits.
b. The Community Economic Betterment Account (CEBA) and Economic Development Set Aside (EDSA) are both loans convertible to grants.
c. One of these is a job-training tax increment financing instrument (TIF).
d. The Michigan Training Incentive Fund is a loan subsidy program.
e. The Texas capital program covers two related programs.

control over these funds once they are disbursed, we count them as a local program, and they do not appear in Table 4.8. Much the same is true in Minnesota, where the state also awards funds to local agencies. Third, the terms and administration of programs—even with a single program class—vary enormously. Obviously, the benefits of loans and other debt instruments are crucially dependent on the rates, terms, and fees applied. Moreover, as we argued in Chapter 3, the administration of programs by state officials can seriously affect the worth of a subsidy.

At the local level, almost all cities claimed that they would provide infrastructure help (including site development) if needed, but in the vast majority of cases, no separate infrastructure program had been established. Almost no cities offered dedicated, customized industrial training incentives. Loans were the most common formally established non-tax subsidy at the local level (slightly under a third had such programs), although a few cities offered grants, convertible loan/grants, and loan guarantees. Most often, local general-use programs were capitalized through CDBG funds. Numerous cities offered Small Business Administration (SBA) financing through local 503/504 investment companies; in fact, many displayed such financing prominently in their economic development literature. As we indicated earlier, these programs were not included in our analysis. Although a number of cities offered some form of tax increment financing subsidy, in the majority of cases these instruments were either reserved for retail development or were less generous than the local property tax abatement subsidy. As a result, TAIM simulates tax increment financing awards for only 10 cities in our sample.

Which are more significant, tax incentives or non-tax incentives? For all 16 firms modeled, state non-tax incentives are vastly more important than state tax incentives. In the most extreme case—the small multistate furniture and fixtures firm—97 percent of the entire incentive package derives from non-tax incentives. Of the 16 firms modeled, the largest contribution of state tax incentives to the entire *state* incentive package is only 18 percent (see the first two columns of Table 4.9). Proportionately, small plants benefit more from state non-tax incentives than do large plants. Nevertheless, the limited contribution of state tax incentives to the entire state incentive package is quite startling. This is particularly so if the state proportions are compared to those of the

Table 4.9 Composition of Incentives (Mean Increment to Cash Flow, %)

Firm	All state incentives		All state and city incentives		All state non-tax incentives		
	Tax	Non-tax	Tax	Non-tax	Infrastructure	Training	General-use
Small, furniture and fixtures	3	97	20	80	13	29	58
Large, furniture and fixtures	11	89	43	57	25	43	32
Small, drugs	10	90	46	54	29	38	34
Large, drugs	18	82	75	25	32	47	22
Small, soaps	10	90	41	59	21	35	44
Large, soaps	15	85	59	41	32	44	24
Small, plastics	4	96	25	75	12	27	60
Large, plastics	12	88	51	49	29	40	31
Small, industrial machinery	7	93	33	67	15	31	54
Large, industrial machinery	15	85	64	36	32	45	23
Small, electronics	9	91	35	65	19	38	43
Large, electronics	16	84	35	65	32	46	23
Small, autos	13	87	64	36	30	46	25
Large, autos	18	82	54	46	30	49	20
Small, instruments	5	95	75	25	13	34	54
Large, instruments	14	86	26	74	32	45	23

NOTE: Numbers in table do not always sum to 100% due to rounding.

combined state and local incentive package (third and fourth columns of Table 4.9), where tax incentives play a much more important role. Indeed, for some firms (large drug firms, small instruments firms), three-quarters of the entire state/local incentive package derives from tax incentives. Of the four cases where the contribution of tax incentives to the entire package is little (a third or less), three involve plants that are themselves mostly of very limited size— small furniture and fixtures with only 67 employees, small plastics with 53, and small industrial machinery with 84. The generosity of local property tax abatements, the availability of certain targeted state tax incentives, and the absence of large locally funded grant and loan programs accounts for the importance of tax incentives at the local level.

At the state level, TAIM is able to distinguish the effects of the three classes of non-tax incentives: infrastructure, training, and general-use. As one would expect, infrastructure incentives are more important for bigger plants, and such incentives never account for more than a third of the entire non-tax state and local package. Training incentives are much more important than infrastructure incentives; in the majority of cases they are the most significant class of non-tax incentives. They range from 27 percent of the entire non-tax package, in the case of small plastics plants, to 49 percent in the case of large auto plants. Mostly, for bigger plants (defined by employment size), training incentives are the leading non-tax incentive. For smaller plants (again defined by employment size), general-use incentives are more significant. The relative size of the three classes of non-tax incentives is a function of the operating ratios associated with the investment in question.

THE SPATIAL PATTERN OF TAXES AND INCENTIVES

Are tax and incentive differences substantively important? Are differences in taxes and incentives among sites large enough to influence business investment and location decisions? As we indicated in the introduction, we will not present any econometric or survey evidence on this issue. We focus on the direct size of tax and incentive differentials across space. Our approach ignores spatial differentials in other factor costs, such as labor, energy, and transportation to markets. More-over, it ignores spatial differentials in the benefits firms receive from state and local government, in other words, differences in what firms receive from paying taxes.[6] Table 4.10 provides data on the mean return after taxes and all incentives across sites (the average increment to cash flow after the firm makes the new investment) and the range of returns. All of the data in this table refer to multistate firms.[7] The coefficient of variation (the ratio of the standard deviation to the mean) provides some sense of the dispersion around that mean. That dispersion is considerable in a few cases: the small furniture and fixtures plants, the small industrial machinery plants, and the large auto/auto parts plant. Here, the range of returns is considerably larger than the mean return. In the case of the small industrial machinery plants, the mean return is $356,586, but the range is over $1.2 million. In these situations it is quite possible that taxes and incentives may have a decisive impact on investment and location decisions. There are also cases with small coefficients of variation and relatively small ranges of returns compared with means: the small and large drug plants, the small and large soap plants, the large plastics plant, and the large instruments plant. The major reasons for these differences across sectors (and to a lesser extent, across firm sizes) are straightforward: 1) varying effective tax rates due to, among other things, varying profitability across sectors (and sizes) and 2) varying eligibility for tax and non-tax incentives due to varying factor mixes and amounts across sectors (and sizes).

Are the differences among returns across the 112 cities in the analysis important? Consider the small furniture and fixtures firm. The mean increment to cash flow generated by the new plant investment is actually negative. However, if the firm decides to invest at one of the best standing offer sites, then returns become positive. In the instance of the large drug plant, the range is a relatively small fraction of the mean return. Nevertheless, the difference in returns between the best and worst site is a very significant $58 million on an initial investment of $470 million. As far as improvements to the firm's internal rate of return, a movement from the worst site to the best site rate represents an increase of 5.3 percentage points.[8]

**Table 4.10 Project Returns after All Taxes and Incentives for 16
Multistate Firms Locating in 112 Cities**

Firm	Mean ($)	Coefficient of variation	Range ($)	Hourly, per-employee wage equivalent of range ($)
Small, furniture and fixtures	(18,434)	−9.03	883,219	0.72
Large, furniture and fixtures	9,346,248	0.11	5,461,309	0.48
Small, drugs	18,592,101	0.05	5,237,500	0.95
Large, drugs	272,501,918	0.04	58,097,457	1.82
Small, soaps	8,613,846	0.05	2,363,827	0.94
Large, soaps	53,803,767	0.05	13,344,649	0.82
Small, plastics	320,545	0.48	789,037	0.84
Large, plastics	20,141,723	0.08	9,111,314	0.90
Small, industrial machinery	356,586	0.80	1,266,732	0.86
Large, industrial machinery	24,464,584	0.21	23,877,858	0.66
Small, electronics	1,135,210	0.43	2,425,336	0.66
Large, electronics	7,951,177	0.53	20,631,480	0.76
Small, autos	15,742,613	0.18	16,897,421	0.70
Large, autos	9,189,576	1.35	57,782,121	0.81
Small, instruments	2,024,889	0.12	1,017,677	0.58
Large, instruments	58,935,884	0.05	15,861,121	0.65

NOTE: "Hourly, per-employee wage equivalent of range" assumes that each employee in the plant works a 40-hour week over a 50-week year, for a 20-year period. The numbers reported are the present value equivalents (discounted using the firm-specific discount rates) of the ranges.

In order to make greater intuitive sense of these data, the last column of Table 4.10 presents the hourly wage rate equivalent of the range. This is calculated by dividing the range by the number of employees at the new plant, then taking the annual present value of this number.[9] Dividing by 2,000—that is, assuming a 40-hour work week over a 50-

week year—gives the wage equivalent of the range. It measures the range in terms of equivalent savings in wages. In the case of the small furniture and fixtures plant, the saving is worth 72 cents per hour. In other words, the difference between the best and worst sites is equivalent to paying all employees 72 cents an hour less, for each hour worked over the 20-year life span of the plant. In most instances, the wage equivalent data are in the 60 to 80 cents an hour range. Two cases are lower than this and four—small and large drug firms, small soap firms, and large plastics firms—higher. We now focus on these four plants that have greater spatial differentials.

Figure 4.1 plots project returns after all taxes and incentives for multistate small drug firms in the 112 city locations. For most cities, a rank position change of a few places makes little substantive difference. The cities at the 50th and 51st best locations, for instance, are separated in hourly wage equivalent amounts by much less than a penny. In such cases, it seems highly unlikely that taxes and incentives are large enough to overcome spatial differentials in factor costs such as labor, energy, or transportation to markets. The exceptions to this are at the extreme ends of the plot. Here, a rank order change of one place sometimes makes a large difference, although seldom by more than 25 cents in hourly wage equivalent terms. Figures 4.2 through 4.4 provide similar plots for large drug, small soap, and large plastics manufacturing firms. A pattern similar to that found with small drug firms is discernible. Overall, the difference between the best and worst sites is substantial, but, except at the extremes, small rank position changes do not appear to matter much. Although the plots are not shown here, the same is true of the other 12 firm types simulated.

This raises a much broader issue: To what extent do taxes and other incentives increase (or decrease) a city's overall locational competitiveness? Figures 4.5 through 4.8 plot returns at the top 20 locations with standing offers. Returns after basic taxes, after basic taxes and tax incentives, and after basic taxes and all incentives are graphed. In the case of the small drug plant, both tax and non-tax incentives do alter substantially the competitive position of cites. The most competitive city (listed as no. 1 in Figure 4.5) has a reasonably competitive basic state and local tax position, roughly similar to that of cities 5, 6 and 7 in the figure. Tax incentives improve no. 1's competitiveness, but not as much as they improve the competitiveness of cities 5, 6, and 7. How-

146

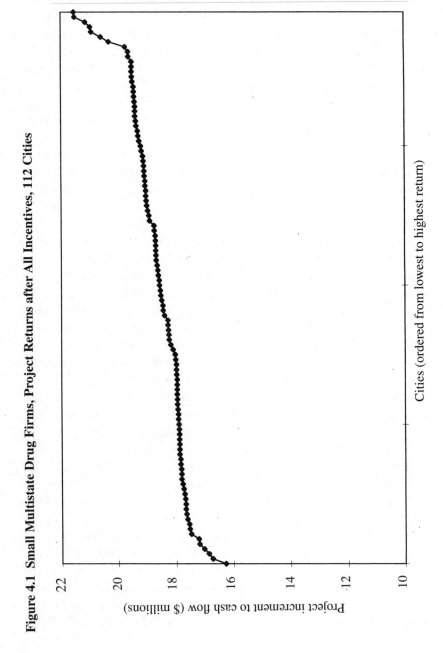

Figure 4.1 Small Multistate Drug Firms, Project Returns after All Incentives, 112 Cities

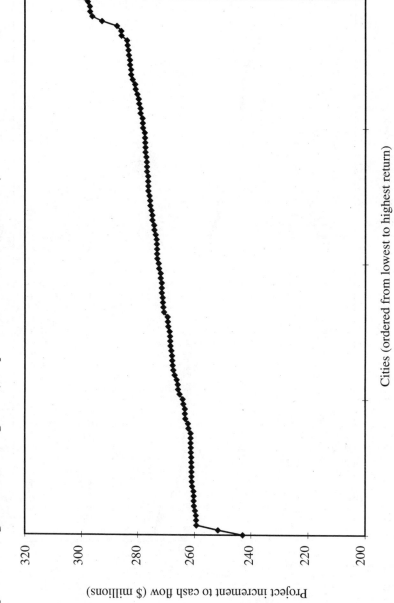

Figure 4.2 Large Multistate Drug Firms, Project Returns after All Incentives, 112 Cities

Cities (ordered from lowest to highest return)

Project increment to cash flow ($ millions)

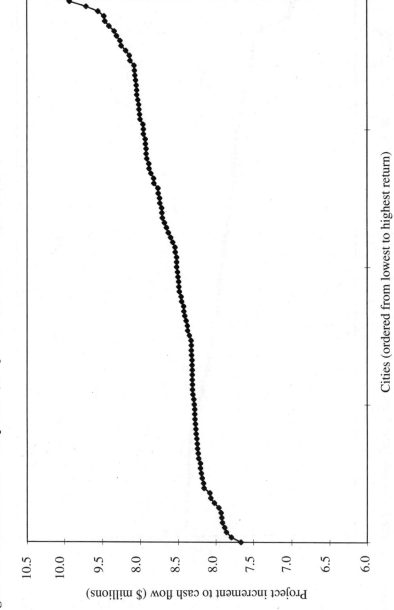

Figure 4.3. Small Multistate Soap Firms, Project Returns after All Incentives, 112 Cities

Cities (ordered from lowest to highest return)

Project increment to cash flow ($ millions)

Figure 4.4 Large Multistate Plastics Firms, Project Returns after All Incentives, 112 Cities

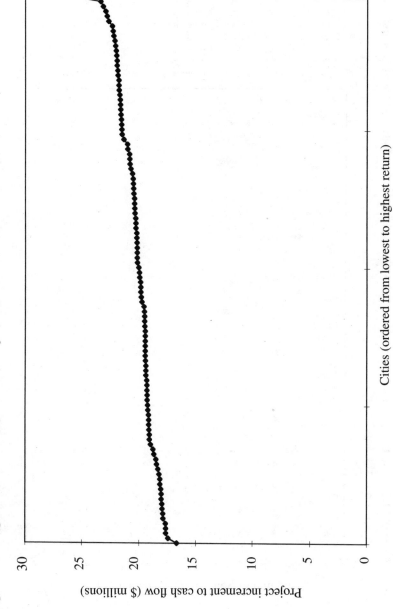

Project increment to cash flow ($ millions)

Cities (ordered from lowest to highest return)

150

Figure 4.5 Small Multistate Drug Firms Investing in a $50 Million Plant, Project Returns after Taxes and All Incentives in the Top 20 Cities

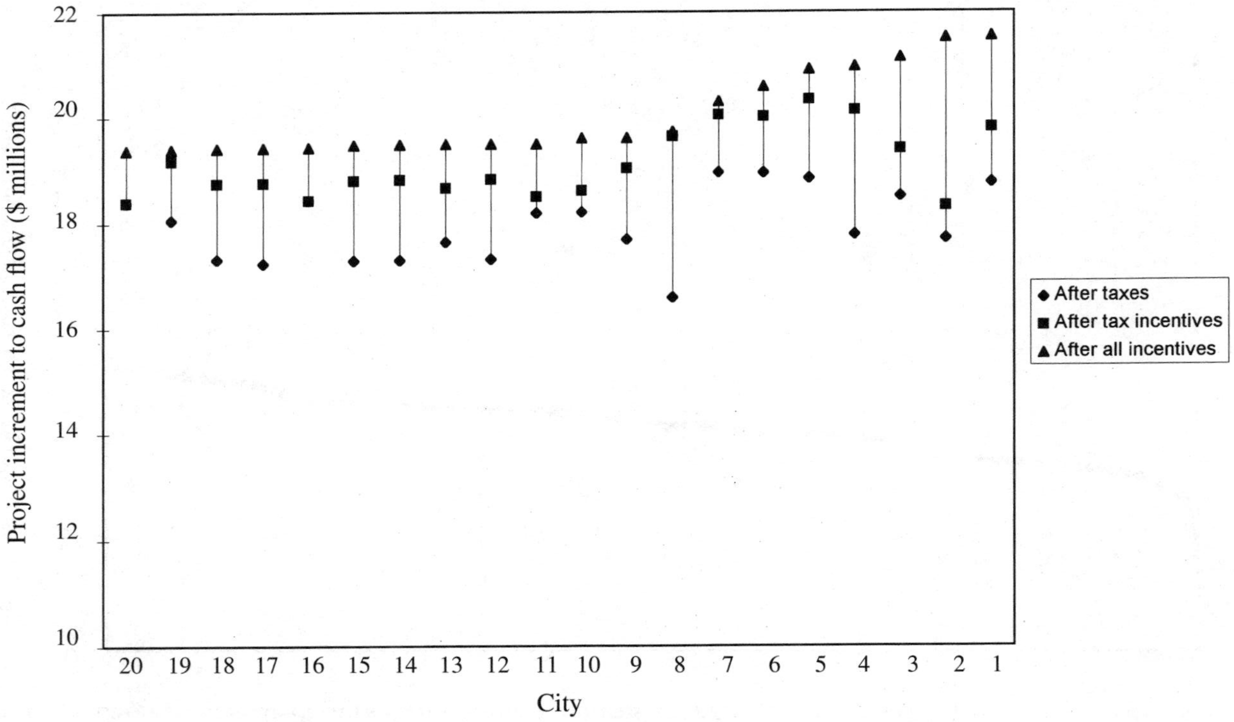

Figure 4.6 Large Multistate Drug Firms Investing in a $470 Million Plant, Project Returns after Taxes and All Incentives in the Top 20 Cities

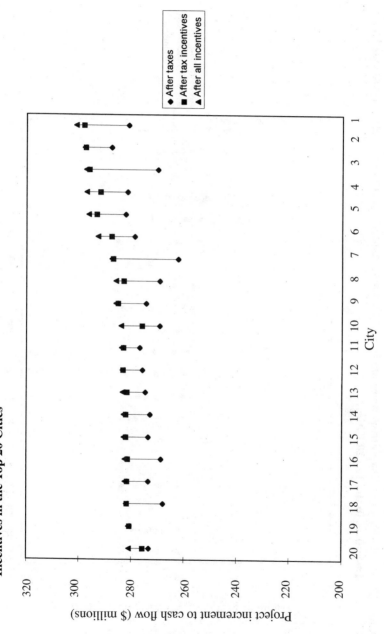

152

Figure 4.7 Small Multistate Soap Firms Investing in a $20 Million Plant, Project Returns after Taxes and All Incentives in the Top 20 Cities

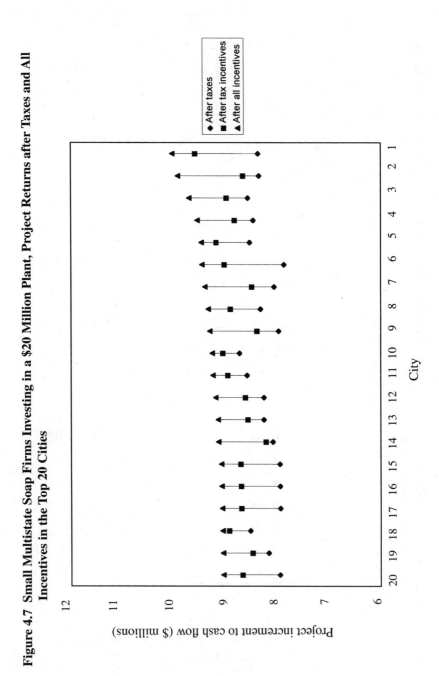

153

Figure 4.8 Large Multistate Plastics Firms Investing in a $70 Million Plant, Project Returns after Taxes and All Incentives in the Top 20 Cities

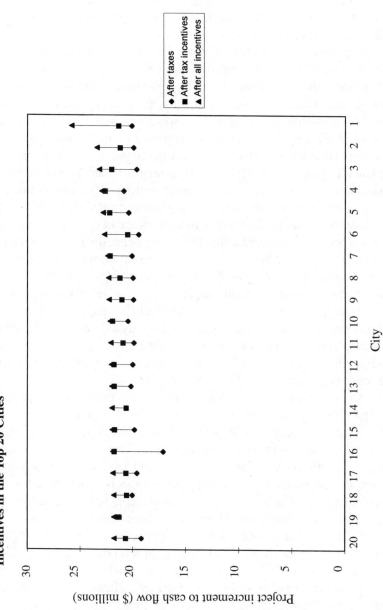

ever, no. 5, 6, and 7 provide relatively meager non-tax incentives compared to no. 1. Thus, it is the particular combination of basic tax
structure and of tax and other incentives that gives city no. 1 its special
locational competitiveness.

Large plants benefit from non-tax incentives to a much lesser extent
than do small plants. The reason for this is that most non-tax incentives
have strict threshold limits (such as a maximum loan size of $0.5 mil-
lion); large businesses come up against these limits much more swiftly
than small businesses. This is clear in Figure 4.6, the plot for large drug
firms. While tax incentives clearly improve returns, non-tax incentives
seldom raise significantly the competitiveness of a city. For small soap
plants (Figure 4.7), non-tax incentives are important. Both tax and non-
tax incentives do enhance the competitiveness of the top 20 cities. For
large plastics plants, the situation is more complex. Although the firm
is categorized as large, non-tax incentives are nevertheless important;
this is because compared to the large drug plant, the large plastics plant
is quite small. The new large plastics plant employs 572 workers versus the drug plant's 2,056. Thus, the "large" plastics plant is really a
medium-sized firm, and this explains the relative importance of non-
tax incentives to it. On the whole, the results for the other 12 firm types
(again not presented here) confirm this analysis. Small- and medium-
sized plants (defined in terms of their absolute size) benefit in terms of
rank position competitiveness from both tax and non-tax incentives.
Larger firms benefit more from tax incentives.

A comparison with the least competitive locations is instructive.
Figure 4.9 plots returns after taxes, tax incentives, and other incentives
for small soap firms. On the whole, the worst locations have a poor tax
structure and also provide poor incentives. There are a few exceptions
to this: in this figure, cities 3, 5, 12, 13, and 17. The exceptions tend to
provide reasonable tax incentives but not much in the way of non-tax
incentives. Although we do not present the data here, this pattern tends
to be generally true for all 16 firm types simulated.

We now examine more closely the impact of incentives on the competitiveness of locations. The focus is again on those sectors that show
greater spatial variation in project returns: small and large drug, small
soap, and large plastics firms. With the four plants, the range between
the best and worst city increases after tax incentives have been added to
basic taxes and after non-tax incentives have been added to taxes and

155

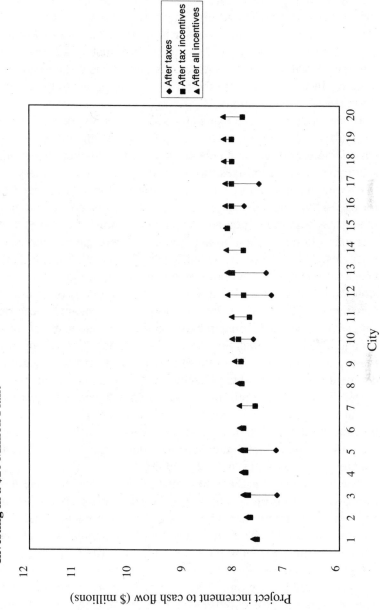

Figure 4.9 Project Returns after Taxes and All Incentives in the Worst 20 Cities for Small Multistate Soap Firms Investing in a $20 Million Plant

tax incentives. This is also true for 10 of the other 12 firm types (large soap and small plastics firms are the two exceptions). In other words, the provision of state and city incentives does not, as some have claimed, tend to make up for poor basic tax structure of a state and city.[10] Rather, overall incentives actually accentuate rather than ameliorate the spatial differentials in returns due to basic state and city tax regimes. Incentives increase the differences in project returns between the best and worst locations.

However, it is not true that states and cities with poor tax structures generally offer poor incentives and that states and cities with good basic structures offer good incentives. In order to better understand the relationship between taxes, tax incentives, and discretionary incentives, we ran regressions for each industrial sector and firm size (that is, for the 16 hypothetical firms). The increment in income due to non-tax incentives was the dependent variable; income after taxes and the increment in income due to tax incentives were the two independent variables. The regressions tested for any linear relationship between taxes, tax incentives, and non-tax incentives. In all instances, regression R^2 values were well below 10 percent, and most often close to 1 percent. F- and t-scores were almost never significant. These results suggest no linear relationship between the three elements of the local tax and incentive regime. So, while at the extremes (comparing cities at the top and bottom of the range) incentives do tend to magnify the competitiveness of local tax systems (as the discussion in the last paragraph illustrated), overall, the relationship between the generosity of incentives offered and the generosity of the basic tax system appears to be quite random. Certainly—and this does support the conclusion of the previous paragraph—there is no evidence that non-tax incentives tend to neutralize high state and local taxes.

The mean (over the 24 states and 112 cities) tax-incentive-derived improvement to project returns for the small drug firm is just under $0.5 million; the non-tax-incentive-derived increment is nearly $0.6 million (Table 4.11). Thus, tax incentives have an hourly wage equivalence of 9 cents (meaning the plant could absorb higher wages to the extent of 9 cents an hour for all employees over the 20-year period). Non-tax incentives are on average worth 11 cents an hour per worker. The difference in project returns between the best and worst tax incentive package across the 112 cities amounts to just over $3 million, as does the difference between the best and worst non-tax incentive package. This is equivalent to paying workers 55 cents an hour less due to tax incentives and 57 cents an hour less due to non-tax incentives.

In the case of the large drug plant (Table 4.12), on average tax incentives increase returns by $4.4 million, non-tax incentives by only $1.5 million. All incentives together are worth an hourly wage equivalent of 19 cents. For small soap plants (Table 4.13), non-tax incentives are more important than tax incentives, all incentives together adding about $0.56 million to returns for the average city. For large plastics firms (Table 4.14), tax incentives are only slightly more important than non-tax incentives. Together, these add about $1.4 million to returns in the average city. Most startling is how consistent the hourly wage equivalents are across these four firm types. The average total incentive package amounts to an equivalent of 20 cents an hour decline in wages for the small drug firms, 19 cents for the large drug firms, 22 cents for the small soap firms, and 14 cents for the large plastics firms. For all 16 firms, the smallest average incentive is worth the equivalent of 9 cents an hour (for large industrial machinery firms), and the largest 24 cents an hour (for small plastics and small industrial machinery firms).

In summary, spatial differentials across the American economy due to basic taxes are large, but so are differentials due to tax and non-tax incentives. Whether these differentials are large enough to really matter depends, of course, on whether differentials in other factor costs are greater, and also on the quantity and quality of goods and services produced by state and local government. Not all firms experience the incentive system equally. In general, larger firms gain less from non-tax incentives and more from tax incentives, whereas for small- and medium-sized firms, non-tax incentives are often of greater significance. The relationship between the burdensomeness of the basic tax regime and the generosity of tax and non-tax incentives is random, except that, at the extremes, incentives tend to exaggerate differentials in the basic tax structure of states and cities. States and cities with very good basic tax structures tend also to offer very generous incentives. Certainly, there is no evidence to suggest that incentives nullify differences in basic tax loads.

Why don't incentives narrow the gap between the best states and the worst states in relation to returns on investment? Why don't high-tax places use large incentives to offset those high taxes, and low-tax

Table 4.11 The Impact of Taxes and Incentives on Project Returns for Small Drug Firms, 112 Cities

	Mean ($)	Coefficient of variation	Range ($)	Hourly, per-employee wage equivalent of range ($)
Project returns				
After basic taxes	17,501,175	0.043	3,838,025	0.70
After tax incentives	17,998,358	0.047	5,175,001	0.94
After all incentives	18,592,101	0.051	5,237,500	0.95
Increment in project returns due to				
Tax incentives	497,183	1.270	3,027,054	
Non-tax incentives	593,743	0.711	3,111,253	
Hourly, per-employee wage equivalent of				
Tax incentives	0.09		0.55	
Non-tax incentives	0.11		0.57	

Table 4.12 The Impact of Taxes and Incentives on Project Returns for Large Drug Firms, 112 Cities

	Mean ($)	Coefficient of variation	Range ($)	Hourly, per-employee wage equivalent of range ($)
Project returns				
After basic taxes	266,613,589	0.032	46,054,414	1.45
After tax incentives	271,023,541	0.036	56,128,561	1.76
After all incentives	272,501,918	0.037	58,097,457	1.82
Increment in project returns due to				
Tax incentives	4,409,952	1.357	25,842,961	
Non-tax incentives	1,478,377	1.043	7,896,833	
Hourly, per-employee wage equivalent of				
Tax incentives	0.14		0.81	
Non-tax incentives	0.05		0.25	

Table 4.13 The Impact of Taxes and Incentives on Project Returns for Small Soap Firms, 112 Cities

	Mean ($)	Coefficient of variation	Range ($)	Hourly, per-employee wage equivalent of range ($)
Project returns				
After basic taxes	8,054,323	0.038	1,518,079	0.60
After tax incentives	8,284,947	0.046	2,053,569	0.82
After all incentives	8,613,846	0.054	2,363,827	0.94
Increment in project returns due to				
Tax incentives	230,624	1.261	1,232,605	
Non-tax incentives	328,899	0.690	1,232,187	
Hourly, per-employee wage equivalent of				
Tax incentives	0.09		0.49	
Non-tax incentives	0.13		0.50	

Table 4.14 The Impact of Taxes and Incentives on Project Returns for Large Plastics Firms, 112 Cities

	Mean ($)	Coefficient of variation	Range ($)	Hourly, per-employee wage equivalent of range ($)
Project returns				
After basic taxes	18,703,065	0.068	6,571,132	0.65
After tax incentives	19,436,782	0.070	6,607,726	0.65
After all incentives	20,141,723	0.076	9,111,314	0.90
Increment in project returns due to				
Tax incentives	733,717	1.237	4,577,488	
Non-tax incentives	704,942	0.768	4,370,217	
Hourly, per-employee wage equivalent of				
Tax incentives	0.07		0.45	
Non-tax incentives	0.07		0.43	

places forego incentives because they are unnecessary? After all, the rationale for enacting incentives is usually couched in terms of the need to "remain competitive." One plausible hypothesis is that the competition for jobs is focused primarily on visible and explicit incentive programs and not on overall after-tax returns. States and cities probably do not have good knowledge of the effective tax rates on various kinds of firms to begin with, and, from descriptions of the battles for particular firms, it does appear that states are trying to match other states' incentive packages, not after-tax returns. The same approach may well apply to the enactment of ongoing incentive programs, where one state feels compelled to offer a loan program because its competitor states have one. In that case, a high-tax state and a low-tax state would be expected to be equally likely to enact, for example, a $2,000 per job tax credit, and in so doing to believe that they are simply matching each others' bids. The result of this process, repeated many times in many states, would be a pattern of incentive offers that bears no relation to basic tax burdens and that leaves the substantial variation among states in after-tax returns little changed.

The importance of incentives in defining the generosity of local tax and incentive regimes is contrary to other established results in the hypothetical firm literature. In particular, in recent work using the AFTAX model, J. Papke (1995, p. 1710) concludes that "the differential cost imposed by these diverse [tax and tax incentive] systems is surprisingly small." Why should the two hypothetical firm models produce such different answers? The crude answer is that the two models (TAIM and AFTAX) operate in different ways, and, in some regards, make different assumptions about firm behavior. The crux of the detailed answer is that the multistate version of the AFTAX model simulates two states (or two locations) at a time, as it is mainly concerned with cross-border competition, and that it imposes some restrictive assumptions regarding the destination of sales (10 percent of sales are destined for the home state) and headquarters location. TAIM distributes sales across the United States in accordance with population size, simultaneously taxing across multiple states (in fact, all of the states in the model) and cities, and allows headquarters location both within and outside the states under consideration. In fact, Papke's work suggests that loosening the AFTAX assumptions results in greater differentials among competing locations. Indeed, even the cross-border simulations of AFTAX indicate much greater spatial differentials than the single-state (home-state expansion) simulations of the model.

We argued earlier that there is reason to believe that the state is more important than the locality in defining a site's tax and tax incentive regime. On average, firms pay a little more in state income and sales taxes than they do in local taxes. Moreover, the states play a key role in setting the parameters of local taxation and in providing or limiting the use of tax incentives. The same argument may be applied to non-tax incentives; usually, the states define what incentives should be allowed at the local level and how these should be provided. Moreover, most non-tax programs are provided through state, not local, government. What limited evidence we have suggests that, with the important exception of tax increment financing subsidies, the vast majority of non-tax incentive program spending is also done by state rather than local government. Here we return to a question brought up earlier in this chapter, but we now raise it in the context of returns on investment after *all* incentives: Is variation in returns among cities within a state more significant than variation across states?

Despite the importance of states in local financing policy, there remains substantial variation across cities within many of the states in our study. If the 112 cities are ranked from lowest to highest by the project returns after all state and local taxes and incentives, then, in many states, the cities are generally spread across the rankings. At the other extreme, in a few states, the cities are fairly tightly clustered in the rankings. In some states, the particular locality matters a great deal more than in other states. In many cases, it is the presence of an enterprise zone that sets one or more cities well apart from others in the same state. This is true in Georgia, Ohio, California (where the cities are grouped in two tight clusters, one containing cities without enterprise zones, the other with), and to an extent in Pennsylvania.

We used a simple one-way analysis of variance to explore the variation of cities across and within states. States with only one city in our sample (there were three of these) were excluded from the analysis. For each of the 16 multistate hypothetical firms, project returns at the 109 city locations were the dependent variable, and the state in which the city is located was the grouping factor. In all cases, F-scores were significant at the 0.0005 probability level. In the main, then, states are an important determinant of city rankings.

Before proceeding any further, it is crucial to point out that, while many of the following figures and maps identify directly the performance of individual states (and indirectly individual cities), the results are for single hypothetical firms only. Best and worst cities (and states) vary greatly by the hypothetical firm under consideration. As an illustration, for small drug firms, cities in New Jersey do not look competitive; however, for many other sectors modeled, some cities in New Jersey perform very well. Thus, the data should not be interpreted as providing a measure of the overall relative competitiveness of a state or city.

Still, it is important not to minimize the level of variation within states. Map 4.1 plots the 20 best and 20 worst city returns, after all taxes and all incentives, for the small drug firm. A few states—Illinois, Iowa, Missouri, New York, and Florida—have a number of cities in the best 20 and none in the worst 20. Indiana, New Jersey, Pennsylvania, Michigan, and Texas have more than one city in the worst 20 and none in the best. Some states manage to have cities in both the top and bottom 20: California, Georgia, and Ohio. Figure 4.10, which plots returns for the *best* and *worst* city in each of the 24 states for the small multistate drug firm, illustrates the wide variability in returns within some individual states, particularly Georgia, Ohio, Pennsylvania, and Wisconsin. Other states are relatively tightly packed, in this case Illinois, New Jersey, Virginia, and Washington (these are states with a number of cities in our sample). Figure 4.11 plots similar information, but for all the cities in a state, not just best and worst; Figure 4.11 gives some sense of the distribution, and thus clustering, of returns within states. Three elements are clearly visible:

- Many states are clustered into one group (for instance, New Jersey and Washington) or two (for instance, California, Pennsylvania, Virginia, and possibly Michigan).
- A few states show no signs of clustering (such as Georgia, Texas, and Wisconsin). It is possible that the lack of any visible evidence of clustering is a function of the small number of cities modeled in some of these states (although this argument does not seem to apply to Texas).
- Putting the clustering issue aside, there tends to be a tremendous range in returns within individual states.

Map 4.1 Best and Worst Locations for Small Multistate Drug Firms

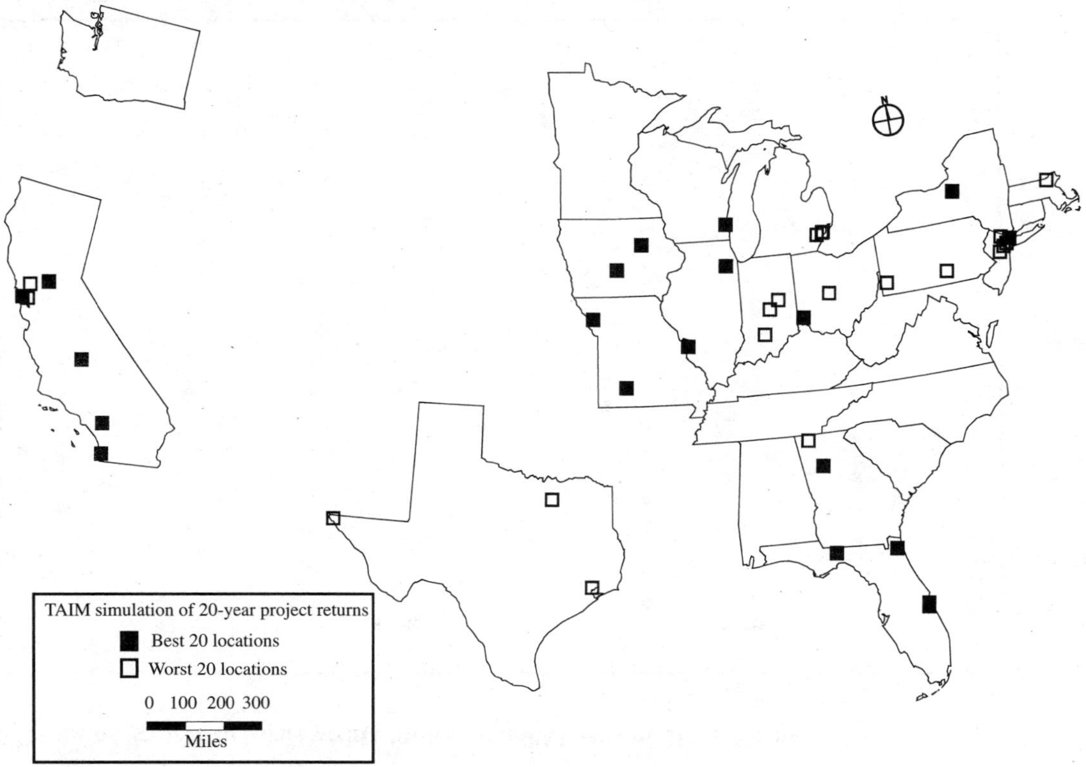

TAIM simulation of 20-year project returns

■ Best 20 locations
□ Worst 20 locations

0 100 200 300

Miles

164

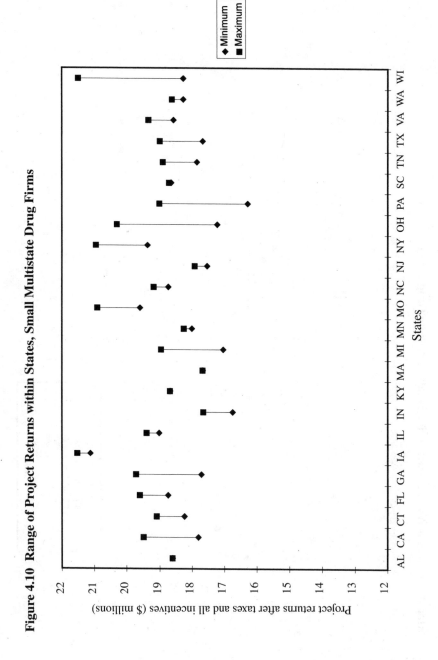

Figure 4.10 Range of Project Returns within States, Small Multistate Drug Firms

165

Figure 4.11 Project Returns Rank Position over 112 Locations, Small Multistate Drug Firms

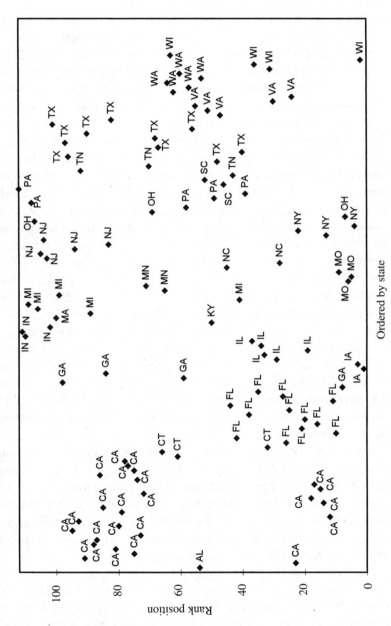

Ordered by state

Similar plots for the three other firms under consideration are provided in Appendix D. They confirm these three points.

This raises a still more general question: which are the best and worst locations for the small drug firm modeled? The best locations are scattered quite widely across the nation. Moreover, there is little geographic coherence to our results. Parts of the Midwest are clearly good for small drug firms, but other parts are clearly not. Similarly, bits of the Sunbelt (California, Georgia, Florida) are good for small drug firms, but other spots are quite bad (Texas). In order to develop a better sense of the regional coherence of project returns for small drug firms, complete results (for 112 cities in 24 states) are presented in Map 4.2. Here, project returns are plotted as contour relief using a triangulated irregular network (TIN) digital elevation model (DEM). Essentially, TIN structures are based on triangular elements with vertices at sample elevations and are derived through a form of interpolation that assumes the surface between three points to be a plane. In Map 4.2, vertices are returns at each of the 112 sites. The map has some rather obvious limitations. There are only 112 vertices, with none, for example, between western Iowa and eastern California. Nevertheless, the map provides a sense of regional bunching not seen in Map 4.1. In particular, a highest peak region in an area around parts of Iowa and Missouri is visible, and a lowest trough region centered on the eastern Midwest is also clear. Otherwise—and this is the important point—no clear regional pattern of elevation contours emerges: the nation does not neatly divide itself into broad sections generally good for or bad for small drug firms. This same lack of regional patterning is apparent in similar TIN plots for the other 15 firms modeled.

Some dramatic changes are visible if Map 4.1 is compared to equivalent maps for the other sectors (see Maps 4.3–4.5). California changes from being a highly competitive state for small drug firms (Map 4.1) to an uncompetitive one for large drug firms (Map 4.3); Florida moves from being a competitive state for small drug firms to a middling state for large drug firms; and the competitiveness of the western Midwest improves substantially from small to large drug firms.

Compare small drug firms (Map 4.1) to small soap firms (Map 4.4). Pennsylvania moves from being a state with a couple of cities in the bottom 20 (small drug firms, Map 4.1) to a state with none in the bottom 20 and three in the top 20 (small soap firms, Map 4.4), and Wash-

Map 4.2 Small Multistate Drug Firms, TIN Digital Elevation Model of Project Returns

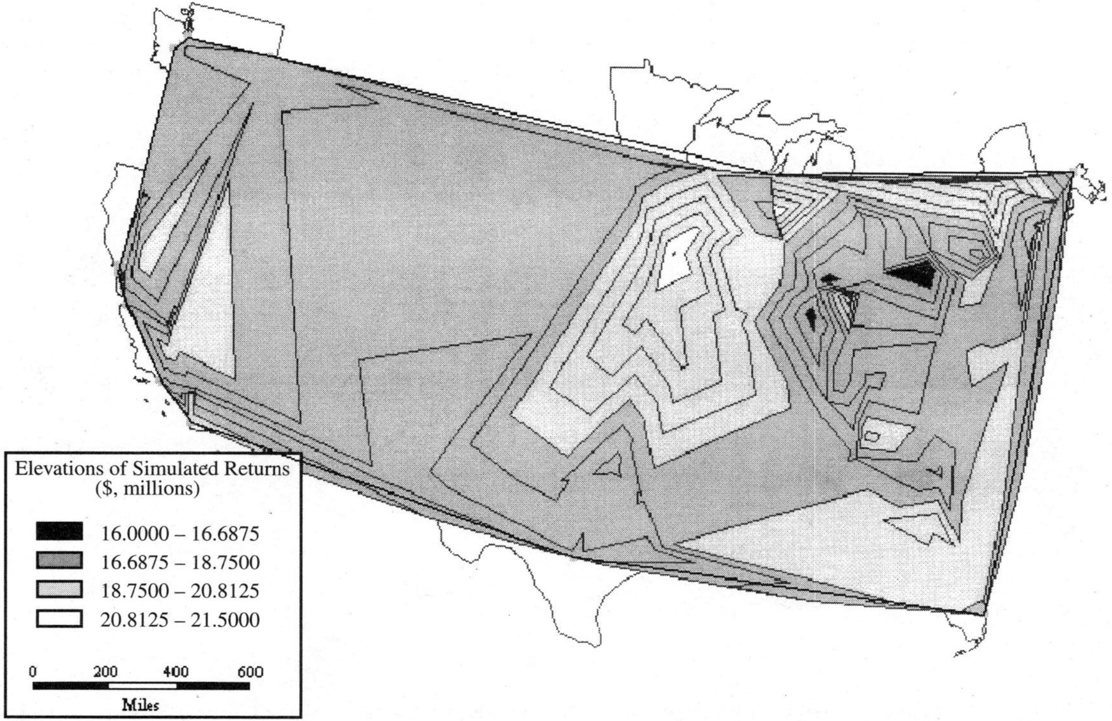

Elevations of Simulated Returns
($, millions)

16.0000 – 16.6875
16.6875 – 18.7500
18.7500 – 20.8125
20.8125 – 21.5000

0   200   400   600
Miles

168

Map 4.3 TAIM Simulation of Best and Worst Locations for Large Multistate Drug Firms

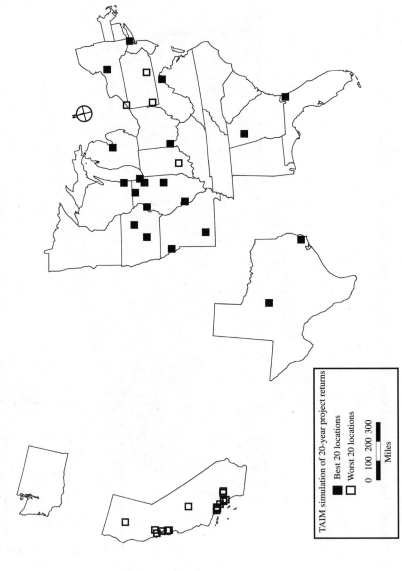

TAIM simulation of 20-year project returns

■ Best 20 locations

□ Worst 20 locations

0 100 200 300

Miles

Map 4.4 TAIM Simulation of Best and Worst 20 Locations for Small Multistate Soap Firms

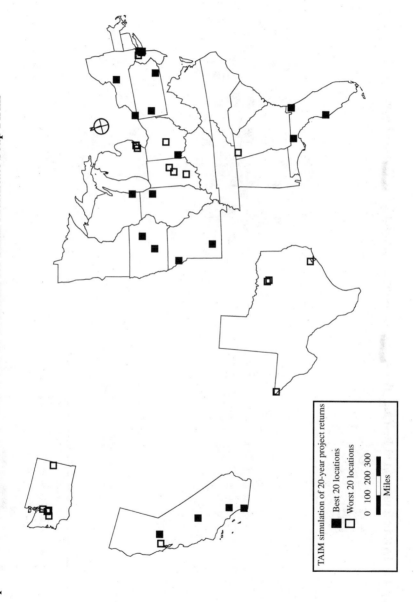

TAIM simulation of 20-year project returns

■ Best 20 locations

□ Worst 20 locations

0 100 200 300

Miles

170

Map 4.5 TAIM Simulation of Best and Worst Locations for Large Multistate Plastics Firms

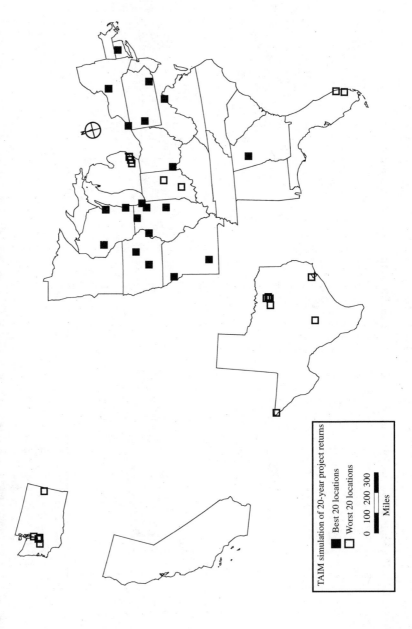

TAIM simulation of 20-year project returns

■ Best 20 locations

□ Worst 20 locations

0 100 200 300

Miles

ington shifts from being a state with no cities in the top or bottom 20 (Map 4.1), to a state with three cities in the bottom 20 (Map 4.4). Comparing large drug to large plastics firms, California changes from being a highly uncompetitive state (large drug firms, Map 4.3) to a state with no cities in the bottom 20 (large plastics firms, Map 4.5); Pennsylvania moves from being highly uncompetitive, with a number of cities in the bottom 20 (Map 4.3) to a highly competitive state with a number of cities in the top 20 (Map 4.5).

In summary, some cities and states do consistently well, and some consistently poorly, but mostly there is a large degree of variation across sectors. Moreover, no obvious regional pattern of results is discernible, even within a single sector. This conclusion provides no support to those who have argued that states are involved in spiraling intraregional wars over new investment. If individual states were copying the incentives offered by their neighbors and making their overall tax burdens no greater than that of neighboring states, one would expect to see a regional pattern of standing offers. Furthermore, the variation in spatial results across sectors *suggests* that whether policy makers in states and cities have thought about it or not, they operate a de facto industrial policy, favoring some sorts of manufacturing investment and disfavoring others.

CONCLUSIONS

There are very wide differences in returns on investment after basic taxes among states and cities. These differences tend to be exaggerated if state taxes are considered alone because states with high state income and sales taxes have tended to have lower local property and sales taxes. The highest tax state placed a tax burden on manufacturers that was typically about three times as large as that of the lowest tax state. Eight states offered investment or jobs tax credits to firms anywhere in the state; in 14 of the 24 states, local property tax abatements are offered. These incentive packages ranged from zero to as high as 40 percent to 45 percent of the before-incentive state and local tax burden. Tax incentives generally did not reduce the variation across states; large investment or jobs credits, for example, were not used primarily to offset high basic taxes. While enterprise zone incentives tended to be larger in states that offered less in the way of general incentives, the effect of enterprise zones was to increase the variation in after-tax returns across states, not to compensate for high basic taxes.

The discretionary incentives included infrastructure subsidies and customized job training at the state level, and general purpose grants, loans, and loan guarantees at both the state and local levels. Averaged over the 16 firm types and 112 cities in 24 states, the mean package of discretionary incentives, expressed in terms of present value wage equivalence, was worth about 9 cents an hour per employee. By comparison, tax incentives had a wage equivalence of 7 cents an hour. Non-tax incentives were a major part of a state's entire incentive package (in fact, in some cases over 90 percent of state incentives derived from non-tax programs), but when local incentives were combined with state ones, the role of discretionary non-tax incentives within the overall package of incentives declined markedly. The reasons for this include the provision of very generous tax incentives—such as the property tax abatement—at the local level, the availability of certain state tax incentives at the local level only, and the dearth of many large local non-tax incentive programs.

For the handful of cities/states at the top or at the bottom of the rankings for any particular firm type, there were quite substantial divergences in returns between one city/state and the next due to tax and incentive differences. However, the inclusion of non-tax incentives very often did little to change the majority of cities in the top or bottom 10. Mostly, cities that were highly competitive after taxes and tax incentives were also highly competitive after the inclusion of non-tax incentives. Overall, non-tax incentives did not ameliorate, but actually accentuated, the tax differentials between the best and worst cities.

Our research has not looked at spatial differentials in other factor costs (such as labor, energy, and transportation) or at the benefits firms receive from taxes, so we are not able to say whether a state's and city's tax and incentive regime could reasonably be expected to alter a firm's location decisions. However, our results suggest that, for the firm types simulated by TAIM, the range of results across all 112 cities (and 24 states) is not trivial. It is of course quite possible that factor cost differentials—in labor, energy, and transportation—could amount to much more than tax and incentive differentials. It is possible that labor costs in a bottom-ranked city may be much lower than in a top-ranked city. However, if tax and incentive regimes were designed to make up for locally high labor costs (or other factor costs), it would be logical to suppose that states in the South would tend to have burdensome tax and incentive regimes, while California and states in the Northeast and Midwest would tend to have much lighter loads. As the maps in this chapter show, no regional pattern of taxes and incentives is discernible. Spatial variation in the tax and incentive burden looks to be quite random. Given that the severity of local tax and incentive regimes does not appear to bear an inverse relationship to factor costs, it seems reasonable to assume that in some cases tax and incentive differentials between top- and bottom-ranked locations could sway plant location decisions.

NOTES

1. Texas is sometimes referred to as a no-income-tax state, but in fact the Texas franchise tax is based in part on federal taxable income and so is rightly classified as an income tax.

2. Iowa, however, exempts computing equipment.

3. Manufacturing corporations filing income taxes in the state of Wisconsin are required to report total sales tax paid on fuel and electricity, and the portion of the tax that applies to fuel and electricity used directly in manufacturing. They then receive a credit for the latter portion of the tax. According to the Wisconsin Department of Revenue, the average manufacturer reports that about 82% of fuel and electricity purchases are used directly in manufacturing. We impute this same percentage to the fuel and electricity purchases of the 16 firms in our model.

4. Without sales throwback, corporations selling in states where they have no tax nexus would be taxed on less than 100% of their income, since a portion of their total U.S. income would not be apportioned to any state for tax purposes. If all or most states applied the throwback rule, on the other hand, the corporation could pay state taxes on more than 100% of its income, since the sales to non-taxing states would become part of the numerator in the sales factor of every state in which the firm is taxed so that the sum of the sales factors in the various states would exceed 100%.

5. This hypothetical state had the same population as the state in question; this was necessary because population affects the apportionment of income to the median state, which in turn affects the firm's taxes paid to the median state.

6. Oakland and Testa (1996) have argued that it is crucial to measure not only the size of the tax burden, but also the benefits firms derive from the state and local goods and services paid for by business taxes. We agree; unfortunately the modeling of tax benefits is still in its infancy.

7. Our interpretation of the data for single-location firms is not much different to that of multistate firms.

8. From 29.3% in Washington, Pennsylvania to 34.6 in Des Moines, Iowa, for the multistate simulation of firm #4 (large drugs) at level 6 (including all taxes and incentives).

9. Present value is calculated using firm-specific discount rates.

10. Eisinger (1988) argues that tax incentives often ameliorate burdensome basic taxes.

5 The Effects of Taxes and Incentives on the Spatial Distribution of Investment Returns

A central question posed at the beginning of this book was the following: Are taxes lower, or incentives higher, in places with higher rates of unemployment? Previous work in this area has focused only on the incentive part of the question; further, the methods have been flawed and the results somewhat contradictory. We have shown that a proper analysis must include state and local tax systems as well as economic development programs for a variety of reasons: because incentives must be measured net of their state and federal income tax effects, because larger incentives in some places may simply be offsetting higher taxes, and because many exemptions and rules incorporated into the tax code could themselves be viewed as incentives. We have also made the case that the hypothetical firm approach provides a superior method for measuring the magnitude of tax differences and financial incentive programs.

The previous chapter established that incentives can be quite large relative to tax burdens and that differences in taxes and incentives across states and cities are substantial. While we do not test a causal model in this study, the magnitude of differences in returns on investment, before and after taxes and incentives, appears to be sufficient to make a difference in business location decisions at the margin. The question to be addressed in this chapter is a spatial one: How do taxes and incentives alter the geographic pattern of returns on investment in new manufacturing facilities? In particular, are the places that generate the highest rates of return the locations that have experienced the highest rates of unemployment and poverty or the lowest rates of job growth? In other words, is the spatial pattern of returns such as to draw investment towards the places where new jobs are most needed?

There are three ways in which the pattern of taxes and incentives could come to favor higher unemployment locations:

- States with higher average levels of unemployment may offer lower taxes or larger state-funded incentives, on a statewide basis, than do states with lower unemployment.

- Localities (cities and counties) with higher levels of unemployment may offer lower taxes or larger local incentives, such as property tax abatements or locally operated loan funds, than do cities with lower unemployment.

- States may target incentives at high-unemployment places, through enterprise zone programs and the like, so that state-funded incentives are larger in higher-unemployment cities.

We will examine how taxes and incentives—statewide, local, and targeted—affect the spatial pattern of returns on investment. We consider the spatial effects at two geographic scales: among the 24 states and among the 112 cities. At the state level, the role of local and targeted incentives can be examined only by developing an "average locality" for each state, and each state is given equal weight in the correlation analyses. At the city level of analysis, each city is given equal weight, and the contribution of a particular state's taxes and incentives to overall correlation coefficients is governed by the number of cities from that state that ended up in our sample. More populous states such as California, Texas, and Florida have greater influence on the relationships calculated, as arguably they should.

THE PATTERN OF RETURNS AMONG STATES

To isolate the effects of state taxes and incentives, we first computed returns on investment in each of the 24 states as if there were no local tax system. We measured separately the effects of the basic state tax system and of four kinds of state incentive programs. Basic state taxes include all features of income and net worth taxes except investment and jobs tax credits, plus state property taxes (if any) and state sales taxes on manufacturing machinery and fuel and electricity. The value of state tax incentives (investment and jobs tax credits) is defined as net project returns after basic state taxes and tax incentives, less net returns after basic taxes only. Non-tax incentives are grouped into three categories: 1) infrastructure subsidies, 2) job training and wage subsidies, and 3) general purpose grants, loans, and loan guarantees. Each of these three types of incentives was evaluated separately by comparing returns after taxes and tax incentives (taking tax incentive programs as entitlements) with returns after taxes, tax incentives, and the non-tax incentives of interest. The increment in returns provided the worth of the incentive to the firm.

The 16 firms modeled represent large and small firms in 8 industries. Each firm was further modeled as a multistate firm initially located in the median state and as a single-location firm with all of its operations (including the new plant) within the sample state. We present results for 5 of the 16 firms, selected to display the range of variation in project returns and the range of new plant sizes.[1] Table 5.1 shows how returns and incentives for these five firms correlated with the state average unemployment rate in 1992. We also show the simple average of the correlation rates for all 16 firms.

Returns after basic state taxes were strongly negatively correlated with the state unemployment rate: the higher the unemployment rate, the lower were returns on new investment in that state. State tax systems, in other words, are "perverse" in their effects, tending to attract jobs to the states that need them the least. State tax incentives, on the other hand, were positively correlated with unemployment, but the correlations were quite weak, ranging from 0.06 to 0.14 for multistate firms, 0.05 to 0.23 for single-location firms. Project returns after state taxes and tax incentives remained negatively correlated with unemployment. These patterns held true for both location assumptions, although the negative correlations were stronger for the multistate firms.

The value of non-tax incentives is highly dependent on firm characteristics; in part, this is due to program eligibility standards and ceilings related to firm or plant size. As a result, there is more variability in the unemployment correlations. Overall, non-tax incentives, for both single-location and multistate firms, bear only a weak relation to unemployment rates, although if anything they are lower in higher-unemployment states. However, for job training subsidies and general loans and grants, the results differ dramatically by plant size. For the six smallest plant sizes, with assets of $5 million to $20 million, these kinds of subsidies were very weakly but positively correlated with

Table 5.1 Correlation between State Average 1992 Unemployment Rate and Firm's Net Return on New Plant Investment in Each State (State Taxes and Incentives Only)[a]

Firm (plant size, in millions)	Net project returns			Value of incentives				
	After basic taxes	After tax incentives	After all incentives	Tax incentives	Infra-structure subsidies	Job training subsidies	General financing programs	All incentives
Multistate firms								
#2: Furniture ($40)	(0.63)	(0.51)	(0.52)	0.08	(0.08)	(0.33)	(0.20)	(0.25)
#5: Soaps ($20)	(0.56)	(0.45)	(0.36)	0.11	(0.15)	0.08	(0.01)	0.04
#7: Plastics ($5)	(0.63)	(0.58)	(0.18)	0.06	(0.24)	0.06	0.14	0.09
#14 Autos ($600)	(0.51)	(0.39)	(0.48)	0.14	(0.19)	(0.50)	(0.20)	(0.26)
#16: Instruments ($180)	(0.61)	(0.54)	(0.57)	0.10	(0.13)	(0.45)	(0.19)	(0.27)
Average: 6 smallest firms	(0.61)	(0.51)	(0.24)	0.11	(0.15)	0.07	0.09	0.09
Average: 7 largest firms	(0.58)	(0.48)	(0.52)	0.12	(0.14)	(0.46)	(0.22)	(0.23)
Average: all 16 firms	(0.60)	(0.50)	(0.42)	0.11	(0.14)	(0.22)	(0.10)	(0.11)
Single-location firms								
#2: Furniture ($40)	(0.34)	(0.23)	(0.34)	0.17	(0.07)	(0.34)	(0.21)	(0.19)
#5: Soaps ($20)	(0.27)	(0.18)	(0.17)	0.22	(0.14)	0.06	(0.02)	0.09

#7: Plastics ($5)	(0.44)	(0.36)	(0.11)	0.05	(0.23)	0.05	0.14	0.08
#14: Autos ($600)	(0.42)	(0.17)	(0.28)	0.23	(0.18)	(0.50)	(0.21)	(0.03)
#16: Instruments ($180)	(0.27)	(0.23)	(0.29)	0.06	(0.12)	(0.45)	(0.20)	(0.21)
Average: 6 smallest firms	(0.36)	(0.27)	(0.12)	0.07	(0.15)	0.05	0.09	0.09
Average: 7 largest firms	(0.34)	(0.20)	(0.29)	0.15	(0.13)	(0.46)	(0.23)	(0.11)
Average: all 16 firms	(0.34)	(0.23)	(0.23)	0.11	(0.14)	(0.23)	(0.11)	(0.04)

a. Negative correlations are shown in parentheses. Basic taxes include state corporate income and net worth taxes, state sales taxes on machinery and equipment and on fuel and utilities, and state property taxes. Tax incentives consist of state income or net worth tax investment and jobs credits. The value of tax incentives is measured by the net project returns after taxes and tax incentives, less project returns after basic taxes only. The value of other incentives is measured by the net project returns after taxes, tax incentives, and the other incentives, minus net project returns after taxes and tax incentives only. The six smallest firms are numbers 1, 5, 7, 9, 11, and 15, with new plant assets of $5 million to $20 million. The seven largest firms are numbers 4, 6, 10, 12, 13, 14, and 16, with new plant assets of $110 million to $600 million.

unemployment. For the largest seven plants, on the other hand, with assets of $110 million to $600 million, the correlation between unemployment and job subsidies was quite negative, ranging from −0.41 to −0.50, and the correlation between unemployment and general loans and grants ranged from −0.18 to −0.30. (These correlation figures include single-location and multistate firms.) The job training and general programs in high-unemployment states apparently are targeted at small firms or have low ceilings on the grant or loan amounts, enabling those states to compete successfully (with low-unemployment states) for small firms but not for large firms.

The end result, considering net project returns after taking all state tax and other incentives into account, is that returns remain negatively correlated with unemployment, statewide incentives offsetting only slightly the perverse effects of state tax systems. To the extent that the classification of some features of the tax system as "basic" rather than as development incentives was arbitrary, the more important conclusion is probably not that certain incentives exhibited a slight tendency to redistribute jobs to high-unemployment states: it is rather that the state income and sales tax systems as a whole, including all incentives whether explicit or not, had the opposite effect. This perverse effect is much stronger for multistate firms, which are probably the more relevant for purposes of evaluating economic development competition among the states. For 12 of the 16 multistate firms, the correlation was −0.36 or stronger. Overall, it appears that, at the state level at least, decades of interstate competition have not produced a pattern of returns on investment that could plausibly contribute to a redistribution of jobs to states in most need, but rather the opposite.

It is possible that these results are sensitive to our choice of year for determining the state unemployment rate. We chose 1992 for obvious reasons: the project returns calculated by the model reflect tax law and incentive programs as of 1992, and we wished to test the hypothesis that the pattern of returns in that year favored states that had higher unemployment at that time. Nonetheless, it is worth testing an alternative measure of unemployment; 1992, after all, was a recession year when unemployment peaked. We calculated as an alternative the average unemployment rate over the five-year period 1989 through 1993. This included two years of relatively low unemployment (which nationally averaged 5.3 percent and 5.5 percent in 1989 and 1990, respectively) and the two years surrounding the unemployment peak in 1992. The correlation for our 24 states between the 1992 rate and the five-year average rate was quite high (0.88); in all but one state (Missouri), the 1992 rate was higher than the five-year average. For each of the 16 multistate firms, we then correlated project returns and the value of incentives in each state with this five-year average unemployment rate. The results, shown in Appendix Table E.2, mirror the figures in Table 5.1 quite closely, with the exception that the basic tax systems were not as strongly negatively correlated with unemployment when the five-year average was used (with correlations at about 75 percent of the values in Table 5.1). The correlations with tax incentives, non-tax incentives, and all incentives taken together were very similar, with very comparable variation across firms as well.

Interestingly, the picture is quite different if we consider the relationship between taxes and job growth, rather than unemployment rates. We measured the percentage increase in state private nonfarm employment between 1980 and 1990, two years that represented approximately the same point in the business cycle. Although one might expect higher job growth to be associated with lower unemployment rates, this was not the case. The three states with the lowest unemployment rates (below 5.2 percent) also had below average job growth (from 11 to 23 percent). These were the Midwestern states of Iowa, Minnesota, and Wisconsin, which basically stagnated, with population growth occurring even slower than job growth, or the out-migration of people matching the out-migration of jobs. At the other extreme were three states (New Jersey, California, and Florida) with high 1992 unemployment rates (above 8.1 percent) despite high growth rates in employment during the previous decade (from 28 to 55 percent).

As shown in Table 5.2, for multistate firms the value of incentives is negatively correlated with job growth. In other words, there is a mild tendency for state tax and other incentives to tilt the incentive surface towards states that experienced slow job growth during the 1980s. This effect is present both for tax incentives and for non-tax incentives; given a basic tax system that is approximately neutral, this produces a pattern of returns after taxes and incentives somewhat favoring slow-growth states.

Table 5.2 Correlation between State Employment Growth and Poverty Rates and Firm's Net Return on New Plant Investment in Each State in 1992 (State Taxes and Incentives Only, Multistate Firms Only)[a]

Firm (plant size in $ millions)	Net project returns			Value of incentives		
	After basic taxes	After tax incentives	After all incentives	Tax incentives	Other incentives	All incentives
Correlation with job growth						
#2: Furniture ($40)	(0.08)	(0.16)	(0.22)	(0.27)	(0.21)	(0.29)
#5: Soaps ($20)	(0.08)	(0.16)	(0.21)	(0.26)	(0.16)	(0.24)
#7: Plastics ($5)	(0.19)	(0.22)	(0.35)	(0.24)	(0.31)	(0.33)
#14: Autos ($600)	(0.14)	(0.23)	(0.25)	(0.31)	(0.20)	(0.33)
#16: Instruments ($180)	(0.01)	(0.08)	(0.12)	(0.28)	(0.19)	(0.29)
Average: all 16 firms	(0.08)	(0.15)	(0.21)	(0.27)	(0.20)	(0.28)
Correlation with poverty rate						
#2: Furniture ($40)	0.31	0.29	0.13	0.06	(0.11)	(0.08)
#5: Soaps ($20)	0.37	0.34	0.22	0.03	(0.09)	(0.06)
#7: Plastics ($5)	0.13	0.14	(0.01)	0.07	(0.09)	(0.08)
#14: Autos ($600)	0.13	0.12	0.13	0.01	0.13	0.09
#16: Instruments ($180)	0.33	0.32	0.30	0.05	0.14	0.13
Average: all 16 firms	0.27	0.25	0.16	0.04	0.01	0.01

a. Negative correlations are shown in parentheses. Job growth is the percentage increase in state employment between 1980 and 1990. Poverty rate is the percentage of persons in poverty from the 1990 census (1989 income).

The preceding results suggest two hypotheses (with opposite direction of causality) for further research, beyond the scope of the current project: 1) it is slow economic growth that drives states to adopt tax and incentive policies more favorable towards business, and 2) the geographic pattern of returns found in 1992 is similar to the pattern that existed at the beginning of the 1980s, so that lower taxes (and hence higher returns) on new investment helped cause greater state job growth during the 1980s. The first hypothesis is consistent with arguments about "growth coalitions" and their effect on public policy at the state and local level, and with the view that the constituency concerned with growth is broader and more influential than the constituency concerned with the unemployed. This hypothesis could be tested using our net project returns for 1992 as the dependent variable and with job growth during some prior period as one of the independent variables.

The second hypothesis could be tested only by constructing a state tax database for 1980 identical in structure to our 1992 database; this is a monumental task, more arduous than constructing the 1992 database because information on each state's tax laws as of 1980 is much more difficult to come by now. On the other hand, our 1992 results could be used in the future as the explanatory tax variable in a regression model predicting job growth from 1992 to some later year.

The poverty rate (percentage of persons in poverty as of 1989, from the 1990 census) is an alternative measure of economic distress. It is interesting that there is a small positive correlation between returns after basic taxes and the poverty rate: the higher a state's poverty rate, the higher the return on new investment (see Table 5.2). State tax policies may have the effect, then, of pulling new jobs towards states with higher concentrations of the poor. There is virtually no relationship between the value of tax or other incentives and poverty, however.

So far, we have considered the effects of state taxes and incentives only. Most tax-burden studies conducted by states have focused on states as the units of analysis rather than cities, but some have incorporated statewide average local property tax burdens into their comparisons. The problems entailed in doing so, and our imperfect solution, were described in the previous chapter, where we presented a comparison of effective state and local tax and tax incentive rates in the 24 states. This was accomplished by constructing a representative city in each state, with a local tax system and property tax abatements typical of cities in that state. The representative cities were not given state or local non-tax incentives; the results that follow thus incorporate only the effects of state and local tax and tax incentive programs (including enterprise zone tax credits).[2] The correlations between these various tax rates (or incentive rates, which are like negative tax rates) and state average unemployment rates are presented in Table 5.3. This simplified table shows only the average correlation coefficient for the 16 multi-state firms.

Effective tax rates are defined as the reduction in the present value of project cash flow resulting from the introduction of state or local taxes at the location of the new plant, divided by the present value of income before all taxes. There is a very strong correlation between basic state tax rates and unemployment (reinforcing the results of Table 5.1): the highest tax rates occur in the states with the highest unemployment rates. Because states with higher state taxes tend to have lower local taxes, as shown in Chapter 4, the effective local tax rate is negatively correlated with unemployment. The combined state plus local tax rate, however, is working to draw investment towards the lower-unemployment states.

With tax incentives, the meaning of the signs is reversed; that is, a positive correlation indicates that the incentive is operating as we might hope, with larger incentives in higher-unemployment states. This is in fact the case, although it is primarily the state incentives that produce this result (and rather weakly at that). Moreover, it appears that this effect is largely attributable to the enterprise zone incentives provided by the states. This effect, weak as it is, may not be particularly relevant. Since the representative cities are given enterprise zone incentives wherever the state allows enterprise zones or the like, these state comparisons grossly exaggerate the prevalence and importance of such zones. In most states, a small minority of potential sites for new industry will be located within an enterprise zone. Thus, the most salient comparisons across states are those that exclude enterprise zone incentives. Focusing on those numbers, we see that state and local tax incentives together bear virtually no systematic relationship to unemployment and do nothing to offset the strong perverse effects of state tax systems. The effective state plus local tax rates calculated after those tax incentives that are generally available (i.e., excluding

**Table 5.3 Correlations of Effective Tax and Incentive Rates in a
Representative City in Each State with State Unemployment,
Job Growth, and Poverty Rates**

Tax and incentive rates	Unemployment rate	Job growth rate	Poverty rate
Basic tax rates before incentives			
State	0.73	0.10	(0.17)
Local	(0.13)	(0.15)	0.24
Combined state and local	0.44	(0.05)	0.06
Tax incentives			
State	0.28	0.10	(0.08)
Local	0.08	(0.26)	0.08
State and local: total	0.26	(0.15)	0.02
State and local: EZ incentives only	0.23	0.12	(0.03)
State and local: non-EZ incentives only	0.06	(0.40)	0.07
State and local tax rates after tax incentives			
After non-EZ tax incentives only	0.46	0.12	0.05
After all tax incentives	0.07	0.07	0.13

NOTE: EZ = enterprise zone. Negative correlations are shown in parentheses. See Tables 4.6 and 4.7 for definitions of effective tax and tax incentive rates. The correlations shown here are a simple average of the correlation coefficients for each of the 16 multistate firms. The unemployment rate is the state rate for 1992; the job growth rate is the percentage increase in employment between 1980 and 1990; the poverty rate is the percentage of persons in poverty, 1989.

enterprise zone incentives) are strongly positively correlated with unemployment.

The correlations between tax rates and job growth or poverty incidence are mixed, with most correlations very weak. The only exception is the tendency for non-enterprise zone tax incentives at the state and local level to be higher in states with lower job growth. Local incentives appear to be reinforcing this tendency found for state incentives alone in Table 5.2.[3]

THE PATTERN OF RETURNS AMONG CITIES

Business location decisions, in the end, are choices between particular places, not entire states. Local taxes and tax incentives, which are on average about equal in magnitude to state taxes and tax incentives, exhibit considerable variation within states. Arguably, then, the best test of the hypothesis that taxes and incentives redistribute jobs to high unemployment places is conducted at the city level. Our sample of cities was stratified into four city population size classes: 1) over 500,000, 2) 100,000 to 499,999, 3) 25,000 to 99,999, and 4) 10,000 to 24,999. Since the sampling percentages and response rates varied by size class, results are shown separately for each of the four classes, although an average of the coefficients for the four classes is also computed.[4] The cities in the sample are listed, by size class and then by state, in Appendix Table B.2, along with data on city population characteristics, tax rates, and tax incentives.

At the state level of analysis, employing representative cities, state/local effective tax rates exhibited a strong tendency to be higher in higher-unemployment states. A similar, but less strong, relationship occurs when we shift to the city level of analysis, as shown in Table 5.4: cities with higher unemployment rates tend to have higher state/local tax rates (producing lower returns after basic taxes). Two factors no doubt explain the difference in the strength of the correlation: the use of city rather than statewide average unemployment rates, and the fact that more populous states are represented at the city level by more cities.

When we shift to the city level of analysis, tax incentives are much more prevalent and of greater magnitude. At the state level, they include only statewide investment and jobs credits, offered in just 8 of the 24 states. In the city analysis, these incentives are included along with state incentives targeted at enterprise zones or the like (where the city contains such a zone) and local property tax abatements, in enterprise zones or generally. Property tax abatements are allowed in 14 of the 24 states, and 22 permit enterprise zones (although such zones are so limited in two of the states that they play no significant role). State tax incentives now include state-funded enterprise zone incentives in 43 of our 112 cities.[5]

Table 5.4 Correlation between City 1992 Unemployment Rate and Firm's Net Returns from New Plant Investment in Each City (Multistate Firms)[a]

Firm (plant size, in millions)	Net project returns			Value of incentives				
	After basic taxes	After tax incentives	After all incentives	State tax incentives	Local tax incentives	State and local tax incentives	Other incentives	All incentives
Average for all city sizes								
#2: Furniture ($40)	(0.23)	(0.02)	(0.05)	0.18	0.21	0.27	(0.04)	0.21
#5: Soaps ($20)	(0.21)	0.00[b]	0.00[b]	0.19	0.21	0.28	(0.04)	0.22
#7: Plastics ($5)	(0.18)	(0.02)	0.04	0.22	0.22	0.27	0.03	0.18
#14 Autos ($600)	(0.15)	(0.04)	(0.06)	0.23	0.17	0.24	(0.14)	0.19
#16: Instruments ($180)	(0.24)	(0.04)	(0.06)	0.21	0.20	0.28	(0.06)	0.24
Average of 16 firms by city size								
500,000 or more	(0.37)	(0.26)	(0.16)	(0.11)	0.32	0.20	0.04	0.17
100,000 - 499,999	(0.09)	0.18	0.10	0.16	0.35	0.30	(0.17)	0.19
25,000 - 99,999	(0.09)	0.17	0.10	0.40	0.23	0.44	(0.10)	0.29
10,000 - 24,999	(0.34)	(0.35)	(0.24)	0.10	0.02	0.17	0.09	0.13
Average: all cities	(0.20)	(0.03)	(0.03)	0.21	0.20	.024	(0.04)	0.21

a. Negative correlations are shown in parentheses. Basic taxes include state and city corporate income and net worth taxes, state and local sales taxes on machinery and equipment and fuel and utilities, and state and local property taxes. Tax incentives consist of state income/net worth tax investment and jobs credits, sales tax exemptions or credits available only in enterprise zones, state property tax credits available only in enterprise zones, and local property tax abatements. The value of incentives is measured by the net project returns after taxes and incentives, less project returns after basic taxes only. The average correlation for all city sizes is a weighted average of the coefficients for the four city size classes; the weight for a size class is the U.S. population living in cities of that size divided by the total U.S. population living in cities of 10,000 or more.
b. Value less than 0.005.

As a result, state tax incentives are more strongly (and positively) correlated with unemployment at the city level, and this pattern is reinforced by local tax incentives. The net effect of state and local tax incentives is to offset the perverse effects of basic state and local taxes. This fundamental pattern is not altered by the addition of state and local non-tax incentives, which bear no discernible relationship to unemployment. (Infrastructure subsidies, job training subsidies, and general-purpose grants and loans are not treated separately here because of the paucity of such programs at the local level.) The combined effect of local taxes, local tax incentives, and targeted incentives is to negate, but not reverse, the perverse pattern exhibited by returns after statewide taxes and incentives. That is, returns no longer bear any relationship to local unemployment rates; correlations are near zero.

The relationship between incentive size and the city unemployment rate does vary substantially by city size class. For the largest and smallest cities, the tax systems significantly favor low-unemployment places, and incentives do not contribute as much to the alleviation of this problem. For the middle two groups, on the other hand, there is virtually no relationship between unemployment and returns after basic taxes, but the tax incentives favor the high-unemployment cities to a much larger degree. Returns after all incentives are negatively correlated with unemployment for the largest and smallest cities, positively correlated for the medium-size cities. This is the case for both single-location and multistate firms. The results for the largest city size class should be interpreted with caution. The number of cities is small (12), and the correlations are heavily influenced by one outlier city, Detroit, which has by far the highest unemployment rate (19.7 percent) but also has high state and local taxes, and so ends up near or at the bottom of the large city group in project returns.

The overall conclusion is that the spatial pattern of state and local taxes and incentives may well result in a spatial redistribution of jobs, but this redistribution will not bear any consistent relationship with local employment conditions. The winning cities will include those with high unemployment and those with low unemployment; the same will be true of the cities losing jobs.

Do taxes and incentives tend to draw investment to cities with higher poverty rates? Once again, the answer depends on the city size (see Table 5.5). Among the middle two size classes (cities with popula-

Table 5.5 Correlation between City 1990 Poverty Rate and Firm's Net Returns from New Plant Investment in Each City: Multistate Firms Only[a]

Firm (plant size, in millions)	Net project returns			Value of incentives		
	After basic taxes	After tax incentives	After all incentives	Tax incentives	Other incentives	All incentives
Average for all city sizes						
#2: Furniture ($40)	(0.04)	0.18	0.17	0.31	0.03	0.29
#5: Soaps ($20)	(0.01)	0.24	0.24	0.35	0.02	0.31
#7: Plastics ($5)	(0.04)	0.18	0.21	0.35	0.10	0.28
#14: Autos ($600)	0.01	0.15	0.15	0.28	0.01	0.26
#16: Instruments ($180)	(0.05)	0.16	0.15	0.32	0.05	0.32
Average of 16 firms by city size						
500,000 or more	(0.35)	(0.32)	(0.16)	0.04	0.12	0.14
100,000 - 499,999	(0.01)	0.33	0.28	0.42	0.00[b]	0.35
25,000 - 99,999	0.07	0.30	0.23	0.42	(0.05)	0.29
10,000 - 24,999	(0.09)	(0.03)	0.06	0.15	0.17	0.22
Average: all cities	(0.03)	0.18	0.17	0.32	0.04	0.29

a. Negative correlations are shown in parentheses. Poverty rate is based on the 1990 census (1989 income). See also notes to Table 5.4.
b. Value less than 0.005.

tions between 25,000 and 499,999) there is a significant tendency for investment returns to favor higher-poverty cities, and this is due entirely to the effects of tax incentives. For the largest and smallest cities, the results are quite ambiguous. (There is a small negative correlation for the largest class, but, again, the small number of cities in this class and the effect of Detroit, with a very high poverty rate, lead one to interpret the correlations for this size class with caution.)

THE EFFECTS OF ENTERPRISE ZONES

While the employment data cited have suggested that only a small share of job growth occurs within enterprise zones, our sample of cities included 44 that contained enterprise zones or were located in a high-unemployment county that qualified for special state tax incentives. This group represented nearly 40 percent of the cities in our sample. This is not necessarily inconsistent with the jobs data; it could be that much job growth occurs in rural areas, smaller cities, and in enterprise zone cities but not within the zones themselves. Nonetheless, the prevalence of enterprise zones, particularly in the larger cities that also tend to have higher unemployment and poverty rates, suggests that further exploration is needed of the effects of zone incentives on the spatial distribution of investment returns.

We divided each city size class into cities without enterprise zones and cities with enterprise zones or similar designations (which include cities in distressed counties). For the three smaller size classes, and for all cities pooled, the enterprise zone cities had substantially higher concentrations of the unemployed, the poor, and blacks (see Table 5.6). This was not the case in the largest city size class, again due in part to the effect of Detroit, which was one of only two non-enterprise zone cities in the largest class. (The other is Seattle, with an unemployment rate of only 4.9 percent.) Enterprise zones are clearly concentrated in larger cities.

Table 5.7 compares cities of 25,000 population or more with and without enterprise zones. (There were enterprise zones in only 2 of the 21 cities of 10,000 to 24,999 population.) The enterprise zone cities provided returns on investment after basic state and local taxes that

Table 5.6 Characteristics of Cities with and without Enterprise Zones, 1992[a]

Characteristics	City population				
	500,000 or more	100,000– 499,999	25,000– 99,999	10,000– 24,999	All
Cities without enterprise zones					
Number of cities	2	20	27	19	68
Average unemployment rate (%)	12.3	6.3	5.9	6.0	6.2
Average poverty rate (%)	22.4	13.2	11.0	13.6	12.7
Average black pop. (%)	42.9	14.8	10.4	6.9	11.7
Cities with enterprise zones					
Number of cities	10	21	11	2	44
Average unemployment rate (%)	8.0	8.1	7.3	8.4	7.9
Average poverty rate (%)	18.1	18.7	17.0	25.4	18.4
Average black pop. (%)	20.6	25.3	12.1	38.6	21.6
All cities					
Number of cities	12	41	38	21	112
Average unemployment rate (%)	8.7	7.2	6.3	6.2	6.9
Average poverty rate (%)	18.8	16.0	12.7	14.7	14.9
Average black pop. (%)	24.3	20.2	10.9	9.9	15.6
Cities with enterprise zone (%)	83.3	51.2	28.9	9.5	39.3
Ratio: EZ cities/non-EZ cities					
Average unemployment rate (%)	0.65	1.28	1.24	1.40	1.27
Average poverty rate (%)	0.81	1.42	1.54	1.87	1.45
Average black pop. (%)	0.48	1.71	1.16	5.57	1.84

a. The term "enterprise zones" is used here to include programs in three states that provide state incentives in selected distressed counties. EZ = enterprise zone.

were slightly lower than returns in the other cities. Interestingly, the enterprise zone cities provided far more regular tax incentives (not limited to enterprise zones) as well as generous enterprise zone incentives. The total tax incentive package in the enterprise zone cities was on average 6 to 10 times as large as the tax incentives offered in the other cities. Other (non-tax) incentives were comparable in the cities with and without enterprise zones. The result of the more generous tax incentives was that returns on investment after all taxes and incentives were from 4 to 136 percent greater (considering the five firms in Table 5.7) in the enterprise zone cities than in the other cities.

State-funded tax incentives provided only to firms locating in enterprise zones (investment and jobs credits for the most part, but also sales tax exemptions) account for most (about 80 percent on average) of the total state/local enterprise zone benefits. Furthermore, in cities with enterprise zones, the enterprise zone incentives account for 29 to 51 percent of the total incentive package, including loans and grants. Thus it is due in part to the state-funded targeted incentives that the tax incentives overall are able to largely offset the perverse effects of state/ local taxes. Table 5.8 shows that, for all city sizes on average, enterprise zone incentives are positively correlated with the unemployment rate. This is hardly surprising, given that an above-average local unemployment rate is generally one of the criteria for enterprise zone eligibility. It is surprising, actually, that the correlation is not higher. This is due to the fact that some high-unemployment places have no enterprise zones, while some states permit enterprise zones in cities with unemployment rates that are only average (at least among our sample). Interestingly, non-enterprise zone tax incentives are also positively correlated with unemployment, and the relationship is more consistent across city sizes.

Thus, while property tax abatement is by no means limited to enterprise zones, the prevalence of additional state tax incentives in such zones appears to be enough to give zone cities a competitive edge (other things equal) that helps tilt the investment return surface towards higher-unemployment places. The exception appears to be the large city class, but once again the average unemployment rate figure is skewed by Detroit, one of only two large cities without an enterprise zone but with a very high unemployment rate.[6] More important is the fact that the 10 large cities with enterprise zones have unemployment

Table 5.7 The Importance of Enterprise Zone (EZ) Incentives: Average Value among Cities of 25,000 or More for Selected Multistate Firms[a]

	#2, Furniture $40[b]	#5, Soap $20	#7, Plastics $5	#14, Auto $600	#16, Instruments $180
	Cities with enterprise zones				
Project returns ($)					
After basic taxes only	8,178,094	8,044,876	81,864	1,692,898	56,067,884
After all incentives	9,883,505	8,873,916	390,703	13,359,831	60,418,974
Value of incentives ($)					
State EZ tax incentives	588,014	302,579	71,339	3,667,208	1,582,707
Local EZ tax incentives	155,697	63,926	17,429	2,255,746	613,479
Total EZ package	743,711	366,505	88,768	5,922,955	2,196,186
Non-EZ tax incentives	306,551	136,328	31,560	4,176,537	1,119,438
Total tax incentive package	1,050,262	502,833	120,327	10,099,492	3,315,624
Non-tax incentives	655,149	326,207	188,512	1,567,440	1,035,466
Total incentive package	1,705,411	829,040	308,840	11,666,932	4,351,090
Percentages					
State EZ incentives/total EZ pkg.	79.1	82.6	80.4	61.9	72.1
EZ tax incentives/all tax incentives	70.8	72.9	73.8	58.6	66.2
EZ tax incentives/total incentive pkg.	43.6	44.2	28.7	50.8	50.5
	Cities without enterprise zones				
Project returns ($)					
After basic taxes only	8,253,901	8,065,024	103,904	2,331,201	56,614,836

(continued)

Table 5.7 (continued)

	#2, Furniture $40[b]	#5, Soap $20	#7, Plastics $5	#14, Auto $600	#16, Instruments $180
After all incentives	9,053,221	8,463,266	267,499	5,666,855	58,090,749
Value of incentives ($)					
Total tax incentive package	109,933	53,659	11,858	1,592,400	384,845
Non-tax incentives	689,387	344,583	151,737	1,743,254	1,091,068
Total incentive package	799,320	398,242	163,595	3,335,654	1,475,913
Ratios: EZ cities to non-EZ cities					
Project returns					
After basic taxes only	0.99	1.00	0.79	0.73	0.99
After all incentives	1.09	1.05	1.46	2.36	1.04
Value of incentives					
Non-EZ tax incentives	2.79	2.54	2.66	2.62	2.91
Total tax incentive package	9.55	9.37	10.15	6.34	8.62
Non-tax incentives	0.95	0.95	1.24	0.90	0.95
Total incentive package	2.13	2.08	1.89	3.50	2.95

a. EZ = enterprise zone. Because only 2 of the 21 cities under 25,000 population had enterprise zones, we confined the analysis to cities of 25,000 or more. The value of state enterprise zone incentives is measured by the difference between the present value of new plant cash flow after all tax incentives and the present value of new plant cash flow given all tax incentives except state enterprise zone incentives. The value of the total enterprise zone package is the difference between the present value of new plant cash flow after all taxes and tax incentives and the present value of new plant cash flow after all taxes and non-enterprise zone tax incentives. The value of local enterprise zone incentives is the difference between the value of the total enterprise zone package and the value of state enterprise zone incentives. The total incentive package includes job training, infrastructure, and general financing programs. Items may not add to total due to rounding.
b. Firm size in millions of dollars.

Table 5.8 Correlation between City Unemployment Rate and Value of Incentives: Enterprise Zone versus Other Incentives (Multistate Firms)

Firm (plant size in millions)	Value of enterprise zone tax incentives		Value of state and local non-EZ incentives		Returns without EZ incentives	
	State	State and local	Tax incentives	All incentives	After tax incentives	After all incentives
Average for all city sizes						
#2: Furniture ($40)	0.22	0.22	0.18	0.08	(0.15)	(0.16)
#5: Soaps ($20)	0.25	0.24	0.16	0.07	(0.13)	(0.12)
#7: Plastics ($5)	0.15	0.17	0.21	0.10	(0.11)	(0.03)
#14: Autos ($600)	0.09	0.07	0.20	0.14	(0.08)	(0.10)
#16: Instruments ($180)	0.23	0.20	0.20	0.12	(0.16)	(0.17)
Average of 16 firms by city size						
500,000 or more	(0.37)	(0.33)	0.45	0.38	(0.12)	(0.05)
100,000 - 499,999	0.17	0.20	0.25	0.06	0.04	(0.02)
25,000 - 99,999	0.45	0.36	0.24	0.08	0.01	(0.04)
10,000 - 24,999	0.00[a]	0.00[a]	0.06	0.12	(0.36)	(0.25)
Average: all cities	0.19	0.18	0.19	0.11	(0.13)	(0.11)

Note: For definitions, see notes to previous tables.
a. Value less than 0.005.

and poverty rates similar to those of the smaller cities with zones and higher than most cities without zones; these large zone cities also provide project returns that on average are higher than returns in the smaller nonzone cities. Consequently, then, the large cities as a group, excluding Detroit, reinforce the preceding conclusions that enterprise zone incentives, if effective, would tend to pull jobs towards high-unemployment places.

Nonetheless, the targeting of tax incentives alone is not sufficient to produce a pattern of returns on investment, after all taxes and incentives, that favors higher-unemployment places, as we showed earlier. A comparison of Table 5.4 and Table 5.8 is instructive. The last column in Table 5.8 shows that, in the absence of enterprise zone incentives, returns on investment would be negatively correlated with unemployment rates, although the correlations are quite weak. An examination of the third column in Table 5.4, showing project returns with enterprise zone incentives included, reveals that the effect of enterprise zones is to offset, but not reverse, the perverse distributional pattern of returns (though, again, this is true on average for all cities but not the largest size class).

Remember that, in those 42 cities where the enterprise zone is just a part of the city, we have allowed the incentives that apply to firms locating within the zones to represent the incentive package for the entire city; this exaggerates the role of enterprise zones. (For the two enterprise zone cities that are actually part of a distressed county, the "zone" incentives do apply throughout the city.) At the same time, the distributional effects are muted by the use of citywide unemployment rates, which are presumably lower than rates within the zones. This seems a reasonable procedure on the grounds that the labor market effects will be felt well beyond the zone itself, even if direct hiring by the new enterprise zone firm is concentrated on zone residents due to statutory restrictions. Nonetheless, if only a small share of job growth occurs within enterprise zones, the correlations that include enterprise zone effects in 40 percent of our cities do exaggerate the role of enterprise zone incentives. The pattern of returns shown in the last two columns of Table 5.8 may more accurately reflect the overall pattern.

Figure 5.1 illustrates the lack of any consistent pattern by focusing on a firm typical in terms of the correlation of taxes and incentives with unemployment—the instruments manufacturer building a $180 million

197

Figure 5.1 Rate of Return on New Plant Investment in Top 25 Cities: Multistate Instruments Manufacturer, $180 Million Plant

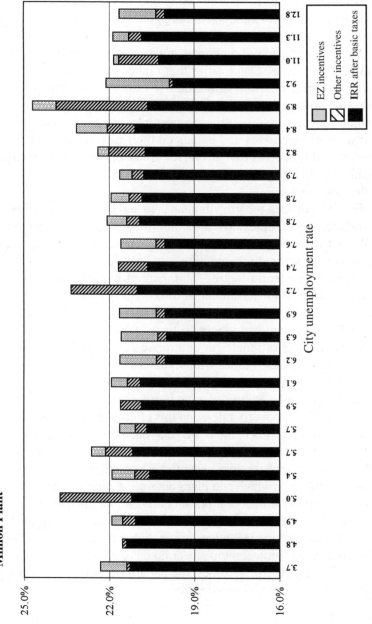

plant. We show only the top 25 cities (those with the highest internal rate of return for this plant after taking into account all taxes and incentives), ordered by unemployment rate. For each city, the graph displays the rate of return after basic taxes and how this rate of return is bettered through the provision of enterprise zone incentives and other (tax and non-tax) incentives. Some cities that ranked poorly after basic taxes improved their position dramatically though non-enterprise zone incentives; others did so through enterprise zone credits. Certain cities, including some with relatively low unemployment, were very competitive without incentives and enhanced their position further through incentives. In other words, incentives are not primarily compensating for high basic taxes, nor are they able to offset the tax disadvantage of high-unemployment cities.

The link between job growth in an area and the incidence of poverty is undoubtedly complex, given the interrelationships between poverty and the factors that contribute to it—unemployment, low-wage employment, wage discrimination, occupational segregation by race and gender, residential segregation, lack of human capital, and mismatches between jobs available and the skills or location of the poor. The attraction of new investment to poverty areas or poorer cities may well be an important part of an effective antipoverty strategy and is certainly part of the rationale for enterprise zones. Are enterprise zone incentives advantaging cities with high rates of poverty? Are the incentives large enough to plausibly make a difference?

Not surprisingly, enterprise zone incentives are noticeably larger in cities with higher poverty rates, and this effect is amplified by the addition of local incentives to the more generous state incentives (see Table 5.9). A comparison of the third and fourth columns of Table 5.9 (the value of non-enterprise zone incentives) and the fourth and sixth columns of Table 5.5 (which combines enterprise zone and non-enterprise zone incentives) shows that tax incentives, and all incentives taken together, favor high poverty places to a substantially larger degree when enterprise zone incentives are included in the analysis. Without enterprise zones, project returns bear no consistent relationship to poverty rates; with enterprise zones, the pattern of returns after all incentives favors poorer cities to a degree.

Table 5.9 Correlation between City Poverty Rate and Value of Incentives: Enterprise Zone versus Other Incentives (Multistate Firms)

Firm (plant size in millions)	Value of enterprise zone tax incentives		Value of state and local non-EZ incentives		Returns without EZ incentives	
	State	State and local	Tax incentives	All incentives	After tax incentives	After all incentives
Average for all city sizes						
#2: Furniture ($40)	0.27	0.30	0.17	0.12	0.05	0.04
#5: Soaps ($20)	0.35	0.36	0.15	0.11	0.07	0.09
#7: Plastics ($5)	0.20	0.25	0.21	0.17	0.05	0.11
#14: Autos ($600)	0.04	0.05	0.21	0.20	0.11	0.11
#16: Instruments ($180)	0.26	0.27	0.18	0.17	0.04	0.03
Average of 16 firms by city size						
500,000 or more	(0.42)	(0.39)	0.36	0.38	(0.14)	(0.02)
100,000 - 499,999	0.20	0.36	0.23	0.14	0.10	0.08
25,000 - 99,999	0.47	0.35	0.22	0.10	0.18	0.11
10,000 - 24,999	0.04	0.04	0.10	0.19	(0.05)	0.05
Average: all cities	0.22	0.24	0.19	0.15	0.06	0.07

Note: For definitions, see notes to previous tables.

CONCLUSIONS

State tax systems exhibit a strong tendency to skew returns on new industrial investment in a perverse direction, producing higher after-tax returns in states with lower unemployment rates, other things equal. This perverse pattern is largely offset by state tax credits and by local taxes and tax incentives, which tend to be more favorable in states and cities with higher unemployment. Non-tax incentives, on the other hand, vary dramatically with firm characteristics; for large plants, such incentives at the state level very clearly favor low-unemployment cities, while for smaller plants the relationship is nonexistent. The large versus small distinction fails to hold up at the city level of analysis, however. The end result is a spatial pattern of returns on new invest-ment that has little or no bearing to the spatial pattern of unemploy-ment among cities.

The *explicit* development incentives are indeed laid out so as to make investment more attractive in the places most in need of jobs. It may be that, in the absence of state and local concern with develop-ment, such incentives would not have been adopted and the state and local tax system overall would have remained perverse in its effects. We could then conclude that incentive competition has produced a neu-tral (or random) spatial distribution of returns, which at least is better than what would have prevailed in the absence of incentives. However, that is the most we could say. Furthermore, to the extent that much of the focus of state level policy has been on features of the tax system that we have included in the "basic" tax, rather than as incentives, it is not clear that even this much can be said. The only firm conclusion is that, after at least a decade and a half of intense competition for invest-ment and jobs, and the widespread adoption of pro-development tax policies and incentives, states and cities have produced a tax and incen-tive system that provides no clear inducement for firms to invest in higher-unemployment places.

These results are consistent with the thesis that state and local eco-nomic development incentives are adopted for a variety of reasons—high unemployment being but one, simple imitation of other states being another—and that such incentives are likely to persist even if state economic performance (and state unemployment rates) improve.

Furthermore, to the extent that slow economic growth is the driving force, the relationship between incentives and unemployment will be a weak one, because slow growth, at least as measured by net job gains, is not clearly associated with high unemployment rates.

NOTES

1. From the 16 firms, we selected 5 that represent prototypes with distinct characteristics, such as size, profitability, and capital intensity. Each of the five is representative of a set of firms whose after-tax returns across states are highly correlated (0.9 or better). Firm 2, the large furniture manufacturer, is a good proxy for firms 8, 10, 11, and 13. Firm 5, the small soap and toiletries firm, is a good proxy for firms 6, 9, 11, and 15. Firm 7 (plastics, small) is a stand-in for firms 1 and 9. Firm 14 (the large automobile manufacturer) is a proxy for 8, 10, 12, and 13; and firm 16 (instruments, large) is a proxy for 3, 4, 6, and 12.

2. Given the small number of cities in our sample in many states, and given the substantial variation across cities in the use of non-tax incentive programs, there was no way to establish with any confidence a representative package of local non-tax incentives for each state. While a state non-tax incentive package could obviously have been specified in the representative city analyses, this would not have provided us any additional information beyond the state-level analysis already conducted with state taxes and incentives only.

3. The positive correlation of 0.10 between state tax incentives and job growth in Table 5.3 seems to be at odds with the negative correlation of –0.27 in Table 5.2. The apparent discrepancy is due to the inclusion of state enterprise zone incentives in Table 5.3.

4. In order to summarize the results across city size classes, we computed an average of the correlation coefficients for each size class. (An overall correlation coefficient for all of the cities pooled would not be valid because of the different sampling rates.) If the importance of the results for a city size class is a function of the portion of the U.S. population living in cities of that size, then the logical weights are population proportions. This is the method we chose: to compute a weighted average of the four correlation coefficients, where the weight is the total U.S. population in that city size class divided by the total U.S. population in the four city size classes together.

5. Enterprise zones existed in 44 of the cities, but the Ohio city with an enterprise zone does not benefit from any state enterprise zone incentives.

6. After 1992, Detroit won federal Empowerment Zone status.

6 .Incentive Competition and Public Policy

State and local economic development policy has been the subject of much debate in the press in recent years, with most of the criticism focused on the large subsidy packages resulting from interstate bidding wars for major plants. It is important to remember that these bidding wars have been occurring against a backdrop of state and local tax policies and ongoing incentive programs that have been on the books for many years, themselves subject to escalation as a result of competitive pressures. The Urban Institute and the National Association of State Development Agencies first published their *Directory of Incentives for Business Investment and Development in the United States* in 1981; it catalogued the major tax incentives, loan and grant programs, loan guarantees, customized job training, and other programs offered routinely by the states. It is these kinds of programs, both at the state and at the local level, that have been the subject of our research, along with the overall effects of state and local tax regimes.

In this chapter, we review the major findings of our study and their implications for public policy at the local, state, and national level. Are the tax and incentive differences across locations significant enough that they should even be a concern of policymakers? Do the results of this study shed any light on the debate over the effects of incentive competition on the efficiency of industrial location and hence on national productivity? What have we learned about the possible national benefits of state and local competition as a result of the redistribution of jobs? Should Congress intervene to limit competition, and how could this be done?

ARE TAX AND INCENTIVE DIFFERENCES IMPORTANT?

Most of the programs and policies that we call explicit economic development incentives—investment and jobs tax credits, property tax abatements, infrastructure subsidies, customized job training programs, business loans, grants, and loan guarantees—have become widespread only in the past 20 years, as states and cities have attempted to respond to a more uncertain and competitive economic environment. These incentives operate against a backdrop of state and local taxes that themselves have been changed in response to those same economic pressures, but in ways that are much more difficult to identify. We have chosen to define a basic state and local tax system— including income, net worth, sales, and property taxes—that initially determines the competitiveness of a site for new business investment, by establishing the after-tax return on investment available at that site, given a particular firm and plant size and a particular technology and set of input prices. We then determine how the various explicit incentives offered by states and localities alter that after-tax return and affect the relative profitability of different kinds of locations.

When we examined returns on investment at the starting point of our analysis—after basic taxes only—we found very wide differences among states and cities. The divergences were exaggerated when we examined state taxes only, for the simple reason that states with high state income and sales taxes tend to have lower local property and sales taxes. However, even when we looked at the results after paying all state and local taxes (but before receiving any incentives) we found very large differences between the returns available at the "best" locations and those available at the "worst" locations. Tax differences have very substantial effects on the spatial pattern of returns. Even when we ignored variation within states (by focusing on a representative city in each state), we found effective state/local tax rates on new investment that ranged, for example, from 3 percent to 13 percent for a small but profitable manufacturer of soaps and toiletries, and from 7 percent to 27 percent for a large but low-profit automobile manufacturer (Table 4.6). The highest tax state placed a tax burden on manufacturers that was typically about three times as large as the lowest tax state. When we looked at particular localities, the differences were more extreme.

Eight states offered investment or jobs tax credits to firms anywhere in the state (Table 4.4); in 14 of the 24 states, local property tax abatements were offered (Table 4.3). Together, these defined the explicit tax incentives generally available as entitlements (although in a minority of places with abatements, they were discretionary); these incentive packages ranged from zero to as high as 40 percent to 45 percent of the before-incentive state and local tax burden. When enterprise zone incentives were added to the picture, an even larger share of state and local taxes (as high as 65 percent) was forgiven as an economic development incentive in the cities with enterprise zones or similar programs.

Tax incentives generally do not reduce the variation across states; large investment or jobs credits, for example, are not used primarily to offset high basic taxes. Enterprise zone incentives tend to be larger in states that offer less in the way of general incentives. Nonetheless, the effect of enterprise zones is to increase the variation in after-tax returns across states, not to compensate for high basic taxes.

Many of the features of what we call the basic tax system have in fact been listed as tax incentives in the *Directory of Incentives for Business Investment and Development* and have no doubt been enacted in some states for economic development purposes. To a firm building a new plant, some of these tax features, such as the exemption of manufacturing machinery and equipment from the sales tax, the exemption of inventories from the property tax, or the double-weighting of sales in the income tax apportionment formula, provide benefits comparable in size to the benefits from explicit incentives such as a new jobs tax credit.

The non-tax incentives included infrastructure subsidies and customized job training at the state level and general purpose grants, loans, and loan guarantees at both the state and local levels. Averaged over the 16 firm types and 112 cities in 24 states, non-tax incentives, expressed in terms of present value wage equivalence, were worth about 9 cents an hour per employee, for each of 40 hours a week, for 50 weeks a year, for 20 years. In other words, state and local non-tax incentives were worth the equivalent of paying all workers in the new plant 9 cents an hour less over the life of the plant. By comparison, non-tax incentives had a wage equivalence of 7 cents an hour. On the whole, discretionary incentives were larger for small plants (a wage equivalence of 13 cents an hour) than for large plants (5 cents an hour).

Non-tax incentives were a major part of a state's entire incentive package (in fact, in some cases over 90 percent of state incentives derived from non-tax programs). Overall, infrastructure and training programs were of less importance to smaller firms than were general-use subsidies (see Table 4.14). In the case of large firms, infrastructure and training incentives were typically worth more than general-use incentives; in fact, for big firms, training incentives alone were often more substantial than general-use incentives. When local incentives were combined with state ones, the role of discretionary non-tax incentives declined markedly. The combined package of state and local tax incentives was often as large as the combined package of non-tax discretionary incentives. The reasons for this include the provision of very generous tax incentives (such as the property tax abatement) at the local level and the dearth of many large local non-tax incentive programs.[1]

At the local level and averaged over all 16 firm types, 48 percent of the increment in income due to incentives derived from tax incentives, 52 percent derived from non-tax incentives. However, there was substantial variation by firm size. For small firms, non-tax incentives were much more important, making up 65 percent of the incentive offer. In the case of big firms, discretionary incentives were much less significant; only 39 percent of the increment to income derived from non-tax incentives.

Do discretionary incentives change the competitive positions of states and cities? While there were a few notable cases where very large general purpose incentives produced great changes in state or city ranking on the basis of investment returns, overall the answer to this question is "not much." For the handful of cities/states at the top or at the bottom of the rankings, there were very substantial differences in returns between one city or state and the next due to tax and incentive variations; still, the inclusion of incentives very often did little to change the identity of the majority of cities in the top 10 or bottom 10. Mostly, cities that were highly competitive after taxes and tax incentives were also highly competitive after the inclusion of non-tax incentives. Moreover, the majority of cities/states in the middle of the rankings were often separated by very little, at any level of analysis, so that adding or deleting a particular program from the analysis could produce substantial shifts in rankings—but shifts that were of little significance because the size of the differences in income between cities/states was small.

In general, the range (that is, the difference between the best and the worst cities) was greater after the inclusion of non-tax incentives than after basic taxes or basic taxes and tax incentives. Averaged over the 16 firm types, the range after the inclusion of non-tax incentives was 1.4 times that after basic taxes and 1.3 times that after taxes and tax incentives. So non-tax incentives did not ameliorate, but actually accentuated, the differential between the best and worst cities. Also, the degree of accentuation appeared to be greater for small firms than for big firms. However, statistically there was no apparent relationship between the generosity of a particular city/state's non-tax incentive package and the burdensomeness of its taxes. In other words, non-tax incentives exaggerated, at the extremes, spatial disparities in taxes, but for most cities the connection between taxes and non-tax incentives was somewhat random.

Is it reasonable to claim that a city's and state's tax and incentive regime could influence location decisions? Our research has not looked at spatial differentials in other factor costs (such as labor, energy, and transportation) or in the benefits firms receive from taxes, so we are not in a position to give an unequivocal answer to the question. However, our results suggest that, for the firm types simulated by TAIM, the range of results across all 112 cities (and 24 states) is not trivial. Large income differences separated the best and worst locations. In the most extreme case, a hourly wage equivalence of $1.82 divided the top- and bottom-ranked cities (this was for the large drug plant simulation; see Table 4.9). There is a likelihood, of course, that factor cost differentials—in labor, energy, and transportation—could amount to much more than $1.82 an hour. Specifically, it is quite possible that labor costs in our bottom-ranked city could be more than $1.82 an hour lower than in our top-ranked city. As it turns out, they are not. Moreover, if tax and incentive regimes were developed to compensate for locally high labor costs (or other input costs), one would logically expect burdensome tax and incentive regimes in southern states, with much lighter loads in California and states in the Northeast and Midwest. However, the maps in Chapter 4 indicate no regional pattern of taxes and incentives. Since the severity of local tax and incentive regimes does not appear to be inversely related to factor costs, tax and incentive differentials between top- and bottom-ranked locations could reasonably be expected to influence plant location decisions in some situations.

Obviously, most cities are not at the very top or the very bottom of the range, but in the broad middle, where not much separates most locations' tax and incentive regimes. In these cases, tax and incentive differentials may or may not have a decisive impact on plant location decisions; it will all depend on the other factor costs at the various sites competing for the investment. More generally, we are inclined to believe that, unless they have some special factor cost advantage, cities and states with severe tax and incentive regimes will tend to be eliminated from location searches. In other words, the greatest impact of tax and incentive regimes may be to exclude at the outset some cities and states from the game—from competing for a new investment opportunity.

Another way to assess the size of tax and incentive differences is to compare the value of the standing offer in a particular state—the set of such factors as tax incentives, loans, grants, and infrastructure subsidies routinely available to new manufacturing plants—with the incentive packages offered as one-time deals for certain facilities. Since auto plants have frequently been the target of bidding wars by states and cities, we will focus on the recent and much publicized subsidy package offered to Mercedes-Benz for locating a new plant in Vance, Alabama. Table 6.1 shows the nominal value of the initial subsidies and future tax abatements. It is these nominal figures that are promulgated by development officials and subsidy critics and that become the focus of debate. The up-front subsidies equaled $118 million, while the annual tax abatements of $3.1 million totaled $55 million over the first 25 years of the plant's existence. Thus, the entire subsidy package was allegedly worth about $173 million.[2]

For purposes of comparison with the results of this study showing the value to the firm of standing incentive offers, there are two problems with the publicized numbers for the Mercedes plant and with similar figures for incentive deals in other places: 1) the figures show the gross cost of the subsidies to the state and local governments, not the net after-tax value of the subsidies to the firm; 2) future tax subsidies are simply added up instead of discounted. To determine the value of the subsidy package with these problems corrected, we created a new firm to be simulated using TAIM. The new firm is the large multistate auto manufacturer (firm no. 14), but with actual data on the Mercedes plant substituted for our average plant data (in particular, the value of land, infrastructure, plant, machinery and equipment, sales, and employment). Then we created an incentive package in an Alabama

Table 6.1   The Subsidy Package for the Mercedes-Benz Auto Assembly Plant: Gross Value versus Value to the Firm in Alternative Locations[a]

Incentives	Value ($ millions)
Gross undiscounted value of incentives in Vance, Alabama	
Initial subsidies	
Infrastructure	32.0
Site acquisition	17.4
Job training	60.0
Sales tax exemptions	8.2
Miscellaneous	0.7
Subtotal	**118.2**
Tax exemptions	
Property tax abatement: $1.5 million/year for 10 years	15.0
Corporate income tax reduction: $1.6 milion/year for 25 years	40.0
Subtotal	**55.0**
Total value of subsidy package	**173.2**
After-tax present value to the firm of the actual subsidy package	
Initial subsidies	71.6
Tax exemptions	14.3
Total	85.9
After-tax discounted value/gross undiscounted value	49.6%
After-tax present value to the firm of the standing incentive offers provided by selected other cities	
Abilene, Texas	34.0
Atlanta, Georgia	53.5
Bedford, Indiana	42.5
Des Moines, Iowa	29.9
Detroit, Michigan	40.5
Fairfield, Ohio	26.1

(continued)

Table 6.1 (continued)

Huntsville, Alabama	10.9
Joliet, Illinois	33.2
Milwaukee, Wisconsin	16.3
St. Joseph, Missouri	32.9
Syracuse, New York	42.8

a. The figures for the gross undiscounted value of the subsidies are from Ken Blum, *The Mercedes Benz Subsidy Package—Whose Benefits? Whose Losses?* All estimates of the after-tax present value to the firm of the subsidy package or of standing incentive offers were generated by TAIM. The firm simulated was the large, multistate auto plant (no. 14) but with actual data on the value of new plant and equipment and new plant sales and employment for the Mercedes plant (as shown in the cited report) substituted for the average plant data in the usual model runs. Items may not sum to total due to rounding.

city to match the actual package, treating the initial subsidies as grants except for the sales tax exemptions (which were modeled as actual exemptions). The property tax and income tax abatements were treated as annual tax credits of $1.5 million for 10 years and $1.6 million for 25 years, respectively. The value of these subsidies is then measured by TAIM net of the federal and Alabama state income tax effects, and discounted to the present (1992).

The value to the firm of the $173 million nominal package was estimated by TAIM at $86 million, or only about half of its nominal value. This figure can then be compared to the after-tax present value of the standing incentive packages offered in other cities. We selected 11 cities that offered the most generous incentives to large auto plants or that were among the top locations for such plants when cities were ranked by returns after all incentives, and simulated the value of their incentives for the same Mercedes plant. As can be seen in Table 6.1, the best examples of these incentive packages represent about half of the special deal offered in Vance, Alabama (over 60 percent in the case of Atlanta). Still, if Alabama's tax system were relatively burdensome to begin with, the packages in some of the other cities could have been sufficient to make those locations comparable, in terms of after-tax return on investment, to the Alabama site. The important points here are that 1) discussions of incentive packages in the press do not present accurate measures of their true worth to the firm, 2) standing incentive offers are not trivial in comparison with the much publicized one-time deals, and 3) incentive packages must be judged in the context of the basic state and local tax system. It is also important to note that the big deals usually are put together in a fashion to make them appear most attractive to the firms and usually include as part of the package the routine incentives that have been the focus of this study.

THE SPATIAL PATTERN OF INCENTIVES AND THE NATIONAL BENEFITS OF COMPETITIVE ECONOMIC DEVELOPMENT POLICY

If the competition among states and cities for jobs is to produce net gains for the nation as a whole, it must be the case that the overall level of investment is greater as a result (because the competition has raised average after-tax returns on investment and thereby drawn capital from overseas or has increased the nation's rate of savings and capital formation), and/or the redistribution of jobs must be such as to increase employment in the places where it provides the most benefit. Because reservation wages tend to be lower in high-unemployment places, the net benefits of a job (the wage paid minus the reservation wage) are more there. We have been investigating the latter hypothesis, namely that incentives are greater in places of high unemployment, opening up the possibility that incentives redistribute jobs from low-unemployment to high-unemployment states and cities.

The explicit tax incentives that have been the focus of our research do indeed exhibit some tendency to make investment more attractive in the places most in need of jobs. State tax incentives are positively, but very weakly, correlated with state unemployment rates (Table 5.1), and combined state and city tax incentives are positively correlated with city unemployment rates (Table 5.4). For state non-tax incentives, the picture is mixed. For large firms, higher-unemployment states provided *smaller* incentive packages, for most of the firms in our study, but for small firms the relationship was virtually nonexistent. At the city level of analysis, results are also mixed, but the general conclusion is that state and local non-tax incentives exhibit no discernible relation to city unemployment rates.

The results for tax and non-tax incentives together lend only weak support to the hypothesis that incentive competition produces a spatial pattern of returns favoring places with more severe unemployment; the value of all incentives combined is mildly positively correlated with city unemployment rates (Table 5.4). However, this conclusion is tempered, if not negated, by considering the overall pattern of after-tax returns. State tax systems exhibit a strong tendency to skew returns on new industrial investment in a perverse direction, producing higher after-tax returns in states with lower unemployment rates, other things equal (Table 5.1). This perverse pattern is offset to a degree by local taxes, which tend to be more favorable in states and cities with higher unemployment (Table 5.3). Nevertheless, the incentives taken in the aggregate are still not enough to clearly offset the effects of state taxes. The end result is a spatial pattern of returns on new investment that bears little or no relationship to the spatial pattern of unemployment. It appears that, after at least a decade and a half of intense competition for investment and jobs, and the widespread adoption of pro-development tax policies and development programs, states and cities have produced a system of taxes and incentives with no clear inducement for firms to invest in higher-unemployment places.

These results are consistent with the following two arguments (although they certainly cannot be taken as proof of either one): 1) state and local economic development incentives are adopted for a variety of reasons, including high unemployment, but, more importantly, slow growth and simple imitation of other states; and 2) even where economic distress, as measured by high unemployment, provided the original political impetus to incentive adoption, incentives are likely to persist in spite of improvement in state economic performance. The latter point is corroborated by recent experience in Iowa, which has remained a low-unemployment state but which has continued, in the three years since our analysis was conducted, to further enhance its already very competitive position by abolishing property taxes on manufacturing machinery and equipment.

TAXES, INCENTIVES, AND EFFICIENCY

Recent critiques of incentive competition by academic economists have focused on the issue of efficiency in the location of economic activity. The arguments are aimed primarily or exclusively at firm-specific deals on the grounds that they distort the location decision, inducing businesses to choose a site that would otherwise not be the least-cost location and producing a geographic pattern of plant locations that is less efficient for the national economy (Burstein and Rolnick 1995). The conclusion is that competition is a negative-sum game.

These economists begin with the assumption that incentives do make a difference, no doubt in part because they argue from a theoretical perspective that tells them that the decisions of profit-maximizing firms will be affected at the margin by differences in cost. The economists appear to be on reasonably solid empirical grounds in this case. Those who have reviewed the very extensive literature on the effectiveness of tax policy or of incentive competition have concluded that the bulk of the evidence now appears to support the thesis that differences in tax levels do measurably affect rates of economic growth (Bartik 1991b).

Unlike many of the labor and other activists who have been broadly critical of incentives, however, economists may in fact argue that state and local competition for business that focuses on broad tax and fiscal policies is actually beneficial and can increase efficiency in business location. Oates and Schwab (1991), for example, extend the Tiebout hypothesis to business location, arguing that having a variety of localities offering different bundles of taxes and public services will permit a business to choose the optimal tax-service bundle for that firm. Furthermore, competition among governments will force them to be more efficient in providing services and to reduce general taxes on business, eliminating any fiscal surplus derived from the business tax base. Therefore, business taxes will come to approximate prices for each locality's bundle of public services, and efficiency in business location will be enhanced since all inputs will then be priced on the basis of marginal cost. According to such economic models, tax competition is good as long as it is not specific to a firm or sector. Tax prices should reflect only costs, not local preferences for particular kinds of firms, preferences that are often implicit in subsidy programs. The arguments against firm- or sector-specific tax policies are the same as the mainstream economists' arguments against state industrial policy.

This line of thinking has led economists to call for federal intervention to reduce incentive competition. In 1995, for example, a group of over 100 economists and others issued a press release calling for an end to "targeted business incentive programs" (Heartland Institute 1995) but favoring statewide business tax relief. Others have proposed banning the use of federal funds to underwrite competition. There have been frequent calls for states to enact truces, and multistate agreements to cease bidding for firms have actually been reached, although the results so far have not been promising (Council of State Governments 1994).

In reality, the world of industrial incentives runs on a continuum, from the one-time deals tailored to a particular firm that is the object of a bidding war, to such broad-scale tax policies as an across-the-board reduction in the corporate income tax rate. In between is a wide range of policies and programs that are targeted in one sense or another but are available on the same terms to more than one particular firm. These strategies include tax incentives that are actually entitlements: that is, investment tax credits and new jobs tax credits; sales tax exemptions for machinery and equipment, or for fuel and electricity used in manufacturing; and property tax abatements for all new industrial construction. The sectoral targeting here is generally quite broad, including all of manufacturing plus, in some states, categories such as warehousing, research and development, or corporate headquarters. However, the approach is more targeted than a general rate reduction, inducing more investment in areas such as manufacturing and drawing capital from others, such as services. Further, by applying only to income from new investment, the programs introduce additional distortions, lowering the cost of replacement capital relative to the implicit cost of keeping old capital.

Equally important, sectoral and industry targeting is implicit in many state and local tax systems and incentive programs. There is substantial variation among firms even within the manufacturing sector with respect to asset composition (the relative importance of working capital, plant and land, machinery and equipment, and inventories) and cost structure (for example, the share of costs accounted for by wages or energy, or the average wage level). As a result, there is wide variation in tax burdens across industries for any given location. States that rely heavily on local property tax financing for provision of local services will have lighter corporate income and sales tax burdens, which will advantage firms with high profit rates and disadvantage firms with a high proportion of real property (plant and equipment) in their asset base. Similarly, a sales tax exemption for fuel and electricity could be worth several times as much to an energy-intensive operation as to the average manufacturing establishment. Table 4.5 illustrated these effects: the exemption of machinery and equipment from the sales tax represented a savings of 17 percent of total state/local taxes for the auto firm, but only 9.4 percent for the instrument manufacturer, while the exemption of fuel and electricity was worth 1.2 percent of taxes for the large drug firm but 6.6 percent for the small plastics company. Exemption of inventories from the property tax was worth twice as much to the large instruments manufacturer as to the large drug firm, and a similar disparity in value applied to the exemption of manufacturing machinery and equipment, when comparing the instruments and auto firms. In states where real property is taxed but all personal property is exempt by statute and always has been, a firm will benefit from a higher after-tax return on investment than would occur in a city in another state that taxes personal property but that advertises a local exemption for machinery and equipment.

Incentives are never neutral, by sector, by factor of production, by type of capital, by new versus old investment, and certainly not by location. The important point is that state and local tax systems are never neutral either. Thus, the basic premise of Burstein and Rolnick (1996)—that state and local tax systems would exercise a neutral influence on the location of economic activity and the composition of investment in the absence of firm-specific incentives—is faulty. Reschovsky (1991) delineates some problems with the Tiebout model applied to business location; he argues that the prevalence of collective goods makes it difficult to achieve equality between business tax burdens and business service bundles. Our research points up another problem: tax burdens will vary from one firm to another for reasons that probably have little bearing on the service needs of those businesses.

The sectoral patterns that emerge from an examination of state and local taxes and incentives are surely not deliberate on the part of policymakers. It is unlikely that the impacts of particular tax policies or programs on different industrial sectors are even considered, even less that the end result can be taken as the expression of some well-thought-out industrial policy. There is probably as little rhyme or reason to the spatial preferences for different industries embodied in the pattern of returns after taxes and incentives in 1992 as there was in the pattern of these returns in 1972. It is difficult to argue that two decades of competition has produced a more efficient pattern of location inducements. Furthermore, since states and localities appear to engage in incentive competition to provide jobs and benefits to workers and residents at least as much as to gain tax base, there is some reason to believe that incentive competition will proceed beyond the point of efficiency that has been described, with states and cities providing subsidies to business in the interest of job creation even if the long-term fiscal effects are negative. Tax and incentive competition will in all likelihood produce a pattern where a sizable fiscal surplus remains in some places that have sufficient inherent locational advantages to offset a poor tax-service bundle, while other places establish incentives so large that they create a fiscal deficit. The argument that tax burdens (after incentives) will come to represent prices for public services seems optimistic, at best.

If the federal government were to succeed in ending the firm-specific deals, would the outcome be more efficient location patterns, as Burstein and Rolnick maintain? There is reason to be skeptical. States and localities are very likely to respond to such prohibitions by exercising their ingenuity in devising other ways of providing indirect subsidies to particular firms; the provision of free infrastructure and services would very likely become commonplace. It would be very difficult to monitor such activities or to define a practice that could feasibly be prohibited, since much infrastructure is already provided free in many places.

Secondly, states may respond to such restrictions by granting tax breaks to all firms instead of only to certain ones. This has already been happening. A major tax concession, granted in the heat of battle to one firm, becomes a politically contentious issue when other firms, long-time fixtures in the local economic landscape, demand equal treatment.

The solution is to extend the tax concession to all manufacturers. The firm-specific distortion has been exchanged for a sector-wide distortion. This process could be accelerated if firm-specific deals were ended. If so, the loss of state revenues and the erosion of financial support for schools and infrastructure and social services would end up being much greater than it would have been if we had let the states make deals with individual firms.

The other possibility, of course, is that by outlawing firm-specific competition, the mega-deals would be reduced, and the subsequent pressure from other businesses to make the special deal a general entitlement would not develop. It is difficult to say which scenario is the more likely.

Interestingly, one of the arguments made by some critics is that incentives are inefficient because they are given to many firms whose location decisions are unaffected by the incentive. They propose that state and local economic development policy, to be more cost-effective, should be directed at particular firms—those whose decisions are likely to hinge on tax burdens. Programs should be negotiated on a firm-by-firm basis, not be made as entitlements to a broad class of firms. Similarly, since an investment tax credit (ITC) targets new investment, an ITC is preferable to an across-the-board cut in tax rates; the rate cut would affect all firms, whether investing or not, and would have to entail a much larger loss in state revenues in order to influence the investment decision of the same extent as an ITC.

Others take a public balance sheet approach that leads to similar kinds of policies. A cost-benefit analysis of economic development programs should be conducted, with the public weighing the public benefits against the public costs. Public funds should be used, according to these advocates, only for projects or firms that satisfy public-interest performance standards regarding labor practices, workplace safety, environmental record, wage levels, or the provision of health insurance ("responsible employer" legislation). Again, this implies greater targeting and a balancing of objectives, requiring something more like a negotiation process and less like an automatic entitlement such as an ITC.

Could it be that cost-effective use of public funds from a local perspective is exactly the opposite from what economists see as desirable from the standpoint of national economic efficiency? The apparent par-

adox, of course, is just the age-old problem of the appropriate accounting region in benefit-cost analysis. As long as state and local
governments are making decisions based on benefits and costs to their
own state or to their own locality, they will devote public resources to
projects that produce net benefits statewide or locally but merely redistribute benefits when a broader accounting region is used. The federal
government could certainly prohibit the use of federal funds to subsidize these types of projects (while allowing them, perhaps, for such
programs as job training, research and development, or technology
transfer, which appear to enhance productivity instead of shifting the
location of production).

INCENTIVE COMPETITION AND EQUITY

To the extent that tax incentives, considered in isolation, are redistributive in the desired direction, it is in substantial measure due to the
prevalence of incentives targeted at high-unemployment areas, either
enterprise zones or distressed counties. Almost all those who have been
critical of incentive competition have allowed that the least harmful, or
perhaps even beneficial, component of it is the redistributive element.
The efficiency argument here is that there are immobilities of labor or
other barriers that prevent capital from shifting so as to equalize levels
of unemployment; subsidies to high-unemployment locations would
therefore be justified. The equity argument is that high-unemployment
places tend also to be ghetto areas, concentrations of African Ameri-
cans and of the poor. Such population groups face restrictions on
mobility. Subsidization via enterprise zones is justified on just such
grounds.
    Interestingly, the states have been doing far more than the federal
government to address distributional issues through economic development policy. While the federal government finally passed a limited
enterprise zone program focused on a small number of cities, states
over the past decade have established numerous similar programs.
States, in other words, have shown themselves quite ready to fund geographically targeted economic development programs.

This raises the question: Should states and localities be prohibited from using Community Development Block Grant (CDBG) or other federal monies to subsidize businesses even if those subsidies are restricted to high-unemployment or high-poverty areas? To the extent that states are using the state CDBG allocations to underwrite local revolving loan funds for business support, and are targeting those funds at poorer communities, such a use of federal funds appears to be complementing state targeting policies and the federal empowerment zone program. However, many of the CDBG-capitalized revolving loan funds we came across were not explicitly concerned with targeting localized areas of distress. Certainly, the federal government's ability to enforce targeting has been seriously eroded over the past two decades.

CAN AND SHOULD INCENTIVE COMPETITION BE CURBED?

To the degree that tax and incentive competition results in a redistribution of jobs, our research lends little or no support to the argument that this redistribution has beneficial effects for the nation as a whole, shifting jobs from places with low unemployment to places with high unemployment. We also cannot say that it is clearly harmful, providing inducements to redistribute jobs in the opposite direction. Of course, one can only speculate as to what might otherwise have occurred; i.e., what the spatial pattern of returns on investment in 1992 would have looked like had states and cities never undertaken to influence their economic fortunes by offering inducements to industry in competition with one another. If this pattern would have been distinctly counterproductive, with higher returns in lower-unemployment places, then one could conclude that competition has at least nullified such effects.

While the arguments that tax and incentive competition in general enhances national welfare appear to us ill-supported, on redistributive grounds, neither are we persuaded that incentive competition improves locational efficiency. Although our study has not directly addressed this issue, it seems apparent from the magnitude of firm differences in returns that neither the basic tax system, nor the tax system with the standard package of incentives included, is likely to bear any systematic relationship to actual public resource costs associated with different industries at different sites. Is there any reason to expect that the cost of providing services to an auto plant is twice as high in South Carolina as it is in Massachusetts, while the cost of providing services to a small soap manufacturer is higher in Massachusetts than in South Carolina? Or that in Texas, the average public service bundle for an auto plant is four times the service bundle provided a large drug manufacturer?[3] These are the relationships that one would expect if effective state/local tax rates reflect differences in service costs. The effective tax rates on these various kinds of firms in these locations are quite different, and it is difficult to imagine that they represent "tax prices" for services. Further, it is not clear why one would anticipate the pattern to be more related to costs in the absence of incentive competition. Since few places appear to conduct any systematic study of fiscal effects, and since these effects are difficult to measure and far from obvious, it seems very unlikely that competition produces a set of after-tax returns *more* in line with public service cost differences.

It is interesting to note that a recent national conference on "the economic war between the states" was attended by many who had gone on record in opposition to incentive wars and had argued that the federal government should intervene to end such competition.[4] Nevertheless, there were few concrete proposals on how that could be accomplished, beyond the federal government prohibiting the use of federal funds for industrial recruitment. How could the federal government intervene to prevent states and cities from using their own funds for such purposes? The practical difficulties in defining a competitive incentive that is to be prohibited seem insurmountable. If Iowa were to be precluded from enacting a property tax exemption to attract a new steel plant (as it did), would it also be prevented from making the same property tax exemption available to all steel manufacturers, or to all manufacturers, or to all corporations (including insurance companies using computers)? If so, would we then require Pennsylvania, which by state law defines the property tax as a tax only on *real* property, to start mandating that local governments also tax machinery and equipment and other personal property, so that Pennsylvania localities do not have a competitive advantage?

Cooperative agreements among states seem to be the only possibilities for reducing incentive wars, and the history here is not cause for optimism. An important step in that direction, however, is simply to undertake efforts to improve the information on which economic development policy is based, so that policymakers in states and cities have a better understanding of the true costs of incentives and of the long-term fiscal and employment effects.

NOTES

1. The exception here is tax increment financing.

2. For this comparison, we used the estimates of the incentive package cost contained in the report by Blum (1995), which was critical of the incentive deal. These figures are actually more conservative than those reported in the Council of State Governments (1994).

3. Our representative city analysis showed the following effective state/local tax rates on new investment after all tax incentives: for firm 14 (the large auto plant), 7.8 percent in Massachusetts, 13.3 percent in South Carolina, 21.2 percent in Texas; for firm 5 (soaps), 5.6 percent in Massachusetts, 4.7 percent in South Carolina; for firm 4 (drugs)—5.6 percent in Texas.

4. Papers presented at this conference, held at the National Academy of Sciences, Washington, DC, were printed in a special issues of *The Region* (June 1995), published by the Federal Reserve Bank of Minneapolis.

Appendix A

Characteristics of the Sample States and Cities

Table A.1 Characteristics of the 24 Sample States

State	Population, 1990	Percentage of U.S. manufacturing employment, 1990	Employment change, 1980-1990	Employment change (%)	Unemployment rate, 1992 (%)	Percentage of persons in poverty, 1989
Alabama	4,040,587	2.0	269,987	25.2	7.3	18.3
California	29,760,021	11.2	3,043,206	36.8	9.1	12.5
Connecticut	3,287,116	1.8	226,398	18.0	7.5	6.8
Florida	12,937,926	2.6	1,632,070	54.9	8.2	12.7
Georgia	6,478,216	3.0	781,275	45.5	6.9	14.7
Illinois	11,430,602	5.4	459,463	11.0	7.5	11.9
Indiana	5,544,159	3.3	349,316	19.4	6.5	10.7
Iowa	2,776,755	1.2	101,527	11.2	4.6	11.5
Kentucky	3,685,296	1.5	224,827	23.4	6.9	19.0
Massachusetts	6,016,425	2.8	480,835	21.0	8.5	8.9
Michigan	9,295,297	4.9	525,261	18.2	8.8	13.1
Minnesota	4,375,099	2.1	337,476	22.6	5.1	10.2
Missouri	5,117,073	2.2	345,050	20.7	5.7	13.3
New Jersey	7,730,188	3.3	708,345	28.2	8.4	7.6
New York	17,990,455	6.1	1,035,833	17.2	8.5	13.0

(continued)

226

Table A.1 (continued)

State	Population, 1990	Percentage of U.S. manufacturing employment, 1990	Employment change, 1980-1990	Employment change (%)	Unemployment rate, 1992 (%)	Percentage of persons in poverty, 1989
North Carolina	6,628,637	4.4	706,194	35.8	5.9	13.0
Ohio	10,847,115	5.8	515,021	13.8	7.2	12.5
Pennsylvania	11,881,643	5.4	553,381	13.7	7.5	11.1
South Carolina	3,486,703	2.0	298,622	30.9	6.2	15.4
Tennessee	4,877,185	2.7	428,403	29.7	6.4	15.7
Texas	16,986,510	5.0	953,894	19.4	7.5	18.1
Virginia	6,187,358	2.2	750,543	47.8	6.4	10.2
Washington	4,866,692	2.0	482,769	37.7	7.5	10.9
Wisconsin	4,891,769	2.9	338,741	21.0	5.1	10.7
Total[a]	201,118,827	85.6	15,548,437			
Median	6,101,892	2.9	481,802	21.8	7.25	12.5

SOURCE: Population, unemployment rates, and poverty rates: Bernan Press, *County and City Extra 1994*; change in total employment:: U.S. Bureau of the Census 1982 and 1993, *County Business Patterns* 1980 and 1990; "manufacturing employment in 1990: U.S. Bureau of the Census 1992a, *1990 Annual Survey of Manufactures*.

a. Columns may not sum to total due to rounding.

Table A.2 City Sample: Demographic Characteristics and Taxes

City	Population, 1990	Size class	Unemployment rate, 1992 (%)	Poverty rate, 1989 (%)	Black pop., 1990 (%)	Enterprise zone in 1992	Effective property tax rate (%)	Property tax abatement	Local sales tax rate (%)
San Diego, CA	1,110,549	1	6.2	13.4	9.3	Yes	1.05	No	1.25
San Francisco, CA	723,959	1	6.3	12.7	10.9	Yes	1.12	No	1.25
Jacksonville, FL	672,971	1	5.7	13.0	25.3	Yes	2.19	No	0.50
Chicago, IL	2,783,726	1	11.3	21.6	39.0	Yes	3.16	Yes	2.50
Indianapolis, IN	741,952	1	5.6	12.5	22.5	Yes	3.72	Yes	0.00
Detroit, MI	1,027,974	1	19.7	32.4	75.7	No	4.63	Yes	0.00
New York City, NY	7,322,564	1	9.0	19.3	28.8	Yes	1.78	Yes	4.25
Dallas, TX	1,006,877	1	7.4	18.0	29.5	Yes	2.10	Yes	2.00
El Paso, TX	515,342	1	10.3	25.3	3.4	Yes	2.81	Yes	2.00
San Antonio, TX	935,933	1	9.2	22.6	7.0	Yes	2.94	Yes	1.50
Seattle, WA	516,259	1	4.9	12.4	10.0	No	1.21	No	1.70
Milwaukee, WI	628,088	1	8.9	22.2	30.5	Yes	3.67	No	0.50
Huntsville, AL	159,789	2	5.6	11.6	24.4	No	1.16	Yes	3.00
Bakersfield, CA	174,820	2	7.1	15.0	9.4	Yes	1.10	No	1.25
Fullerton, CA	114,144	2	4.7	9.8	1.9	No	1.01	No	1.25
Oakland, CA	372,242	2	9.5	18.8	43.9	No	1.24	No	1.25

(continued)

Table A.2 (continued)

City	Population, 1990	Size class	Unemployment rate, 1992 (%)	Poverty rate, 1989 (%)	Black pop., 1990 (%)	Enterprise zone in 1992	Effective property tax rate (%)	Property tax abatement	Local sales tax rate (%)
Riverside, CA	226,505	2	6.9	11.9	7.4	Yes	1.03	No	1.25
Sacramento, CA	369,365	2	7.6	17.2	15.3	Yes	1.02	No	1.25
Salinas, CA	108,777	2	11.0	15.6	3.0	No	1.00	No	1.25
Santa Ana, CA	293,742	2	8.5	18.1	2.6	No	1.02	No	1.25
Simi Valley, CA	100,217	2	4.1	3.6	1.6	No	1.14	No	1.25
Sunnyvale, CA	117,229	2	4.0	4.7	3.4	No	1.04	No	1.25
Thousand Oaks, CA	104,352	2	4.0	4.2	1.3	No	1.05	No	1.25
Bridgeport, CT	141,686	2	10.6	17.1	26.6	Yes	4.75	Yes	0.00
Hartford, CT	139,739	2	10.7	27.5	38.9	Yes	2.69	Yes	0.00
Hollywood, FL	121,697	2	6.1	11.0	8.4	No	2.69	No	0.00
St. Petersburg, FL	238,629	2	5.2	13.6	19.5	Yes	2.61	No	0.00
Tallahassee, FL	124,773	2	5.6	22.3	29.1	Yes	2.29	No	1.00
Tampa, FL	280,015	2	6.7	19.4	25.0	Yes	2.65	No	0.50
Atlanta, GA	394,017	2	9.2	27.3	67.1	Yes	2.33	Yes	2.00
Savannah, GA	137,560	2	8.3	22.6	51.3	No	1.31	Yes	2.00
Des Moines, IA	193,187	2	5.0	12.9	7.1	No	4.23	Yes	0.00

Rockford, IL	139,426	2	6.1	13.4	14.8	Yes	3.40	Yes	0.00
Lowell, MA	103,439	2	10.7	18.0	2.2	No	2.51	No	0.00
Ann Arbor, MI	109,592	2	3.8	16.1	8.9	No	3.17	No	0.00
Springfield, MO	140,494	2	5.7	17.8	2.4	Yes	1.68	Yes	1.50
St. Louis, MO	396,685	2	11.0	24.6	47.4	Yes	2.68	Yes	0.50
Greensboro, NC	183,521	2	4.5	11.6	34.0	No	1.32	No	2.00
Elizabeth, NJ	110,002	2	9.9	16.1	19.9	Yes	2.57	No	0.00
Newark, NJ	275,221	2	14.7	26.3	58.5	Yes	3.46	Yes	0.00
Syracuse, NY	163,860	2	8.2	22.7	20.2	Yes	3.33	Yes	4.00
Erie, PA	108,718	2	8.9	19.3	12.2	Yes	2.82	Yes	0.00
Knoxville, TN	165,121	2	7.1	20.8	15.6	No	2.33	No	2.25
Abilene, TX	106,654	2	6.9	15.3	7.0	Yes	2.57	Yes	2.00
Beaumont, TX	114,323	2	7.9	21.1	41.2	Yes	1.84	Yes	2.00
Fort Worth, TX	447,619	2	7.5	17.4	22.0	Yes	2.91	Yes	1.50
Garland, TX	180,650	2	4.9	7.8	9.0	Yes	2.46	Yes	2.00
Plano, TX	128,713	2	2.9	3.3	4.0	No	2.34	Yes	2.00
Norfolk, VA	261,229	2	8.8	19.3	39.1	Yes	1.38	No	1.00
Richmond, VA	203,056	2	6.4	20.9	55.4	No	1.45	No	1.00
Virginia Beach, VA	393,069	2	4.7	5.9	13.9	No	1.09	No	1.00
Spokane, WA	177,196	2	8.2	17.3	1.9	No	1.55	No	1.50

(continued)

Table A.2 (continued)

City	Population, 1990	Size class	Unemploy- ment rate, 1992 (%)	Poverty rate, 1989 (%)	Black pop., 1990 (%)	Enterprise zone in 1992	Effective property tax rate (%)	Property tax abatement	Local sales tax rate (%)
Tacoma, WA	176,664	2	7.4	16.8	11.4	No	1.83	No	1.40
Beverly Hills, CA	31,971	3	3.8	6.6	1.4	No	1.20	No	1.25
Camarillo, CA	52,303	3	3.8	4.4	1.7	No	1.04	No	1.25
Campbell, CA	36,048	3	3.4	5.8	2.1	No	1.08	No	1.25
Cerritos, CA	53,240	3	3.7	4.0	7.4	No	1.15	No	1.25
Colton, CA	40,213	3	9.8	15.6	9.0	No	1.14	No	1.25
Napa, CA	61,842	3	4.8	7.7	0.2	No	1.25	No	1.25
Novato, CA	47,585	3	3.1	4.2	2.7	No	1.06	No	1.25
Porterville, CA	29,563	3	12.8	26.8	1.2	Yes	1.01	No	1.25
Redding, CA	66,462	3	8.8	14.3	1.0	No	1.05	No	1.25
Redlands, CA	60,394	3	4.9	9.0	3.9	No	1.13	No	1.25
Visalia, CA	75,636	3	6.8	17.6	1.5	No	1.05	No	1.25
Bristol, CT	60,640	3	5.3	4.4	1.7	No	1.84	Yes	0.00
Cape Coral, FL	74,991	3	4.4	5.9	0.8	No	2.17	No	0.00
Largo, FL	65,674	3	3.9	7.4	0.8	No	2.00	No	1.00
Melbourne, FL	59,646	3	6.5	12.8	9.4	No	1.95	No	0.00

230

City								
Palm Bay, FL	62,632	3	5.9	8.7	7.5	No	2.02	No	0.00
Riviera Beach, FL	27,639	3	9.1	22.6	69.8	No	2.54	No	0.00
Sunrise, FL	64,407	3	4.9	6.5	7.4	No	2.91	No	1.00
West Palm Beach, FL	67,643	3	6.5	16.2	32.6	Yes	2.67	No	0.00
LaGrange, GA	25,597	3	8.9	21.3	42.3	No	0.76	No	2.00
Waterloo, IA	66,467	3	7.2	16.9	12.2	No	4.68	Yes	1.00
Champaign, IL	63,502	3	4.9	22.7	14.2	Yes	2.44	Yes	1.00
Joliet, IL	76,836	3	7.8	13.0	21.5	Yes	3.02	Yes	1.50
Rock Island, IL	40,552	3	7.8	19.3	17.2	Yes	3.55	Yes	0.50
Anderson, IN	59,459	3	8.2	18.0	14.3	Yes	4.34	Yes	0.00
Midland, MI	38,053	3	5.2	9.5	1.6	No	2.31	Yes	0.00
Westland, MI	84,724	3	6.3	7.1	3.3	No	3.45	No	0.00
St. Joseph, MO	71,852	3	8.4	16.7	3.7	Yes	1.82	Yes	1.85
Hoboken, NJ	33,397	3	6.2	16.4	5.5	No	2.35	No	0.00
New Brunswick, NJ	41,711	3	8.9	22.0	29.6	No	2.73	Yes	0.00
Mt. Vernon, NY	67,153	3	7.4	11.8	55.6	No	3.66	No	4.25
Fairfield, OH	39,729	3	3.7	3.8	3.6	Yes	1.45	Yes	0.00
Lancaster, PA	55,551	3	6.5	20.9	12.2	Yes	2.12	Yes	0.00
Baytown, TX	63,850	3	7.9	16.1	12.1	Yes	3.13	Yes	1.00
Olympia, WA	33,840	3	6.8	13.0	1.2	No	1.52	No	1.40

(continued)

Table A.2 (continued)

City	Population, 1990	Size class	Unemployment rate, 1992 (%)	Poverty rate, 1989 (%)	Black pop., 1990 (%)	Enterprise zone in 1992	Effective property tax rate (%)	Property tax abatement	Local sales tax rate (%)
Eau Claire, WI	56,856	3	5.9	18.6	0.6	No	2.87	No	0.50
Green Bay, WI	96,466	3	5.4	13.4	0.6	Yes	3.87	No	0.50
Wauwatosa, WI	49,366	3	2.3	3.3	1.2	No	4.23	No	0.50
Dalton, GA	21,761	4	5.8	14.8	10.7	No	1.43	No	2.00
Bedford, IN	13,817	4	5.9	11.4	0.9	No	4.39	Yes	0.00
Danville, KY	12,420	4	7.9	20.0	15.6	No	0.97	No	0.00
Hamtramck, MI	18,372	4	16.5	28.5	14.0	No	3.90	No	0.00
Marshall, MN	12,023	4	4.4	13.0	0.3	No	4.81	No	0.50
Willmar, MN	17,531	4	5.2	18.1	0.4	No	5.30	No	1.75
Henderson, NC	15,655	4	7.9	24.1	52.9	Yes	1.40	No	2.00
Oakland, NJ	11,997	4	3.0	1.5	1.2	No	2.30	No	0.00
Dublin, OH	16,366	4	1.3	1.0	1.5	No	2.31	No	0.75
Wilmington, OH	11,199	4	6.6	15.1	5.8	No	1.70	Yes	1.00
Butler, PA	15,714	4	7.4	23.2	1.3	No	1.92	Yes	0.00
Carlisle, PA	18,419	4	3.6	9.9	5.4	No	4.21	No	0.00
Washington, PA	15,864	4	11.5	25.5	13.1	No	6.56	No	0.00

Cayce, SC	11,163	4	4.9	9.3	19.4	No	2.93	Yes	0.00
Summerville, SC	22,519	4	4.7	9.8	17.8	No	3.03	Yes	0.00
Cookeville, TN	21,744	4	6.6	18.9	2.5	No	1.15	No	2.25
Tullahoma, TN	16,761	4	5.5	14.2	6.3	No	2.13	No	2.25
Jacksonville, TX	12,765	4	8.8	26.7	24.3	Yes	2.31	Yes	1.50
Salem, VA	23,756	4	2.4	5.2	4.4	No	1.18	No	1.00
Winchester, VA	21,947	4	4.8	11.3	10.0	No	0.50	No	1.00
Puyallup, WA	23,875	4	5.7	7.0	1.1	No	1.70	No	1.40

SOURCE: Population, unemployment rate, poverty rates, and percentage of population black: Berman press, *County and City Extra 1994*; enterprise zone and property tax data: authors' survey; local sales tax rates: Prentice-Hall, *State and Local Taxes*; Commerce Clearing House, *State Tax Guide*, and authors' survey.

NOTE: Poverty rate is percentage of persons in poverty from 1990 Census. Effective property tax rate is the nominal combined rate (city, county, and school) times the assessment ratio. Project returns are the present value of 20-year returns from investment by an out-of-state firm in a new plant in each city, after state and local taxes and tax incentives. Local corporate income taxes existed in the following cities (rates in parentheses): Detroit (2 percent) and Hamtramch (1 percent), Michigan; New York City (8.85 percent); and Dublin (2 percent), Fairfield (1.5 percent), and Wilmington (1 percent), Ohio. Local gross receipts taxes were imposed in the following Washington cities: Olympia (0.1 percent), Seattle (0.215 percent), and Tacoma (0.11 percent).

Table A.3 Average Effective Local Property Tax Rates by State[a]

| State | Our sample data | | | | ACIR: selected cities | | | | Statewide effective rate, 1992 (%) | Median city rate used (%) |
| | Cities | Local tax rates, 1992 (%) | | | Cities | Local tax rates, 1990 (%) | | | | |
		Low	Median	High		Low	Median	High		
Alabama	1		1.16		14	0.62	1.09	1.82		1.09
California	23	1.01	1.05	1.25	43	1.01	1.05	1.27		1.05
Connecticut	3	1.84	2.69	4.75	35	1.24	2.77	6.11		2.77
Florida	12	1.95	2.41	2.91	28	1.63	2.18	2.61	1.75	1.75
Georgia	4	0.76	1.45	2.44	10	0.80	2.80	3.28		1.45
Illinois	5	2.44	3.16	3.55	61	1.05	2.90	5.19	2.57	2.57
Indiana	3	3.72	4.34	4.39	28	1.98	3.63	8.23	3.27	3.27
Iowa	2	4.23	4.45	4.68	17	2.71	3.57	4.50	3.10	3.10
Kentucky	1		0.97		12	0.34	0.98	1.21		0.98
Massachusetts	1		2.51		78	Inadequate data			2.48	2.48
Michigan	3	2.31	3.45	3.90	33	2.39	3.26	3.50		3.26
Minnesota	2	4.81	5.06	5.30	11	4.81	5.20	7.14	4.62	4.62
Missouri	3	1.68	1.82	2.68	13	1.19	1.69	2.24	2.17	2.17
New Jersey	5	2.30	2.57	3.46	32	1.30	2.00	4.73		2.57
New York	3	1.78	3.33	3.66	31	Inadequate data				3.33
North Carolina	2	1.32	1.36	1.40	23	0.39	1.22	1.69		1.36

Ohio	3	1.45	1.70	2.31	54	1.55	2.40	5.41	2.40
Pennsylvania	5	1.92	2.82	6.56	20	Inadequate data			2.82
South Carolina	3	2.93	2.98	3.03	7	Inadequate data			2.98
Tennesssee	2	1.15	2.13	2.33	15	1.04	2.15	2.89	2.15
Texas	10	1.84	2.51	3.13	43	0.41	1.94	2.42	2.51
Virginia	5	0.50	1.18	1.45	44	0.29	0.76	2.38	1.18
Washington	5	1.21	1.55	1.83	19	1.19	1.49	1.76	1.55
Wisconsin	4	2.87	3.77	4.23	21	2.34	3.31	4.22	3.40

a. Where assessment ratios or tax rates vary by class of property, we show the effective rate for real property. Rates are the sum of city, county, and school district tax rates, plus other minor special district taxes in many states. Effective rate is the nominal rate times the assessment ratio.

The property tax rates for the representative cities were determined in three ways. In eight states, it was possible to compute a statewide average effective property tax rate on industrial property. This is simply the total property taxes collected on industrial property divided by the total value of industrial property in the state, where value is equal to assessed value divided by the assessment ratio. In the case of Massachusetts, however, the "statewide average" is actually the unweighted average of the industrial tax rates in the 23 cities that had in excess of $200 million in industrial valuation in fiscal year 1994, as calculated by the authors.

Unfortunately, none of the other 16 states report data on property taxes collected by class of property. For these 16 states, we compared our rates with those for chosen cities reported in Selected Features of Fiscal Federalism (U.S. Advisory Commission on Intergovernmental Relations [ACIR]1992). The ACIR table, in turn, was based on tax rates published in the Commerce Clearing House (CCH) State Tax Reporter 1991. The CCH cities represent a non-random selection of cities of 20,000 population or more. There are problems with the CCH data for 3 of the 16 states. These three states are New York (where nominal rates only were shown, with the erroneous statement that assessment ratios are uniform statewide when in fact there is large variation), Pennsylvania (where some data that could be corroborated were erroneous and produced effective rates as high as 20 percent, and South Carolina (where effective rates appeared far too low). For the remaining 13, the range of tax rates and the median rates corroborate our sample and the validity of our median rates, for the most part. Where there are significant differences, we have substituted the ACIR medians for our own if our sample of cities was quite small.

Appendix B

The Hypothetical Firm Model:
Assumptions and Details of Operation

Appendix B

The Hypothetical Firm Model:
Assumptions and Details of Operation

THE FIRM'S FINANCIAL STATEMENTS
AND NEW PLANT FINANCING

In order to focus on the effects of incentives on returns from a new investment, we assume that each hypothetical firm would have been in a "steady state" but for the expansion. That is, each year the gross value of the depreciable assets in place on January 1, 1992, is maintained by undertaking replacement investment equal to retirements. With straight-line depreciation, annual depreciation of these assets is constant, and therefore accumulated depreciation and the net value of these assets also remain constant. Replacement investment is financed by rolling over long-term debt, so that total long-term debt and interest expense for existing assets remain constant. The result is that the simulation of firm operations in the absence of new plant investment produces a constant net income after taxes each year for the 20-year period; net income is also equal to cash flow. This becomes the baseline cash flow for purposes of computing the addition to cash flow each year attributable to the new plant investment, which is simply the firm's total net cash flow with the new investment less the baseline cash flow.

The model includes one spreadsheet that contains the formulas for calculating the basic financial reports—an income statement, a balance sheet, and a statement of cash flows—for 20 years, as well as supporting statements for calculating the amortization of long-term debt, depreciation, replacement investment, federal income taxes, median state income taxes, and sample state income taxes. The financial statement spreadsheet draws information from four database spreadsheets: 1) a firm database, showing, for each of the 16 hypothetical firms, balance sheet and income statement data for the original firm and the new plant, codes indicating the depreciation schedules appropriate to that industry, and private loan rate assumptions by asset category; 2) a table of federal tax depreciation schedules and straight-line (book) depreciation schedules; 3) a state tax database, including tax rates and other parameter values for all relevant features of state sales and income taxes, including investment and jobs credits (statewide and for enterprise zones only); and 4) a local tax database, including the parameters of the state property tax system (assessment ratios by property class and depreciation schedules applied to personal property

239

valuation), local property tax rates and abatement schedules, an enterprise zone existence variable, and local sales tax rates.

The Excel spreadsheet model begins by constructing a complete set of financial statements for one of the 16 prototype firms. The initial balance sheet is for January 1, 1992; the firm then builds a new establishment, with the plant placed in service on July 1, 1992. Short-term assets and liabilities (inventories, accounts payable and receivable, etc.) are increased proportionately as a result of the expansion. New property, plant, and equipment are added in the same proportions to total assets as for the existing firm. Additional net working capital (current assets minus current liabilities) necessitated by new plant and the new plant fixed assets are financed by a combination of additional long-term debt, retained earnings, and the sale of common stock, in such a way as to maintain the same ratio of debt to equity. Retained earnings generated during 1992 (i.e., net income after taxes) are used first; if additional equity is required, the firm issues common stock. The proportion of debt used to finance the expansion is larger than the proportion of debt in the existing firm's balance sheet, but, as the new debt is retired, the average debt ratio over the 20 years will be equal to the existing debt ratio. That is, we assume that the average capital structure of the firms in the Compustat database for that industry is also the target or ideal capital structure that the firm seeks to maintain in the long run.

The cost of equity varies by firm. Data from ValueLine were used to determine an average beta value (a measure of risk, or stock price volatility relative to the market) for firms in each industry. The cost of common stock for an industry was then computed according to standard portfolio theory as the industry beta value times the average market risk premium for common stock of 7 percent plus the risk-free rate of return in 1992 (estimated at 7 percent). An adjustment was made for the use of preferred stock, which was assumed to carry an interest rate of one percentage point above the firm's cost of long-term debt; this made very little difference, as the ratio of preferred stock to common stock was very small for the firms in our study (based on the Compustat data). Table B.1 shows the resultant weighted cost of equity for each of our firms. From this was deducted an assumed inflation premium of 4.0 percent to arrive at the real discount rate for each firm. This was then used to discount the additional cash flow available to equity investors attributable to the new plant to arrive at the present value of project returns.

New plant private debt financing terms vary by asset class and loan size. (Because of the small-issue industrial revenue bond [IRB] size limits, we do not simulate the use of IRB financing for any of our firms.) The interest rate assumptions are shown in Table B.2. The long-term rates (applied to financing land, plant, and infrastructure) are based on corporate A-rated bond rates for 1992; the short-term rates (3–4 years, for financing short-lived equipment and

Table B.1 Assumed Cost of Equity for Hypothetical Firms

Firm	Industry	Cost of equity (%)
#1, 2	Furniture & fixtures	13.4
#3, 4	Drugs	16.2
#5, 6	Soap, cleaners, toiletries	14.6
#7, 8	Miscellaneous plastic products	14.0
#9, 10	Industrial machinery	13.9
#11, 12	Electronic components	15.0
#13	Motor vehicles & parts	14.1
#14	Motor vehicles & parts	15.8
#15, 16	Instruments	14.5

NOTE: Cost of equity is the same for both firm sizes in an industry because data on beta coefficients by industry did not allow size distinctions. However, for firm number 13 we used the beta for auto parts and supplies; for firm number 14, we used the beta for automobile manufacturers.

working capital) are based on Federal Reserve data on commercial and industrial fixed-rate bank loans in 1992, with interest rates declining substantially as loan size increases. Interpolation was used to derive rates for intermediate-term loans (for equipment lasting 7–12 years).

The new property plant and equipment are depreciated for tax purposes according to the Modified Accelerated Cost Recovery System (MACRS) schedule that applies to buildings (31.5 years, straight-line), infrastructure (15 years, 150 percent declining balance), and machinery and equipment (200 percent declining balance, over a period of 5 or 7 years depending on the industry). The depreciable basis of each asset is its acquisition cost (from the database of firm financial characteristics) plus state and local sales taxes on machinery and equipment, where applicable. Depreciable assets are assumed to have zero salvage value and to be replaced at the end of the appropriate class life (20 years for infrastructure, 40 years for buildings, 5 to 15 years for machinery and equipment). Since we are using a 20-year time horizon, replacement schedules are modeled only for machinery and equipment. Assets are depreciated on the books according to the appropriate Alternative Depreciation System (ADS) straight-line schedule (20 years for infrastructure, 40 years for buildings, 5 to 15 years for machinery and equipment).

Table B.2 Interest Rate and Loan Term Assumptions

Loan characteristics	Working capital	Computers and other nonmanufacturing equipment	Furniture and fixtures	Manufacturing machinery and equipment	Plant, land, and infrastructure
Term (years)	3	4	8	7–10	20
			Interest rate (%)		
Loan size					
Under $1 million	8.00	8.00	10.00	10.00	11.70
$1 to $5 million	7.00	7.00	8.75	8.75	10.25
Over $5 million	6.00	6.00	7.50	7.50	8.80

NOTE: Corporate A-rated bonds carried an interest rate of 8.8 percent on average during the first half of 1992 (*Survey of Current Business*, January 1993), p. S-16). Commercial and industrial bank loans with terms of 3–4 years during the first half of 1992 carried interest notes of 5.9 percent for loans over $1 million, 7.7 percent for loans of $500,000 to $1 million, and 8.8 percent for loans under $500,000 (U.S. Federal Reserve Board 1993 and 1994, Table 19).

INCOME TAXES AND APPORTIONMENT

Using the income statement, federal income taxes are calculated as follows: from income before income taxes, deduct the excess of tax over book depreciation and state income taxes paid. The remainder is federal taxable income; the progressive federal rate structure is applied to this amount. The calculation of state income taxes also begins with net income before income taxes. The excess of state tax depreciation (which in some instances is different from the federal) over book depreciation is then deducted, along with income taxes paid to other states (in a few states) and federal income taxes (in three states). Nonbusiness income is then deducted, and the remaining taxable income of the firm is apportioned to the hypothetical median state and the sample state (one of the 24 actual states in our study) according to those states' apportionment formulas (based on some combination of payroll, property, and sales). Income apportioned to the sample state plus any nonbusiness income allocated to that state are then taxed according to that state's schedule (generally a flat rate in the 24 states). In most states, nonbusiness income, which we assume consists entirely of corporate bond interest, is allocated entirely to the headquarters state (the median state for our multistate firms and the sample state for our single-state firms). From state taxes, we then deduct any state credits for new investment or job creation, carrying them forward to apply against future taxes (as state law allows) if they cannot all be used in 1992.

We assume that income taxes are paid concurrently, that is, that corporations file and remit taxes quarterly and end up paying exactly what they owe each year, so that the income tax actually paid during 1992 exactly equals income tax liability for 1992. Net worth taxes, on the other hand, are usually based on the end-of-year balance sheet and are generally paid only when the corporation files its return in the spring of the following year. Thus, the firm's 1992 income tax payment reflects income and costs from its new plant, which was in operation during the latter half of 1992, but the net worth tax it pays in 1992 is based on the January 1, 1992, balance sheet, before any new plant assets and liabilities were acquired.

Apportionment is based on the shares of the firm's payroll and property located in the sample state and in the median state, and on the destination of sales. For the single-state firm, all payroll and property, before and after the new plant is opened, are located entirely in the sample state. For the multistate firm, all payroll and property of the existing firm are located in the median state, while the new plant payroll and property are located in the sample state.

We assume that the firm is selling in national markets, with sales to each state in proportion to the state's population. All firms have a tax nexus in the sample state and in the median state. The single-state firm has sales offices in the median state that make it taxable there; some of its income will be apportioned to the median state because the sales factor for the median state is positive, even though the payroll and property factors are zero. The multistate firm would pay a small amount of taxes to the sample state even in the absence of the new plant, for the same reason.

All firms are assumed to have 20 percent of their sales destined for the "other" states, in which they are not taxed. A portion of these sales may be thrown back to the sample state if the sample state has a throwback rule. (The median state does not require throwback.) Our assumption is that sales to the sample state come first from production facilities in the sample state. If production there is less than sales to the sample state (which depends on the state's population), goods are exported to the sample state (and to the other non-taxing states) from the firm's median state facilities. In that case, there is no throwback to the sample state because the plant in the sample state is not producing any goods destined for out of state. If sample state production exceeds local sales, the excess is exported to the median state and to the other states in proportion to the assumed populations, with the goods produced in the sample state and exported to the "other" non-taxing states subject to throwback.

The median state and the sample state combined always have 80 percent of the population (approximately the share of the 24 states in our study) and 80 percent of the sales; the larger the sample state population, the smaller the median state population. This has the effect of accentuating the importance of the income tax in the larger states, since more of the firm's income will be apportioned there, but reducing the impact of throwback rules in the larger states (which are more likely to absorb all of the new plant's production). Both effects seem realistic and follow from the assumption that firms will find it profitable to maintain sales offices only in states where there is a substantial market; the 26 smaller states account for only 20 percent of total sales. The assumption is also consistent with data from Wisconsin income tax returns showing that, for apportioning corporations, only about 16 percent of sales were to non-taxing states and therefore subject to throwback.

CALCULATION OF PROPERTY TAXES

Property taxes are paid in one calendar year based on the value of property at the end of the previous calendar year. The multistate firm pays the same property taxes to the median state each year, based on the original firm's constant assets, and begins paying property taxes to the sample state in 1993, based on new plant assets that first appear on the balance sheet at the end of 1992. The calculation of property taxes paid in the sample state begins with the valuation of taxable classes of property. Inventory and land values are constant from 1993 onward, since neither asset depreciates and we assume no inflation. (Both items increase from 1992 to 1993, reflecting the new plant.) Three states tax inventories of raw materials, goods in process, and finished goods differently. We follow the Wisconsin tax study (1990) in assuming that 40 percent of inventories are finished goods; we assume that 25 percent are raw materials, and that 35 percent are goods in process. Plant and infrastructure are valued at book value, which reflects straight-line depreciation over 40 and 20 years, respectively.

Each category of personal property other than inventories is valued according to the state's guidelines for depreciating machinery and equipment, which are usually by category (furniture and fixtures, transportation equipment) and industry (for manufacturing machinery and equipment), just as federal depreciation schedules are. Of the 18 sample states that tax at least some kinds of personal property, 14 publish state depreciation guidelines to be used by local assessors. The other four (Connecticut, Kentucky, Missouri, and Virginia) allow assessors to use whatever guidelines they think appropriate; for these 4 states, we assumed depreciation schedules representing the average of the other states. In the average state, a piece of machinery and equipment will be valued at 48 to 51 percent of acquisition cost on average over the life of the equipment. This figure is as high as 62 to 65 percent in Alabama, and as low as 28 to 35 percent in Indiana, reflecting differences in how rapidly the equipment is depreciated and in the minimum percentage allowed as long as equipment remains in use.

Once property has been valued, the assessment ratio appropriate for each asset category is applied, which may be mandated by state statute or left to local discretion. The assessed value is then multiplied by the local property tax rate. The consolidated local property tax rate is the sum of rates for the city, the school district (if independent of the city), the county in which a majority of the city is located (where counties exist and levy taxes), and other special districts overlying the city. Where the city includes within it more than one school district or other special district, the district rates that apply are the rates in the area of the city representing the most likely location for new industry, where local officials were able to identify such an area, or the average for the city, where such areas could not be identified.

HOW INCENTIVES ARE INCORPORATED INTO FINANCIAL STATEMENTS

Public capital grants lower the portion of the acquisition cost of assets that must be financed from equity; this increases cash and net income in 1992. Public loans at below-market rates, or loan guarantees that reduce interest rates, lower annual interest expense on the income statement, which increases cash

246

flow; public loans do not increase overall long-term debt (the public debt substituting for higher-cost private debt). The availability of job training or of wage subsidies lowers operating costs during 1992 and thus increases net income after taxes. Sales taxes on purchases of machinery and equipment increase the acquisition cost of assets and hence the amount of debt and equity that must be raised to finance the new plant. (For tax purposes, sales taxes cannot be deducted in the year paid but must be capitalized into the cost of the asset and then depreciated.) This occurs in 1992 and in subsequent replacement years. If the state has a sales tax that applies to fuel and utilities, this will increase fuel and utility expense each year.

JOBS CREDITS AND EMPLOYEE ELIGIBILITY

In order to model jobs credits generally and enterprise zone credits in particular, it was necessary to make some assumptions about how many of a firm's new hires met each state's eligibility criteria for these credits. These eligibility criteria relate sometimes to place of residence, sometimes to unemployment status, sometimes to both. Table B.3 shows the assumptions made, based in part on research by Bartik (1991b, p. 95). Bartik found that new establishment hires consisted of 6–7 percent local residents previously unemployed and 16 percent local residents previously not in the labor force. If all such individuals were considered "unemployed" for enterprise zone incentive purposes, then an average expectation would be that about 25 percent of new hires would be local (city) residents who were previously unemployed. We assume that 60 percent of those unemployed had been unemployed 90 days or more, that new hires are disproportionately from the enterprise zone because of proximity, and that the zone accounts for a disproportionate share of the city's unemployed (since high unemployment is a criterion for establishing a zone). One further assumption was required to complete the table: either that 50 percent of new hires are from within the city (regardless of employment status) or that 50 percent of new hires are unemployed (except within the zone).

Table B.3 Unemployment and Residence Assumptions for Enterprise Zone Incentives (New Plant Employees in Each Category, %)

Unemployment status at time of hiring	Residence at time of hiring		
	Anywhere	City	Zone
All	100	50	30
Unemployed	50	25	20
Unemployed 90 days or more	30	15	12

Appendix C

Computational Structure of TAIM

Appendix C

Computational Structure of TAIM

Models of operating ratios, balance sheets, and tax and income statements were built in a single Microsoft Excel workbook (the INCOME workbook), the details of which are provided in Appendix B. These models reference descriptive databases held elsewhere containing information such as firm operating ratios, federal and state tax codes, and the various state asset-depreciation schedules. In order for the INCOME workbook to carry out its various calculations, it must receive information on what state, industrial sector, firm size, spatial structure, and incentive type level are to be modeled. It receives this instruction from a series of Visual Basic procedures (the PROGRAM). Once INCOME has this information, it runs through the spreadsheet model, building a set of operating ratios and calculating balance sheets and income and tax statements for the firm. Finally, INCOME produces a series of output numbers, including the present value of the annual increments to after-tax cash flow over 20 years, the internal rate of return on the incremental cash flow, the present value of taxes paid to federal and various state and local governments, and the nominal value of incentives awarded. PROGRAM then reads the results (after-tax cash flow and so on) of INCOME's calculations into a series of variables and deposits these into a RESULTS file.

The preceding description is true only for simulations of tax regimes without any discretionary incentives. The modeling of discretionary incentives involves some important modifications. As indicated earlier, states have laws and administrative rules that govern the way in which discretionary incentives are dispersed. In order to be eligible for an incentive, a firm must meet certain criteria. Moreover, the amount of discretionary incentives provided to a firm will depend on the sort of investment the firm intends to make. Thus, once INCOME has created the operating ratios and balance sheets for a new investment, this information needs to be made available to a rule-based expert system (the NON-TAX-INCENTIVE-SYSTEM), which determines, for example, the discretionary incentives for which the investment is eligible. Each program, each state, and each city has its own expert system. Information is transferred between INCOME and the NON-TAX-INCENTIVE-SYSTEM by PROGRAM. Based on information it has received, the NON-TAX-INCENTIVE-SYSTEM checks the incentives for which the investment qualifies, calculates a likely incentive amount from each incentive program based on historical ratios for that type of benefit, and then compiles the best (using an algorithm that minimizes the cost of debt) package of incentives available from each state for a firm of that particular type (defined by its sector, size, and headquarters structure), making sure that no incentive program rules are broken by the package.

Once this has been accomplished, the NON-TAX-INCENTIVE-SYSTEM distributes incentives to appropriate asset categories (land, plant, machinery, infrastructure, and working capital). Thus, the NON-TAX-INCENTIVE-SYSTEM must take the entire incentive package and distribute the total public financing to the appropriate (and permitted) asset classes, making sure that no asset class receives more public funding than would have been provided by the private sector. Finally, for incentives in the form of loans, loan guarantees, and linked deposits, future interest and principal payments must be generated in accordance with general program rules. PROGRAM reads this loan schedule information into a series of 5×20 matrices (one for each of five asset classes over a 20-year period). These matrices then replace the existing public financing schedule in INCOME. INCOME subsequently recalculates its financing of assets, taking into account this new public subsidy. It produces a new balance sheet and income statement and applies the relevant tax codes to that income. PROGRAM takes these results and puts them into the RESULTS workbook.

The addition of city-level incentives brings a further level of complexity. Firms receive these incentives on top of—or, in some cases, as replacements for—state programs. Data on city-level incentives are held in a separate database. The INCOME workbook references this database to calculate appropriate abatement and tax increment financing (TIF) awards in each city. Further Visual Basic modules also reference this database to construct city-level grant, loan, and loan guarantee incentives available in each city in each state and to build the best package of city incentives. The detailed operations of TAIM are summarized in Figure C.1.

Figure C.1 Computational Structure of TAIM

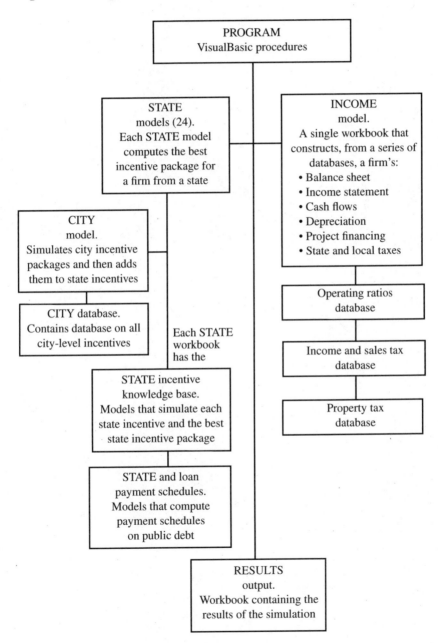

Appendix D

**Additional Results on the Worth and
Spatial Distribution of Taxes and Incentives**

Table D.1 The Impact of Taxes and Incentives on Project Returns, Small Furniture and Fixtures Firms, 112 Cities

	Mean ($)	Coefficient of variation	Size of range ($)	Hourly, per-employee wage equivalent of range ($)
Project returns				
After basic taxes	(255,378)	(0.411)	470,543	0.38
After tax incentives	(207,444)	(0.473)	445,491	0.36
After all incentives	(18,434)	(9.029)	883,219	0.72
Increment in project returns due to				
Tax incentives	47,934	1.282	311,333	
Non-tax incentives	189,010	0.601	558,123	
Hourly, per-employee wage equivalent of				
Tax incentives	0.04		0.25	
Non-tax incentives	0.15		0.46	

NOTE: Negative values are shown in parentheses.

Table D.2 The Impact of Taxes and Incentives on Project Returns, Large Furniture and Fixtures Firms, 112 Cities

	Mean ($)	Coefficient of variation	Size of range ($)	Hourly, per-employee wage equivalent of range ($)
Project returns				
After basic taxes	8,221,983	0.081	3,496,674	0.31
After tax incentives	8,705,916	0.094	3,851,349	0.34
After all incentives	9,346,248	0.107	5,461,309	0.48
Increment in project returns due to				
Tax incentives	483,933	1.266	2,625,554	
Non-tax incentives	640,332	0.690	3,001,269	
Hourly, per-employee wage equivalent of				
Tax incentives	0.04		0.25	
Non-tax incentives	0.06		0.26	

Table D.3 The Impact of Taxes and Incentives on Project Returns, Large Soap Firms, 112 Cities

	Mean ($)	Coefficient of variation	Size of range ($)	Hourly, per-employee wage equivalent of range ($)
Project returns				
After basic taxes	51,627,858	0.035	8,904,319	0.55
After tax incentives	52,919,613	0.044	13,603,234	0.84
After all incentives	53,803,767	0.047	13,344,649	0.82
Increment in project returns due to				
Tax incentives	1,291,755	1.363	8,343,971	
Non-tax incentives	884,154	0.790	5,506,504	
Hourly, per-employee wage equivalent of				
Tax incentives	0.08		0.52	
Non-tax incentives	0.05		0.34	

Table D.4 The Impact of Taxes and Incentives on Project Returns, Small Plastics Firms, 112 Cities

	Mean ($)	Coefficient of variation	Size of range ($)	Hourly, per-employee wage equivalent of range ($)
Project returns				
After basic taxes	97,849	0.992	482,229	0.51
After tax incentives	152,422	0.635	464,937	0.50
After all incentives	320,545	0.479	789,037	0.84
Increment in project returns due to				
Tax incentives	54,574	1.228	311,262	
Non-tax incentives	168,122	0.615	516,917	
Hourly, per-employee wage equivalent of				
Tax incentives	0.06		0.33	
Non-tax incentives	0.18		0.56	

Table D.5 The Impact of Taxes and Incentives on Project Returns, Small Industrial Machinery Firms, 112 Cities

	Mean ($)	Coefficient of variation	Size of range ($)	Hourly, per-employee wage equivalent of range ($)
Project returns				
After basic taxes	(3,830)	(46.284)	790,808	0.53
After tax incentives	116,361	1.711	976,320	0.66
After all incentives	356,586	0.802	1,266,732	0.86
Increment in project returns due to				
Tax incentives	120,192	1.217	646,370	
Non-tax incentives	240,224	0.684	776,537	
Hourly, per-employee wage equivalent of				
Tax incentives	0.08		0.44	
Non-tax incentives	0.16		0.53	

NOTE: Negative values are shown in parentheses.

Table D.6 The Impact of Taxes and Incentives on Project Returns, Large Industrial Machinery Firms, 112 Cities

	Mean ($)	Coefficient of variation	Size of range ($)	Hourly, per-employee wage equivalent of range ($)
Project returns				
After basic taxes	21,075,382	0.216	19,545,516	0.54
After tax incentives	23,261,173	0.201	20,964,961	0.58
After all incentives	24,464,584	0.208	23,877,858	0.66
Increment in project returns due to				
Tax incentives	2,185,791	1.282	14,963,988	
Non-tax incentives	1,203,411	0.928	7,969,315	
Hourly, per-employee wage equivalent of				
Tax incentives	0.06		0.42	
Non-tax incentives	0.03		0.22	

Table D.7 The Impact of Taxes and Incentives on Project Returns, Small Electronic Components Firms, 112 Cities

	Mean ($)	Coefficient of variation	Size of range ($)	Hourly, per-employee wage equivalent of range ($)
Project returns				
After basic taxes	514,484	0.625	1,528,710	0.42
After tax incentives	734,235	0.509	1,701,391	0.46
After all incentives	1,135,210	0.433	2,425,336	0.66
Increment in project returns due to				
Tax incentives	219,751	1.227	1,063,405	
Non-tax incentives	400,975	0.681	1,347,166	
Hourly, per-employee wage equivalent of				
Tax incentives	0.06		0.29	
Non-tax incentives	0.11		0.36	

Table D.8 The Impact of Taxes and Incentives on Project Returns, Large Electronic Components Firms, 112 Cities

	Mean ($)	Coefficient of variation	Size of range ($)	Hourly, per-employee wage equivalent of range ($)
Project returns				
After basic taxes	4,905,744	0.721	16,891,559	0.62
After tax incentives	6,849,499	0.561	17,925,312	0.66
After all incentives	7,951,177	0.526	20,631,480	0.76
Increment in project returns due to				
Tax incentives	1,943,755	1.232	10,675,662	
Non-tax incentives	1,101,678	0.894	7,780,432	
Hourly, per-employee wage equivalent of				
Tax incentives	0.07		0.39	
Non-tax incentives	0.04		0.29	

**Table D.9 The Impact of Taxes and Incentives on Project Returns, Small
Auto/Auto Parts Firms, 112 Cities**

	Mean ($)	Coefficient of variation	Size of range ($)	Hourly, per-employee wage equivalent of range ($)
Project returns				
After basic taxes	13,660,914	0.177	12,218,429	0.51
After tax incentives	14,793,759	0.169	12,247,625	0.51
After all incentives	15,742,613	0.181	16,897,421	0.70
Increment in project returns due to				
Tax incentives	1,132,844	1.271	7,252,643	
Non-tax incentives	948,854	0.909	6,972,737	
Hourly, per-employee wage equivalent of				
Tax incentives	0.05		0.30	
Non-tax incentives	0.04		0.29	

**Table D.10 The Impact of Taxes and Incentives on Project Returns,
Large Auto/Auto Parts Firms, 112 Cities**

	Mean ($)	Coefficient of variation	Size of range ($)	Hourly, per-employee wage equivalent of range ($)
Project returns				
After basic taxes	2,480,101	4.861	54,279,143	0.76
After tax incentives	7,488,671	1.610	58,016,319	0.81
After all incentives	9,189,576	1.353	57,782,121	0.81
Increment in project returns due to				
Tax incentives	5,008,570	1.300	30,599,903	
Non-tax incentives	1,700,906	1.098	9,805,576	
Hourly, per-employee wage equivalent of				
Tax incentives	0.07		0.43	
Non-tax incentives	0.02		0.14	

Table D.11 The Impact of Taxes and Incentives on Project Returns, Small Instruments Firms, 112 Cities

	Mean ($)	Coefficient of variation	Size of range ($)	Hourly, per-employee wage equivalent of range ($)
Project returns				
After basic taxes	1,687,584	0.078	653,044	0.37
After tax incentives	1,774,660	0.085	709,825	0.41
After all incentives	2,024,889	0.117	1,017,677	0.58
Increment in project returns due to				
Tax incentives	87,077	1.241	546,336	
Non-tax incentives	250,229	0.666	716,801	
Hourly, per-employee wage equivalent of				
Tax incentives	0.05		0.31	
Non-tax incentives	0.14		0.42	

Table D.12 The Impact of Taxes and Incentives on Project Returns, Large Instruments Firms, 112 Cities

	Mean ($)	Coefficient of variation	Size of range ($)	Hourly, per-employee wage equivalent of range ($)
Project returns				
After basic taxes	56,344,150	0.045	12,658,540	0.52
After tax incentives	57,904,449	0.048	13,834,561	0.57
After all incentives	58,935,884	0.053	15,861,121	0.65
Increment in project returns due to				
Tax incentives	1,560,299	1.274	10,506,146	
Non-tax incentives	1,031,435	0.897	7,716,225	
Hourly, per-employee wage equivalent of				
Tax incentives	0.06		0.43	
Non-tax incentives	0.04		0.32	

Table D.13 Average Value of Incentives, Multistate Firms ($)

Firm (plant size, in millions)	Value of all tax incentives			Value of enterprise zone tax incentives only			State and local non-enterprise zone incentives		
	State	Local	State and local	State	Local	State and local	Tax incentives	Other incentives	Total incentives
Average for all city sizes									
#2: Furniture ($40)	197,835	192,501	390,336	168,428	49,692	218,120	172,216	612,496	784,712
#5: Soaps ($20)	98,328	85,914	184,242	90,043	20,356	110,399	73,843	323,319	397,162
#7: Plastics ($5)	20,144	24,528	44,673	19,784	5,355	25,138	19,534	166,352	185,886
#14: Autos ($600)	1,305,375	2,873,683	4,179,057	999,233	724,271	1,723,505	2,455,553	1,720,787	4,176,340
#16: Instruments ($180)	557,012	728,300	1,285,312	475,965	196,216	672,181	613,131	981,734	1,594,865
Average of 16 firms by city size									
500,000 or more	1,080,880	1,432,333	2,513,212	1,179,622	84,204	1,263,826	1,249,386	873,035	2,122,422
100,000 - 499,999	767,940	667,664	1,435,604	587,664	262,829	850,493	585,111	673,247	1,258,358
25,000 - 99,999	378,481	609,678	988,159	263,052	249,074	512,126	476,033	803,480	1,279,513
10,000 - 24,999	37,540	604,711	642,251	147,174	0	147,174	495,076	687,868	1,182,945
Average: all cities	391,140	640,839	1,031,979	339,366	161,913	501,279	530,700	723,226	1,253,926

NOTE: Items may not add to totals due to rounding.

262

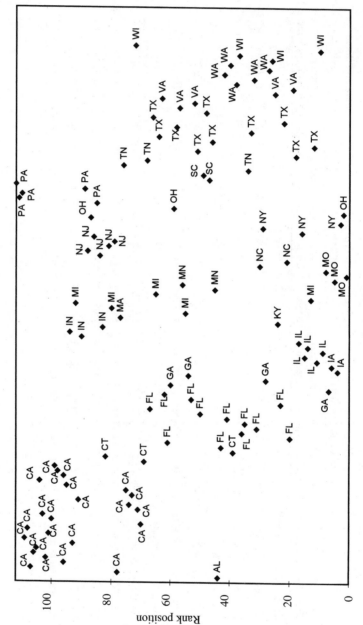

Figure D .1 Project Returns Rank Position over 112 Locations, Large Multistate Drug Firms

Figure D.2 Project Returns Rank Position over 112 Locations, Small Multistate Soap Firms

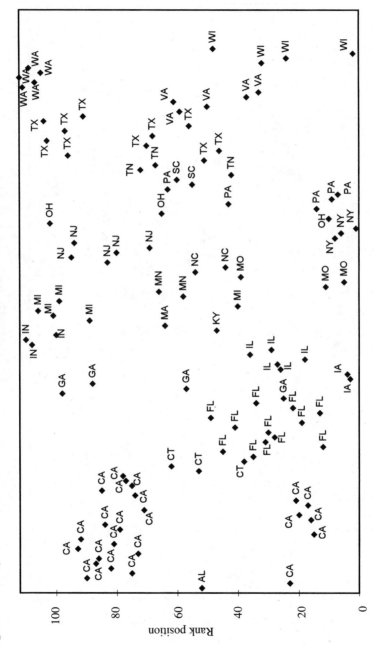

Ordered by state

Figure D.3 Project Returns Rank Position over 112 Locations, Large Multistate Plastics Firms

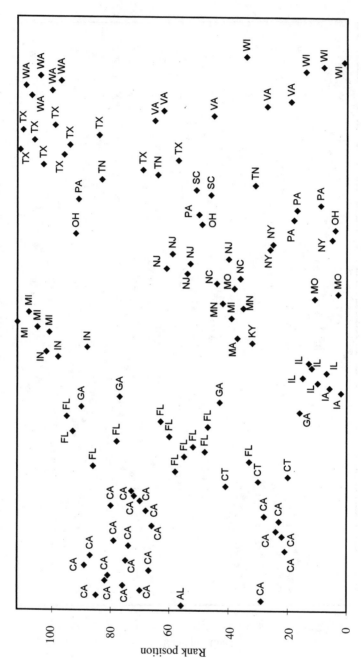

Ordered by state

Appendix E

Detailed Results: Correlations between Project Returns and Unemployment Rates for States and Cities

Table E.1 Correlation between State Average 1992 Unemployment Rate and Firm's Net Return on New Plant Investment in Each State (Multistate Firms, State Taxes and Incentives Only)

Firm (plant size, in millions)	Net project returns			Value of incentives						
	After basic taxes	After tax incentives	After all incentives	Tax incentives	Infra-structure subsidies	Job training subsidies	General financing programs	All non-tax incentives	All incentives
#1: Furniture ($5)	(0.53)	(0.49)	(0.12)	0.18	(0.23)	0.05	0.16	0.10	0.11
#2: Furniture ($40)	(0.63)	(0.51)	(0.52)	0.08	(0.08)	(0.33)	(0.20)	(0.33)	(0.25)
#3: Drugs ($50)	(0.53)	(0.47)	(0.46)	0.08	(0.17)	(0.14)	(0.14)	(0.21)	(0.13)
#4: Drugs ($470)	(0.48)	(0.41)	(0.45)	0.16	(0.19)	(0.49)	(0.20)	(0.51)	(0.09)
#5: Soaps ($20)	(0.56)	(0.45)	(0.36)	0.11	(0.15)	0.08	(0.01)	(0.02)	0.04
#6: Soaps ($110)	(0.58)	(0.44)	(0.48)	0.11	(0.16)	(0.41)	(0.19)	(0.39)	(0.16)
#7: Plastics ($5)	(0.63)	(0.58)	(0.18)	0.06	(0.24)	0.06	0.14	0.08	0.09
#8: Plastics ($70)	(0.63)	(0.55)	(0.56)	0.11	(0.14)	(0.32)	(0.22)	(0.34)	(0.27)
#9: Machinery ($10)	(0.64)	(0.45)	(0.18)	0.11	(0.13)	0.09	0.13	0.11	0.13
#10: Machinery ($250)	(0.61)	(0.48)	(0.54)	0.11	(0.10)	(0.48)	(0.30)	(0.47)	(0.27)
#11: Electronics ($20)	(0.68)	(0.53)	(0.36)	0.12	(0.10)	0.04	(0.01)	(0.01)	0.04
#12: Electronics ($200)	(0.68)	(0.53)	(0.56)	0.12	(0.11)	(0.46)	(0.18)	(0.44)	(0.22)
#13: Autos ($120)	(0.62)	(0.54)	(0.57)	0.09	(0.12)	(0.44)	(0.29)	(0.43)	(0.33)
#14: Autos ($600)	(0.51)	(0.39)	(0.48)	0.14	(0.19)	(0.50)	(0.20)	(0.54)	(0.26)
#15: Instruments ($10)	(0.63)	(0.57)	(0.26)	0.09	(0.09)	0.10	0.13	0.12	0.13
#16: Instruments ($180)	(0.61)	(0.54)	(0.57)	0.10	(0.13)	(0.45)	(0.19)	(0.44)	(0.27)

NOTE: Negative correlations are shown in parentheses.

Table E.2 Correlation between State Average Unemployment Rate 1989–1993 and Firm's Net Return on New Plant Investment in Each State (Multistate Firms, State Taxes and Incentives Only)

Firm (plant size in millions)	Net project returns			Value of incentives		
	After basic taxes	After tax incentives	After all incentives	Tax incentives	Non-tax incentives	All incentives
#1: Furniture ($5)	(0.43)	(0.39)	(0.12)	0.17	0.06	0.07
#2: Furniture ($40)	(0.46)	(0.37)	(0.41)	0.07	(0.30)	(0.23)
#3: Drugs ($50)	(0.32)	(0.28)	(0.32)	0.04	(0.22)	(0.16)
#4: Drugs ($470)	(0.23)	(0.19)	(0.23)	0.10	(0.38)	(0.08)
#5: Soaps ($20)	(0.34)	(0.27)	(0.25)	0.06	(0.06)	(0.02)
#6: Soaps ($110)	(0.36)	(0.28)	(0.32)	0.06	(0.32)	(0.15)
#7: Plastics ($5)	(0.54)	(0.49)	(0.18)	0.13	0.04	0.05
#8: Plastics ($70)	(0.49)	(0.42)	(0.44)	0.14	(0.30)	(0.22)
#9: Machinery ($10)	(0.50)	(0.36)	(0.17)	0.06	0.05	0.06
#10: Machinery ($250)	(0.49)	(0.39)	(0.40)	0.08	(0.29)	(0.15)
#11: Electronics ($20)	(0.52)	(0.41)	(0.32)	0.09	(0.06)	(0.03)
#12: Electronics ($200)	(0.52)	(0.41)	(0.42)	0.10	(0.30)	(0.14)
#13: Autos ($120)	(0.51)	(0.43)	(0.44)	0.11	(0.31)	(0.22)
#14: Autos ($600)	(0.46)	(0.36)	(0.42)	0.09	(0.43)	(0.21)
#15: Instruments ($10)	(0.45)	(0.40)	(0.20)	0.10	0.07	0.08
#16: Instruments ($180)	(0.41)	(0.36)	(0.38)	0.09	(0.31)	(0.18)

NOTE: Negative correlations are shown in parentheses.

Table E.3 Correlation between City 1992 Unemployment Rate and Firm's Net Returns from New Plant Investment in Each City: Selected Multistate Firms, by City Size Class

Firm (plant size in millions)/city population	Net project returns			Value of incentives		
	After basic taxes	After tax incentives	After all incentives	Tax incentives	Other incentives	All incentives
#2: Furniture ($40)						
500,000 or more	(0.40)	(0.30)	(0.21)	0.04	(0.01)	0.01
100,000 - 499,999	(0.14)	0.15	0.08	0.29	(0.11)	0.18
25,000 - 99,999	(0.10)	0.23	0.13	0.49	(0.17)	0.31
10,000 - 24,999	(0.36)	(0.37)	(0.31)	0.06	0.13	0.15
#5: Soaps ($20)						
500,000 or more	(0.25)	(0.16)	(0.11)	0.06	0.00[a]	0.04
100,000 - 499,999	(0.25)	0.08	0.00[a]	0.28	(0.16)	0.16
25,000 - 99,999	(0.10)	0.20	0.11	0.48	(0.17)	0.27
10,000 - 24,999	(0.26)	(0.24)	(0.09)	0.09	0.16	0.21
#7: Plastics ($5)						
500,000 or more	(0.40)	(0.26)	(0.07)	0.33	0.18	0.31
100,000 - 499,999	0.10	0.30	0.20	0.27	0.02	0.17
25,000 - 99,999	(0.11)	0.19	0.05	0.46	(0.14)	0.17
10,000 - 24,999	(0.42)	(0.44)	(0.10)	0.09	0.16	0.18

(continued)

Table E.3 (continued)

Firm (plant size in millions)/city population	After basic taxes	After tax incentives	After all incentives	Tax incentives	Other incentives	All incentives
#14: Autos ($600)						
500,000 or more	(0.34)	(0.14)	(0.13)	0.51	(0.01)	0.49
100,000 - 499,999	0.14	0.31	0.26	0.30	(0.30)	0.21
25,000 - 99,999	(0.09)	0.10	0.11	0.35	0.08	0.35
10,000 - 24,999	(0.39)	(0.42)	(0.45)	0.06	(0.22)	(0.02)
#16: Instruments ($180)						
500,000 or more	(0.48)	(0.38)	(0.24)	0.18	0.04	.016
100,000 - 499,999	(0.22)	0.13	0.05	0.35	(0.26)	0.25
25,000 - 99,999	(0.07)	0.19	0.16	0.43	(0.07)	0.38
10,000 - 24,999	(0.35)	(0.35)	(0.34)	0.06	0.10	0.10

NOTE: Negative correlations are shown in parentheses. For each firm, the number in parentheses is new plant investment in millions of dollars. Basic taxes include state and city corporate income and net worth taxes, state and local sales taxes on machinery and equipment and fuel and utilities, and state and local property taxes. Tax incentives consist of state investment and jobs tax credits, sales tax exemptions or credits in enterprise zones, state property tax credits in enterprise zones, and local property tax abatements. The value of incentives is measured by the net project returns after taxes and incentives, less project returns after basic taxes only. The average correlation for all city sizes is a weighted average of the coefficients for the four city size classes; the weight for a size class is the U.S. population living in cities of that size divided by the total U.S. population living in cities of 10,000 or more.
a. Absolute value less than 0.005.

Table E.4 Correlation between City 1992 Unemployment Rate and Firm's Net Returns from New Plant Investment in Each City: Average for All City Sizes by Firm

Firm (plant size in millions)	Net project returns			Value of incentives		
	After basic taxes	After tax incentives	After all incentives	Tax incentives	Other incentives	All incentives
Multistate firms						
#1: Furniture ($5)	(0.18)	(0.03)	0.01	0.28	0.02	0.16
#2: Furniture ($40)	(0.23)	(0.02)	(0.05)	0.27	(0.04)	0.21
#3: Drugs ($50)	(0.25)	(0.02)	(0.06)	0.29	(0.07)	0.23
#4: Drugs ($470)	(0.21)	(0.02)	(0.05)	0.27	(0.15)	0.22
#5: Soaps ($20)	(0.21)	0.00[a]	0.00[a]	0.28	(0.04)	0.22
#6: Soaps ($110)	(0.23)	(0.01)	(0.04)	0.28	(0.07)	0.24
#7: Plastics ($5)	(0.18)	(0.02)	0.04	0.27	0.03	0.18
#8: Plastics ($70)	(0.19)	(0.04)	(0.06)	0.26	(0.05)	0.22
#9: Machinery ($10)	(0.16)	0.01	0.05	0.26	0.01	0.19
#10: Machinery ($250)	(0.16)	(0.03)	(0.04)	0.25	(0.03)	0.22
#11: Electronics ($20)	(0.19)	(0.02)	0.01	0.27	(0.01)	0.20
#12: Electronics ($200)	(0.17)	(0.02)	(0.05)	0.27	(0.06)	0.23
#13: Autos ($120)	(0.20)	(0.07)	(0.08)	0.26	(0.02)	0.22
#14: Autos ($600)	(0.15)	(0.04)	(0.06)	0.24	(0.14)	0.19
#15: Instruments ($10)	(0.25)	(0.05)	(0.02)	0.27	(0.01)	0.14
#16: Instruments ($180)	(0.24)	(0.04)	(0.06)	0.28	(0.06)	0.24

(continued)

Table E.4 (continued)

Firm (plant size in millions)	Net project returns			Value of incentives		
	After basic taxes	After tax incentives	After all incentives	Tax incentives	Other incentives	All incentives
Single-location firms						
#1: Furniture ($5)	(0.14)	0.03	0.07	0.24	0.02	0.20
#2: Furniture ($40)	(0.16)	0.06	0.05	0.21	(0.03)	0.22
#3: Drugs ($50)	(0.16)	0.06	0.04	0.23	(0.07)	0.23
#4: Drugs ($470)	(0.12)	0.07	0.05	0.23	(0.15)	0.20
#5: Soaps ($20)	(0.11)	0.10	0.11	0.19	(0.04)	0.22
#6: Soaps ($110)	(0.12)	0.09	0.08	0.17	(0.07)	0.18
#7: Plastics ($5)	(0.16)	0.01	0.07	0.24	0.03	0.21
#8: Plastics ($70)	(0.17)	0.00[a]	(0.01)	0.21	(0.04)	0.22
#9: Machinery ($10)	(0.08)	0.09	0.11	0.16	0.01	0.18
#10: Machinery ($250)	(0.11)	0.04	0.04	0.16	(0.03)	0.17
#11: Electronics ($20)	(0.12)	0.06	0.09	0.22	(0.01)	0.24
#12: Electronics ($200)	(0.11)	0.06	0.05	0.21	(0.06)	0.20
#13: Autos ($120)	(0.17)	0.01	0.00[a]	0.22	(0.02)	0.22
#14: Autos ($600)	(0.08)	0.08	0.07	0.16	(0.14)	0.14
#15: Instruments ($10)	(0.17)	0.04	0.05	0.25	(0.01)	0.19
#16: Instruments ($180)	(0.16)	0.04	0.02	0.24	(0.05)	0.23

273

NOTE: Negative correlations are shown in parentheses. For each firm, the number in parentheses is new plant investment in millions of dollars. Basic taxes include state and city corporate income and net worth taxes, state and local sales taxes on machinery and equipment and fuel and utilities, and state and local property taxes. Tax incentives consist of state investment and jobs tax credits, sales tax exemptions or credits in enterprise zones, state property tax credits in enterprise zones, and local property tax abatements. The value of incentives is measured by the net project returns after taxes and incentives, less project returns after basic taxes only.

a. Absolute value less than 0.005.

Table E.5 Effective Tax and Tax Incentive Rates in a Representative City in Each State: Correlations with State Unemployment, Job Growth, and Poverty Rates

Taxes/incentives	Firm	Unemployment	Job growth	Poverty
Basic state taxes	#2: Furniture	0.79	0.10	(0.20)
	#5: Soaps	0.76	0.10	(0.16)
	#7: Plastics	0.68	0.19	(0.12)
	#14: Autos	0.69	0.15	(0.08)
	#16: Instruments	0.73	0.04	(0.27)
Basic local taxes	#2: Furniture	(0.14)	(0.14)	0.23
	#5: Soaps	(0.12)	(0.15)	0.25
	#7: Plastics	(0.13)	(0.09)	0.27
	#14: Autos	(0.12)	(0.05)	0.25
	#16: Instruments	(0.14)	(0.19)	0.23
Basic state and local taxes	#2: Furniture	0.50	(0.04)	0.03
	#5: Soaps	0.64	0.01	0.00
	#7: Plastics	0.24	0.02	0.18
	#14: Autos	0.27	0.04	0.16
	#16: Instruments	0.48	(0.13)	(0.02)
State tax incentives	#2: Furniture	0.35	0.09	(0.07)
	#5: Soaps	0.34	0.07	(0.04)
	#7: Plastics	0.29	0.14	(0.01)
	#14: Autos	0.25	0.00	(0.14)
	#16: Instruments	0.21	0.17	(0.09)
Local tax incentives	#2: Furniture	0.08	(0.28)	0.07
	#5: Soaps	0.08	(0.26)	0.08
	#7: Plastics	0.08	(0.15)	0.09
	#14: Autos	0.09	(0.30)	0.09
	#16: Instruments	0.08	(0.28)	0.06

Taxes/incentives	Firm	Unemployment	Job growth	Poverty
State and local total tax incentives	#2: Furniture	0.33	(0.16)	0.00
	#5: Soaps	0.33	(0.11)	0.02
	#7: Plastics	0.25	(0.05)	0.08
	#14: Autos	0.20	(0.30)	0.03
	#16: Instruments	0.20	(0.15)	0.00
State and local enterprise zone tax incentive package	#2: Furniture	0.30	0.11	(0.05)
	#5: Soaps	0.32	0.16	(0.03)
	#7: Plastics	0.26	0.24	0.03
	#14: Autos	0.16	0.01	(0.03)
	#16: Instruments	0.17	0.11	(0.04)
State and local non-enterprise zone tax incentive package	#2: Furniture	0.05	(0.41)	0.08
	#5: Soaps	0.08	(0.41)	0.07
	#7: Plastics	0.03	(0.34)	0.07
	#14: Autos	0.07	(0.39)	0.07
	#16: Instruments	0.05	(0.41)	0.08
State and local taxes after non-enterprise zone tax incentives	#2: Furniture	0.52	0.14	0.00
	#5: Soaps	0.63	0.14	(0.02)
	#7: Plastics	0.29	0.21	0.20
	#14: Autos	0.30	0.25	0.16
	#16: Instruments	0.51	0.03	(0.06)
State and local taxes after all tax incentives	#2: Furniture	0.33	0.07	0.04
	#5: Soaps	0.54	0.08	(0.01)
	#7: Plastics	0.11	0.05	0.16
	#14: Autos	0.19	0.22	0.16
	#16: Instruments	0.40	(0.05)	(0.03)

NOTE: See Tables 4.6, 4.7, and 5.3 for explanations of terms.

REFERENCES

Allen, Kevin, Hugh Begg, Stuart McDowall, and Gavin Walker. 1986. *Regional Incentives and the Investment Decision of the Firm.* London: Department of Trade and Industry, Her Majesty's Stationary Office.

American Bar Association. Section of Taxation. 1993. *ABA Sales and Use Tax Desk Book,* 1992–93 Edition. Washington, D.C.

Archer, Stephan, and Steven Maser. 1989. "State Export Promotion for Economic Development," *Economic Development Quarterly* 3(3): 235–242.

Area Development. 1993. "Directory of State Incentives," *Area Development* 28(1): 78–138.

Atkinson, Robert. 1991. "Some States Take the Lead: Explaining the Formation of State Technology Policies," *Economic Development Quarterly* 5(1): 33–44.

Bachtler, John. 1990. "Grants for Inward Investors: Giving Away Money?" *National Westminster Bank Quarterly Review* (May): 15–24.

Bartik, Timothy J. 1991a. "The Effects of Property Taxes and Other Local Public Policies on the Intrametropolitan Pattern of Business Location." In *Industry Location and Public Policy,* Henry W. Herzog, Jr. and Alan M. Schlottmann, eds. Knoxville: University of Tennessee Press.

———. 1991b. *Who Benefits from State and Local Economic Development Policies?* Kalamazoo, Michigan: W.E. Upjohn Institute for Employment Research.

Bartik, Timothy J., Charles Becker, Steve Lake, and John Bush. 1987. "Saturn and State Economic Development," *Forum for Applied Research and Public Policy* 2(1): 29–41.

Begg, Hugh, and Stuart McDowall. 1987. "The Effect of Regional Investment Incentives on Company Decisions," *Regional Studies* 21(5): 459–470.

Bernan Press. 1994. *County and City Extra.* Lanham, Maryland.

Blair, John, and Robert Premus. 1987. "Major Factors in Industrial Location: A Review." *Economic Development Quarterly* 1(1): 72–85.

Blum, Ken. 1995. *The Mercedes Benz Subsidy Package: Whose Benefits? Whose Losses?* Chicago: Midwest Center for Labor Research.

Bowman, Ann. 1987. *Tools and Targets: The Mechanics of City Economic Development.* National League of Cities' Research Report on America's Cities. Washington, D.C.: National League of Cities.

Bradshaw, Ted, Nancy Nishikawa. and Edward Blakely. 1992. *State Economic Development Promotions and Incentives: A Comparison of State Efforts and Strategies.* Berkeley: University of California.

Brierly, Allen. 1986. "State Economic Development Policy Choices." Paper presented at the Annual Meeting of the Southwest Political Science Association, Houston, March.

Brigham, Eugene. 1985. *Financial Management: Theory and Practice.* Fourth Edition. New York: Dryden Press.

Brooks, Stephen H. 1993. *Report to the Massachusetts Special Commission on Business Tax Policy.* Waltham, Massachusetts: S. H. Brooks Co., Inc. Cited in Tannenwald and Kendrick, 1995.

Brooks, Stephen, Robert Tannenwald, Hillary Sale, and Sandeep Puri. 1986. *The Competitiveness of the Massachusetts Tax System.* Interim Report of the Massachusetts Special Commission on Tax Reform. House No. 5148. Boston.

Burstein, Melvin L., and Arthur J. Rolnick. 1995. "Congress Should End the Economic War among the States." Federal Reserve Bank of Minneapolis 1994 Annual Report. *The Region* 9(1): 3–20.

————. 1996. "Congress Should End the Economic War for Sports and Other Businesses," *The Region* 10(2): 35–36.

Calzonetti, F.J., and Robert T. Walker. 1991. "Factors Affecting Industrial Location Decisions: A Survey Approach." In *Industry Location and Public Policy,* Henry W. Herzog, Jr., and Alan M. Schlottmann, eds. Knoxville: University of Tennessee Press.

Carroll, Robert, and Michael Wasylenko. 1990. "The Shifting Fate of Fiscal Variables and Their Effect on Economic Development." *Proceedings of the Eighty-Second Annual Conference,* 1989. Washington, D.C.: National Tax Association-Tax Institute of America.

————. 1991. "Economic Growth and Government Fiscal Behavior, 1973–1987." In *State and Local Finance for the 1990s: A Case Study of Arizona,* Therese McGuire and Dana Wolfe, eds. Tempe: Arizona State University Press.

Chapman, Keith, and David Walker. 1990. *Industrial Location.* Oxford, UK: Basil Blackwell.

Clarke, Marianne K. 1986. *Revitalizing State Economies.* Washington, D.C.: National Governors' Association.

Clingermayer, James, and Richard Feiock. 1990. "The Adoption of Economic Development Policies by Large Cities: A Test of Economic, Interest Group, and Institutional Explanantions," *Policy Studies Journal* 18(3): 539–552.

Colgan, Charles. 1995. "Brave New World: International Regulation of Subsidies and the Future of State and Local Economic Development Programs," *Economic Development Quarterly* 9(2): 107–118.

Commerce Clearing House. *State Tax Reporter.* Chicago.

Commerce Clearing House. *Multistate Corporate Income Tax Guide*. Chicago.

Commerce Clearing House. *State Tax Guide*. Chicago.

Cornia, G., W. Testa, and F. Stocker. 1978. *State-Local Fiscal Incentives and Economic Development*. Urban and Regional Development Series No. 4. Columbus, OH: Academy of Contemporary Problems.

Council of State Governments. 1994. "State Business Incentives," *State Trends and Forecasts* 3(June): 1–31.

Diamond, Derek R., and Spence, Nigel A. 1983. *Regional Policy Evaluation*. Farnbrough, Hants: Gower.

Eisinger, Peter. 1988. *The Rise of the Entrepreneurial State*. Madison: University of Wisconsin Press.

———. 1995. "State Economic Development in the 1990s: Politics and Policy Learning." *Economic Development Quarterly* 9(2): 146–158.

Elling, Richard, and Ann Sheldon. 1991. "Determinants of Enterprise Zone Success: A Four State Perspective." In *Enterprise Zones: New Directions in Economic Development*, Roy Green, ed. Newbury Park, California: Sage.

Fainstein, Susan. 1991. "Promoting Economic Growth: Urban Planning in the United States and Great Britain," *Journal of the American Planning Association* 22(1): 22–33.

Federation of Tax Administrators. 1991. *Sales Taxation of Services: Who Taxes What?* Washington, D.C.

Feiock, Richard. 1989. "The Adoption of Economic Development Policies by State and Local Governments: A Review," *Economic Development Quarterly* 3(3): 266–270.

Feiock, Richard, and James Clingermayer. 1986. "Municipal Representation, Executive Power and Economic Development Adoption," *Policy Studies Journal* 15(7): 211–230.

Fisher. Peter S. 1990. "The National Consequencies of Decentralized Industrial Policy in the United States." Paper presented at the Annual Meeting of the Association of Collegiate Schools of Planning, Austin, Texas, November.

———. 1991. "What's Really New about the Economic Role of American States in the 1980s?" Paper presented at the ACSP-AESOP Joint International Congress, Oxford, England, July.

Fosler, R. Scott. 1988. *The New Economic Role of American States: Strategies in a Competitive World Economy*. New York: Oxford University Press.

Foster, Norman, David Forkenbrock, and Thomas Pogue. 1991. "Evaluation of a State-level Road Program to Promote Local Economic Development," *Transportation Quarterly* 45(October): 143–57.

Gerking, Shelby, and William Morgan. 1991. "Measuring Effects of Industrial Location and State Economic Development Policy: A Survey." In *Industry Location and Public Policy*, Henry W. Herzog, Jr. and Alan M. Schlottmann, eds. Knoxville: University of Tennessee Press.

Glickman, Norman, and Douglas Woodward. 1989. *The New Competitors: How Foreign Investors are Changing the U.S. Economy.* New York: Basic Books.

Goss, Ernest. 1994. "The Impact of Infrastructure Spending on New Business Formation: The Importance of State Economic Development Spending," *Review of Regional Studies* 24(3): 265–279.

Goss, Ernest, and Joseph Phillips. 1994. "State Employment Growth: The Impact of Taxes and Economic Development Agency Spending," *Growth and Change* 25(3): 287–300.

Grady, Dennis. 1987. "State Economic Development Incentives: Why Do States Compete?" *State and Local Government Review* 19(Fall): 86–94.

Grasso, Patrick G., and Scott B. Crosse. 1991. "Enterprise Zones: Maryland Case Study." In *Enterprise Zones: New Directions in Economic Development*, Roy Green, ed. Newbury Park, California: Sage.

Gray, Virginia, and David Lowery. 1990. "The Corporatist Foundations of State Industrial Policy," *Social Science Quarterly* 71(March): 3–22.

Green, Gary, and Arnold Fleischman. 1991. "Promoting Economic Development: A Comparison of Central Cities, Suburbs and Nonmetropolitan Communities," *Urban Affairs Quarterly* 27(September): 145–154.

Guskind, Robert. 1990. "The Giveaway Game Continues," *Planning* 56(2): 4–8.

Hanson, Russell. 1993. "Bidding for Business: A Second War between the States?" *Economic Development Quarterly* 7(2): 183–198.

Hanson, Susan B. 1985. "State Industrial Policy." Paper delivered at the Annual Meeting of the Southwest Political Science Association, Houston, Texas, March.

Haug, Peter. 1984. "Regional Policy Incentives in the Scottish Electronics Industry," *Scottish Journal of Political Economy* 31(3): 274–283.

Heartland Institute. 1995. "100+ Economists Urge: End Economic War between the States." News release, September 20. Palatine, Illinois.

Hovey, Harold A. 1986. "Interstate Tax Competition and Economic Development." In *Reforming State Tax Systems*, Steven Gold, ed. Washington, D.C.: National Conference of State Legislatures.

Howland, Marie. 1990. "Measuring Capital Subsidy Costs and Job Creation: The Case of Rural UDAG Grants," *Journal of the American Planning Association* 56(Winter): 166–177.

Hunt, Timothy L. 1985. *Michigan's Business Tax Costs Relative to the Other Great Lakes States*. Kalamazoo, Michigan: W.E. Upjohn Institute for Employment Research.

Hunt, Timothy L., and Christopher J. O'Leary. 1989. *Experience Rating of Unemployment Insurance in Michigan and Other States: A Microeconomic Comparison for 1988*. Kalamazoo, Michigan: W.E. Upjohn Institute for Employment Research.

Jones, Stephan R.G. 1989. "Reservation Wages and the Cost of Unemployment." *Econometrica* 56(May): 225–246.

Kieschnick, Michael. 1981. *Taxes and Growth: Business Incentives and Economic Development*. Washington, D.C.: Council of State Planning Agencies.

KPMG Peat Marwick. 1994. "The Competitiveness of New York's Business Taxes," *State Tax Notes* 7(July 18): 161–190.

Krmenec, Andrew. 1990. "The Employment Impacts of an Investment Incentive: Differential Efficiency of the Industrial Revenue Bond," *Regional Studies* 24(2): 95–107.

Kudrle, Robert, and Cynthia Kite. 1989. "The Evaluation of State Programs for International Business Development," *Economic Development Quarterly* 4(4): 288–300.

Ladd, Helen F. 1995. "The Tax Expenditure Concept after 25 Years," *NTA Forum* No. 20 (Winter): 1–5.

Ladd, Helen F., and John Yinger. 1991. *America's Ailing Cities*. Updated Edition. Baltimore: Johns Hopkins University Press.

Laughlin, James D. 1993. *An Assessment of Indiana's Competitive Position in Business Recruitment*. Indianapolis: Indiana Economic Development Council, Inc.

Ledebur, Larry, and Douglas Woodward. 1990. "Adding a Stick to the Carrot: Location Incentives with Clawbacks, Recisions, and Recalibrations," *Economic Development Quarterly* 4(3): 221–237.

LeRoy, Greg. 1994. *No More Candy Store: States and Cities Making Job Subsidies Accountable*. Chicago: Federation for Industrial Retention and Renewal; and Washington, D.C.: Grassroots Policy Project.

Logan, John, and Harvey Molotch. 1987. *Urban Fortunes: The Political Economy of Place*. Berkeley: University of California Press.

Loh, Eng Seng. 1995. "The Effects of Jobs-Targeted Development Incentive Programs," *Growth and Change* 24(3): 365–383.

Lugar, Michael. 1987. "The States and Industrial Development: Program Mix and Policy Effectiveness." In *Perspectives on Local Public Finance and Public Policy*, Vol. 3, Economic Development, John Quigley, ed. Greenwich, Connecticut: JAI Press.

282

Markusen, Ann, Peter Hall, and Amy Glasmeier. 1986. *High Tech America.* Boston: Allen & Unwin.

Markusen, Ann, Peter Hall, Scott Cambell, and Sabina Deitrick. 1991. *The Rise of the GunBelt.* New York: Oxford University Press.

Marlin, Matthew. 1990. "The Effectiveness of Economic Development Subsidies," *Economic Development Quarterly* 4(1): 15–22.

Marston, Stephen T. 1985. "Two Views of the Geographic Distribution of Unemployment," *Quarterly Journal of Economics* 100(February): 57–79.

McCraw, Thomas K. 1986. "Mercantilism and the Market: Antecedents of American Industrial Policy." In *The Politics of Industrial Policy,* Clause Barfield and William Schambra, eds. Washington, D.C.: American Enterprise Institute.

McGreevy, T., and A. Thomson. 1983. "Regional Policy and Company Investment Behavior," *Regional Studies* 17(5): 347–356.

McGuire, Therese. 1992. Review of *Who Benefits from State and Local Economic Development Policies?* by Timothy J. Bartik. *National Tax Journal* 45(December): 457–459.

———. 1993. "Jobs and Taxes: Do State Taxes Affect Economic Development?" *Institute of Government and Public Affairs Policy Forum* 6(2): 1–4.

McGuire, Therese, and Michael Wasylenko. 1987. "Employment Growth and State Government Fiscal Behavior: A Report on Economic Development for States from 1974 to 1984." Report prepared for the New Jersey State and Local Expenditure and Revenue Policy Commission, July 2.

McMillan, T.E. 1965. "Why Manufacturers Choose Plant Locations vs. Determinants of Plant Location," *Land Economics* 41(August): 239–246.

Milward, H. Brinton, and Heidi Hosbach Newman. 1989. "State Incentive Packages and the Industrial Location Decision," *Economic Development Quarterly* 3(3): 203–222.

Morgan, William. 1964. The Effects of State and Local Taxes and Financial Inducements on Industrial Location. Ph.D. diss., University of Colorado, Boulder.

Morgan, William, John Mutti ,and Mark Partridge. 1989. "A Regional General Equilibrium Model of the United States: Tax Effects on Factor Movements and Regional Production," *Review of Economics and Statistics* 71(November): 626–635.

Muller, Thomas. 1975. *Growing and Declining Urban Areas: A Fiscal Comparison.* Washington, D.C.: Urban Institute.

National Association of State Development Agencies (NASDA). 1988. *1988 NASDA State Economic Development Expenditure and Salary Survey.* Washington, D.C.: NASDA.

————. 1991. *Directory of Incentives for Business Investment and Development in the United States.* Third Edition. Washington, D.C.: Urban Institute Press.

Netzer, Dick. 1991. "An Evaluation of Interjurisdictional Competition through Economic Development Incentives." In *Competition Among States and Local Governments,* Daphne Kenyon and John Kincaid, eds. Washington, D.C.: Urban Institute Press.

Newman, Robert, and Dennis Sullivan. 1988. "Econometric Analysis of Business Tax Impacts on Industrial Location: What Do We Know, and How Do We Know it?" *Journal of Urban Economics* 23(March): 215–34.

Oakland, William, and William Testa. 1996. "State-Local Business Taxation and the Benefits Principle," *Economic Perspectives* 19(2): 2–19.

Oates, Wallace E., and Robert M. Schwab. 1991. "The Allocative and Distributive Implications of Local Fiscal Competition." In *Competition among States and Local Governments,* Daphne Kenyon and John Kincaid, eds. Washington, D.C.: Urban Institute Press.

Owen, James. 1990. "Microgeographic Decisions in an Industrial Plant Location," *Economic Development Quarterly* 4(2): 137–143.

Papke, James. 1995. "Interjurisdictional Business Tax Cost Differentials: Convergence, Divergence and Significance," *State Tax Notes* 9(24): 1701–1711.

————. 1996. *Cross Firm-Size Variation in Subnational Taxation under Federal Consumption-Based Taxation: Impacts and Implications.* West Lafayette, Indiana: Purdue University, Center for Tax Policy Studies.

Papke, James, and Leslie Papke. 1984. "State Tax Incentives and Investment Location Decisions: Microanalytic Simulations." In *Indiana's Revenue Structure: Major Components and Issues,* Part II, James Papke, ed. West Lafayette, Indiana: Purdue University, Center for Tax Policy Studies.

————. 1986. "Measuring Differential State and Local Tax Liabilities and Their Implications for Business Investment Location," *National Tax Journal* 39: 357–366.

Papke, Leslie. 1987. "Subnational Taxation and Capital Mobility: Estimates of Tax-Price Elasticities," *National Tax Journal* 40(2): 191–203.

————. 1991. "The Responsiveness of Industrial Activity to Interstate Tax Differentials: A Comparison of Elasticities." In *Industry Location and Public Policy,* Henry W. Herzog, Jr. and Alan M. Schlottmann, eds. Knoxville: University of Tennessee Press.

Peters, Alan H. 1993. "Clawbacks and the Administration of Economic Development Policy in the Midwest," *Economic Development Quarterly* 7(4): 328–340.

Peters, Alan H., and Peter S. Fisher. 1995. "Measuring the Competitiveness of State and Local Economic Development Incentives," *Computers, Environment and Urban Systems* 19(4): 261–274.

———. 1997. "Do High Unemployment States Offer the Biggest Business Incentives? Results for Eight States Using the 'Hypothetical Firm' Method," *Economic Development Quarterly* 11(2):107–122.

Premus, Robert. 1982. "The Location of High Technology Firms and Regional Economic Development." Staff study prepared for use by the Subcommittee on Monetary and Fiscal Policy of the Joint Economic Committee, Congress of the United States, June 1.

Prentice-Hall. *State and Local Taxes: All States Tax Guide.* New York: Maxwell Macmillan.

Price, Waterhouse, & Co. 1978. *State Tax Comparison Study.* Cited in Kieschnick, 1981, p. 42.

Rasmussen, David, Marc Bendick, and Larry Ledebur. 1984. "A Methodology for Developing Economic Development Incentives," *Growth and Change* 15(2): 18–25.

Ray, D. Michael. 1971. "The Location of United States Manufacturing Subsidiaries in Canada," *Economic Geography* 47(3): 389–400.

Reese, Laura. 1991. "Municipal Fiscal Health and Tax Abatement Policy," *Economic Development Quarterly* 5(1): 23–32.

Reschovsky, Andrew. 1991. "How Closely Does State and Local Government Behavior Conform to a Perfectly Competitive Model?" In *Competition among States and Local Governments,* Daphne Kenyon and John Kincaid, eds. Washington, D.C.: Urban Institute Press.

Rinehart, James R., and William E. Laird. 1972. "Community Inducements to Industry and the Zero-sum Game," *Scottish Journal of Political Economy* 9(February): 73–90.

Rubin, Barry, and Kurt Zorn. 1985. "Sensible State and Local Economic Development," *Public Administration Review* 45(March/April): 333–339.

Rubin, Irene, and Herbert Rubin. 1987. "Economic Development Incentives: The Poor (Cities) Pay More," *Urban Affairs Quarterly* 23(1): 37–62.

Rubin, Marilyn Marks. 1991. "Urban Enterprise Zones in New Jersey: Have They Made a Difference?" In *Enterprise Zones: New Directions in Economic Development*, Roy Green, ed. Newbury Park, California: Sage.

Schmenner, Roger W. 1982. *Making Business Location Decisions.* Englewood Cliffs, New Jersey: Prentice-Hall.

Schneider, Mark. 1985. "Suburban Fiscal Disparities and the Location Decisions of Firms," *American Journal of Political Science* 29(August): 587–605.

Schweke, William, Carl Rist, and Brian Dabson. 1994. *Bidding for Business: Are Cities and States Selling Themselves Short?* Washington, D.C.: Corporation for Enterprise Development.

Shannon, John. 1991. "Federalism's 'Invisible Regulator': Interjurisdictional Competition." In *Competition among States and Local Governments,* Daphne Kenyon and John Kincaid, eds. Washington, D.C.: Urban Institute Press.

Sharp, Elaine. 1986. "The Politics and the Economics of the New City Debt," *American Political Science Review* 80(4): 1271–1288.

Sharp, Elaine, and David Elkins. 1991. "The Politics of Economic Development Policy," *Economic Development Quarterly* 5(2): 126–39.

Singletary, Loretta, Mark Henry, Kerry Brooks, and James London. 1995. "The Impact of Highway Investment on New Manufacturing Employment in South Carolina: A Small Region Spatial Analysis," *Review of Regional Studies* 25(1): 37–55.

Site Selection. 1993. "20th Annual Survey: '50 Legislative Climates'," *Site Selection and Industrial Development* 38(5): 1096–1169.

Skoro, Charles. 1988. "Rankings of State Business Climates: An Evaluation of Their Usefulness in Forecasting." *Economic Development Quarterly* 2(2): 138–152.

Smith, Tim, and William Fox. 1990. "Economic Development Programs for States in the 1990s," *Economic Review* (Federal Reserve Bank of Kansas City) 75(July/August): 25–35.

Spiegel, Mark, and Charles de Bartolome. Forthcoming. *Journal of Urban Economics.*

Sridhar, Kala S. 1993. Tax Costs and Employment Benefits of Enterprise Zones. Master's thesis submitted to the Graduate Program in Urban and Regional Planning, University of Iowa.

———. 1996. "Tax Costs and Employment Benefits in Enterprise Zones," *Economic Development Quarterly* 10(1): 69–90.

Stafford, Howard. 1974. "The Anatomy of the Location Decision: Content Analysis of Case Studies." In *Spatial Perspectives on Industrial Organization and Decision Making,* F.E. Ian Hamilton, ed. New York: John Wiley.

Steinnes, Donald N. 1984. "Business Climate, Tax Incentives, and Regional Economic Development," *Growth and Change* 15(2): 38–47.

Stevens, Gladstone T., Jr. 1979. *Economic and Financial Analysis of Capital Investments.* New York: John Wiley.

Swales, J. 1989. "Are Discretionary Regional Subsidies Cost-Effective?" *Regional Studies* 23(4): 361–374.

Swanstrom, Todd. 1985. *The Crisis of Growth Politics: Cleveland, Kucinich, and the Challenge of Urban Populism.* Philadephia: Temple University Press.

Tannenwald, Robert. 1996. "State Business Tax Climate: How Should It Be Measured and How Important Is It?" *New England Economic Review* (January/February): 23–38.

Tannenwald, Robert, and Christine Kendrick. 1995. "Taxes and Capital Spending: Some New Evidence." In *1994 Proceedings of the 87th Annual Conference on Taxation,* Frederick Stocker, ed. Columbus, Ohio: National Tax Association.

Taylor, M.J. 1975. "Organizational Growth, Spatial Interaction and Location Decision Making" *Regional Studies* 9(4): 313–23.

U.S. Advisory Commission on Intergovernmental Relations (ACIR). 1992. *Significant Features of Fiscal Federalism, 1992.* Vol. 1. Washington, D.C.: U.S. Advisory Commission on Intergovernmental Relations.

U.S. Bureau of the Census. 1982. *County Business Patterns, 1980, No. 1: United States.* Washington, D.C.: U.S. Government Printing Office.

———. 1990. *1987 Census of Manufactures: Industry Series.* Washington, D.C.: U.S. Government Printing Office.

———. 1991. *1987 Census of Manufactures: General Summary.* Washington, D.C.: U.S. Government Printing Office

———. 1992a. *1990 Annual Survey of Manufactures: Geographic Area Statistics.* Washington, D.C.: U.S. Government Printing Office.

———. 1992b. *1991 Annual Survey of Manufactures: Statistics for Industry Groups and Industries.* Washington, D.C.: U.S. Government Printing Office.

———. 1993a. *County Business Patterns, 1990, No. 1: United States.* Washington, D.C.: U.S. Government Printing Office.

———. 1993b. *1991 Annual Survey of Manufactures: Geographic Area Statistics.* Washington, D.C.: U.S. Government Printing Office.

U.S. Department of Commerce. 1992. *Survey of Current Business.* January.

———. 1993. *Survey of Current Business.* January.

———. 1994. *U.S. Industrial Outlook 1994.* Washington, D.C.: U.S. Government Printing Office.

U.S. Department of Housing and Urban Development. 1992. *State Enterprise Zone Update.* August. Washington, D.C.

U.S. Department of Labor. Bureau of Labor Statistics. 1992. *Unemployment in States and Local Areas.* 1992. Annual Supplement. Washington, D.C.

U.S. Federal Reserve Board. 1993. *Annual Statistical Digest.* Washington, D.C.

———. 1994. *Annual Statistical Digest.* Washington, D.C.

U.S. Internal Revenue Service. 1992. *Corporation Source Book of Statistics of Income 1990.* Washington, D.C.: U.S. Government Printing Office.

U.S. Office of Management and Budget (OMB). 1989. *Special Analyses: Budget of the United States Government, Fiscal Year 1989.* Part F, Federal Credit Programs. Washington, D.C.: Executive Office of the President.

Walker, Robert, and David Greenstreet. 1989. "Public Policy and Job Growth in Manufacturing: An Analysis of Incentive and Assistance Programs." Paper presented at the 36th North American Meeting of the Regional Science Association, Santa Barbara, California, November 10–12.

Wardrep, Bruce N. 1985. "Factors Which Play Major Roles in Location Decisions," *Industrial Development* 154(July/August): 73–74.

Wasylenko, Michael J. 1981. "The Location of Firms: The Role of Taxes and Fiscal Incentives." In *Urban Government Finance*, Roy Bahl, ed. Beverly Hills, California: Sage.

———. 1991. "Empirical Evidence on Interregional Business Location Decisions and the Role of Fiscal Incentives in Economic Development." In *Industry Location and Public Policy*, Henry W. Herzog, Jr., and Alan M. Schlottmann, eds. Knoxville: University of Tennessee Press.

Wasylenko, Michael, and Therese McGuire. 1985. "Jobs and Taxes: The Effect of Business Climate on State's Employment Growth Rates," *National Tax Journal* 38(4): 497–511.

Watts, H.D. 1980. *The Large Industrial Enterprise.* London: Croom Helm.

Wheaton, William. 1983. "Interstate Differences in the Level of Business Taxation," *National Tax Journal* 36(1): 83–94.

Williams, William. 1967. "A Measure of the Impact of State and Local Taxes on Industry Location." *Journal of Regional Science* 7(1): 49–59.

Wisconsin, Department of Revenue. 1973. *Corporate Tax Climate: A Comparison of Nineteen States.* Madison, Wisconsin.

Wisconsin, Department of Revenue. 1990. *Corporate Tax Climate: A Comparison of Nineteen States.* Madison, Wisconsin.

Wisconsin, Department of Revenue. 1995. *Corporate Tax Climate: A Comparison of Nineteen States.* Madison, Wisconsin.

Wolkoff, Michael J. 1990. "New Directions in the Analysis of Economic Development Policy," *Economic Development Quarterly* 4(4): 334–44.

Young, Ken, and Charlie Mason. 1983. *Urban Economic Development: New Roles and Relationships.* London: Macmillan.

Zuckerman, Dror. 1984. "On Preserving the Reservation Wage Property in a Continuous Job Search Model," *Journal of Economic Theory* 34(October): 175–179.

AUTHOR INDEX

Allen, Kevin, 107n
Archer, Stephan, 11
Atkinson, Robert, 23

Bachtler, John, 108n
Bartik, Timothy J., 11–12, 16–17, 18, 20, 26, 29n, 30n, 56, 213, 246
Becker, Charles, 277
Begg, Hugh, 107n
Bendick, Marc, 27n, 107n
Blair, John, 2, 7, 30n, 107n
Blakely, Edward, 6, 53n
Blum, Ken, 210, 221n
Bowman, Ann, 23
Bradshaw, Ted, 6, 53n
Brierly, Allen, 23
Brigham, Eugene, 79
Brooks, Kerry, 285
Brooks, Stephen H., 19, 59, 60, 64, 67, 78, 79, 81–82, 106n
Burstein, Melvin L., 1, 213, 215, 216
Bush, John, 277

Calzonetti, F.J., 14, 30n
Cambell, Scott, 282
Carroll, Robert, 30n
Chapman, Keith, 2, 7
Clarke, Marianne K., 22
Clingermayer, James, 22, 23
Colgan, Charles, 101
Cornia, G., 13
Crosse, Scott B., 15

Dabson, Brian, 1
De Bartolome, Charles, 30n
Deitrick, Sabina, 282
Diamond, Derek R., 13, 29n

Eisinger, Peter, 5–6, 16, 21, 30n, 173n
Elkins, David, 285
Elling, Richard, 15

Fainstein, Susan, 21
Feiock, Richard, 22, 23, 24
Fisher, Peter S., 6, 18, 23, 106n
Fleischman, Arnold, 22
Forkenbrock, David, 28n
Fosler, R. Scott, 21
Foster, Norman, 28n
Fox, William, 1

Gerking, Shelby, 7
Glasmeier, Amy, 282
Glickman, Norman, 8, 11, 28n
Goss, Ernest, 30n
Grady, Dennis, 23
Grasso, Patrick G., 15
Gray, Virginia, 22
Green, Gary, 22
Greenstreet, David, 14
Guskind, Robert, 8, 21

Hall, Peter, 282
Hanson, Russell, 11, 21, 23, 30n
Hanson, Susan B., 30n
Haug, Peter, 52n
Henry, Mark, 285
Hovey, Harold A., 8, 32
Howland, Marie, 108n
Hunt, Timothy L., 37, 52n, 59, 64, 65, 67

Jones, Stephan R.G., 29n

Kendrick, Christine, 19, 60, 61, 75
Kieschnick, Michael, 28n, 52n, 60, 61, 63, 78
Kite, Cynthia, 11
Krmenec, Andrew, 30n
Kudrle, Robert, 11

Ladd, Helen F., 8, 106n
Laird, William E., 28n
Lake, Steve, 277

Laughlin, James D., 19, 52n, 59, 64
Ledebur, Larry, 27n, 99, 107n
LeRoy, Greg, 1
Logan, John, 9
Loh, Eng Seng, 30n
London, James, 285
Lowery, David, 22
Lugar, Michael, 22

Malloy, Joe, 106n
Markusen, Ann, 27n
Marlin, Matthew, 30n
Marston, Stephen T., 8
Maser, Steven, 11
Mason, Charlie, 30n
McCraw, Thomas K., 5
McDowall, Stuart, 107n
McGreevy, T., 107n
McGuire, Therese, 17, 30n
McMillan, T.E., 61
Milward, H. Brinton, 3
Molotch, Harvey, 9
Morgan, William, 7, 15, 17
Muller, Thomas, 8
Mutti, John, 17

Netzer, Dick, 5, 10–11, 28n
Newman, Heidi Hosbach, 3
Newman, Robert, 16, 17
Nishikawa, Nancy, 6, 53n

Oakland, William, 173n
Oates, Wallace E., 10, 213
O'Leary, Christopher J., 52n
Owen, James, 102, 107n

Papke, James, 29n, 30n, 35, 52n, 59, 64,
    67, 78, 79, 106n, 160
Papke, Leslie, 19, 35, 52n, 57, 59, 61,
    64, 67, 78, 79, 106n
Partridge, Mark, 17
Peters, Alan H., 18, 30n, 100, 106n
Phillips, Joseph, 30n
Pogue, Thomas, 28n

Premus, Robert, 2, 7, 14, 30n, 107n
Puri, Sandeep, 277

Rasmussen, David, 27n, 107n
Ray, D. Michael, 27n
Reese, Laura, 23
Reschovsky, Andrew, 215
Rinehart, James R., 28n
Rist, Carl, 1
Rolnick, Arthur J., 1, 213, 215, 216
Rubin, Barry, 9, 28n
Rubin, Herbert, 23
Rubin, Irene, 23
Rubin, Marilyn Marks, 15

Sale, Hillary, 277
Schmenner, Roger W., 14, 15, 62, 108n
Schneider, Mark, 13
Schwab, Robert M., 10, 213
Schweke, William, 1
Shannon, John, 34, 38, 41
Sharp, Elaine, 30n
Sheldon, Ann, 15
Singletary, Loretta, 30n
Skoro, Charles, 30n
Smith, Tim, 1
Spence, Nigel A., 13, 29n
Spiegel, Mark, 30n
Sridhar, Kala S., 23, 29n
Stafford, Howard, 15
Steinnes, Donald N., 19, 60
Stevens, Gladstone T., Jr., 79
Stocker, F., 13
Sullivan, Dennis, 16, 17
Swales, J., 33, 107n
Swanstrom, Todd, 30n

Tannenwald, Robert, 19, 60, 61, 75
Taylor, M.J., 28n
Testa, William, 13, 173n
Thomson, A., 107n

Walker, David, 2, 7
Walker, Gavin, 277

Walker, Robert, 14, 30n
Wardrep, Bruce N., 62
Wasylenko, Michael J., 6, 17, 28n, 30n
Watts, H.D., 287
Wheaton, William, 57
Williams, William, 59
Wolkoff, Michael J., 28n
Woodward, Douglas, 8, 11, 28n, 99

Yinger, John, 8
Young, Ken, 30n

Zorn, Kurt, 9, 28n
Zuckerman, Dror, 29n

SUBJECT INDEX

Abatements, 6, 22, 23, 34
  by state, 120–121 (table)
  See also Property taxes
Accelerated Cost Recovery System
  (ACRS) depreciation, 81
Administration, of incentives, 98–103
Administrative history, of incentive
  program, 49
Administrative ratios, for non-tax
  incentives, 84
ADS. *See* Alternative Depreciation
  System (ADS)
Advertising, 22
  as economic development instrument,
  106n2, 106n6
AFTAX model, 79–80, 106n2, 106n6,
  160–161
Aggregate tax measures
  as incentive analysis approach, 56–57
  disaggregating results and, 82–83
Alabama, 106n5
  Mercedes-Benz incentives, 1, 2,
  208–211
  tax system in, 126n, 127
Allocation of resources. *See* Resources
Alternative Depreciation System (ADS),
  241
Annual Survey of Manufactures, 50
Apportionment of income, 113–117
  income taxes and, 243–244
Appropriations, for state economic
  development agencies, 6
Area Development (periodical), 39, 51,
  103
Assets
  distributing incentives across classes
  of, 95
  and hypothetical firm method, 67–68
Automobile industry
  Japanese investment in United States,
  3

standing offers and, 208
See also specific manufacturers

"Balance Agriculture with Industry"
  program (Mississippi), 5
Basic tax rate, 132n
Benefits
  of incentives, 10–13
  lack of, from state and local incentive
  programs, 9
  of Mazda investment, 3
  of state and city incentives, 3
BMW, in South Carolina, 1, 2–3
Britain. *See* Great Britain
Bureau of Indian Affairs programs, 32
Business. *See* Firm
Business assistance centers, 22
Business income, 36
  See also Corporate income taxes and
  credits
Business purchases, sales tax and, 37,
  110–112, 111–112 (table)
Business taxation
  interstate differences in, 55
  See also Corporate income taxes and
  credits

California, tax system in, 126n, 127
Capital, impact of incentives on, 25
Capital budgeting decisions, 80
Case study technique, evaluating
  incentive impact using, 15
Cash flow
  capital budgeting and, 80
  hypothetical firm model summary
  measure, 48
CDBG. *See* Community Development
  Block Grants (CDBG)
CEBA. *See* Community Economic
  Betterment Account (CEBA)
Census of Manufactures, 68

Cities
  characteristics of sample, 227–233
    (table)
  information on non-tax incentives
    and, 104
  locational competitiveness of,
    145–154
  project returns and unemployment
    rates for, 265–275
  ranked by returns on investment,
    73 (table)
  returns on investment among,
    186–190, 200–201
  TAIM study choice of, 50–51
  TAIM study population classes,
    51 (table)
  tax and incentive variations within,
    76
  taxes and tax incentives compared
    with state variations, 129–134,
    131–132 (table)
  See also Enterprise zones; Variations
    in economic development incentives
City government, site location and, 7
City modeling, 69
Clawbacks, administration of, 99–102
Climate indexes, 27n3
Community Development Block Grants
    (CDBG), 219
  city-level, 108n16
  funds, 42, 44
  revolving loan funds and, 93
Community Economic Betterment
    Account (CEBA), 22, 105
Comparative tax burdens, 18
Competitive incentives
  as defined for study, 31–33
  federal limits called for, 1
  net benefits to nation, 4
  valuation of, 46
Competitiveness, of cities, 145–154
Compustat database, 63–65
Constant proportions, hypothetical firm
    method and, 61

Corporate income taxes and credits, 110,
    113–117
  apportionment of, 243–244
  simulation treatment of, 35–36, 52n3
  1992 state, 114–116 (table)
Corporation
  domestic vs. foreign, 106n5
  See also Corporate income taxes and
    credits; Firm
Corporation Source Book, 68
Cost-benefit analysis, of economic
    development programs, 217, 218
Costs, processing, 7
Council of State Governments, on
    slowdown of economic development,
    6
Credits
  general, 116n
  as incentives, 6
  job and investment, 117
  for stimulating private investment,
    33–34
  See also Investment credits; Tax
    credits; Taxes and tax incentives
Customized job training and wage
    subsidies, 40–41
  See also Job training

Databases
  TAIM, 108n24
Debt, subordination of public, 91
Debt instruments, 90–91
Demographic characteristics and taxes,
    of city sample, 227–233 (table)
Department of Agriculture programs, 32
Department of Transportation (DOT),
    infrastructure subsidies and, 42
Deposits. See Linked-deposit programs
Depreciation on assets, 116n, 241
  MACRS and ACRS, 81, 116n
Development. See Economic
    development

Directory of Incentives for Business Investment and Development in the United States, 38, 51, 203, 205
Discretionary incentives. *See* Non-tax incentives
Distribution of investment returns, effects of taxes and incentives on spatial, 175–201
DOT. *See* Department of Transportation (DOT)

Econometric technique, evaluating incentive impact using, 15–17
Economic development
agency spending and, 30n16
federal funds for, 43–44
history of, 5–6
regressive impact on local distribution of income, 9
size of effort, 1–2
state spending on, 6
See also Economic development incentives; Variations in economic development incentives
Economic Development Administration (EDA), 44
Economic development competition
benefits of, 211–212
criticisms of, 1, 7–10
curbing, 219–221
among localities, 6–7
interstate or interlocal, 75–78
Economic development incentives
administration altering worth of, 98–103
benefits of, 3, 10–13
to BMW, 1, 2–3
as business cost, 13
business location decisions and, 12, 13–20
competitive, study definition of, 31–33
composition of, 141 (table)
distributing across asset classes, 95

expansion of and justification for state and local, 5–7
expenditures on, as incentive analysis approach, 58
explicit, 203–204, 211
in financial statements, 245–246
foreign direct investment and, 11
impact on growth, 13–19, 25–26
impact on investment decisions, 107n11
impact on location decisions, 13, 109
infrastructure, 87–89
job creation and, 7–8
judged by new employment, 7
justification for, 6–7
location decisions affected by, 4, 207–208
measuring, 3–4, 13, 24–26
to Mercedes-Benz, 1, 2, 208–210
quasi-governmental, 45
research on usefulness of, 10–13
spatial distribution of, 12, 20–24
TAIM results, 203–211
targeted tax incentives, 118
training, 89–90
unemployment and, 12
value of, 2, 3–4, 82, 98–103
worth across sectors, 136–137
See also Non-tax incentives; Standing incentive offer; Taxes and tax incentives; Variations in economic development incentives
Economic development instruments, regression models for, 22
Economic development policy. *See* Public policy
Economic development tax expenditures, 33–39
Economic need measures, 22
EDA. *See* Economic Development Administration (EDA)
Education, 41

Effective tax rates (ETRs), 16, 30n17,
131–132 (table), 133, 184,
185 (table)
Efficiency
in resource allocation, 10
taxes, incentives and, 213–218
Electricity, sales tax on, 37
Employees
jobs credits and, 77–78, 246
training incentives for, 89–90
See also Labor; Unemployed persons
Employment
growth, poverty rates, and net return
on new plant investment,
182 (table)
incentives judged by, 7
as justification for incentives, 4, 6
labor mobility and, 8–9
in manufacturing, 50–51
spatial patterns of incentives and, 20
value of incentive-induced growth,
11–12
See also Job training; Unemployment
Employment performance. See Job
creation
Employment size, and hypothetical firm
method, 68–69
England. See Great Britain
Enterprise zones, 5, 77, 109
in cities, 186, 190–199, 191 (fig.)
general credits for, 116n
importance of, 193–194 (table)
spatial distribution of investment and,
190–199
tax incentives and, 119, 122–124,
134, 205
unemployment and, 184
Equilibrium, 28n7
incentive competition and, 10
Equity, incentive competition and, 218–
219
ETRs. See Effective tax rates (ETRs)

Exemptions
from sales tax, 37–38
See also Taxes and tax incentives
Expenditure(s)
hypothetical firm method and, 61
program or tax, 58
Expert systems
TAIM use of, 49, 84–85, 91–92

Factor proportions problem, hypothetical
firm method and, 61–62
FDI. See Foreign direct investment (FDI)
Federal Aviation Authority, 44
Federal government
competitive incentives and, 220
firm-specific incentives and, 216
incentives financed by, 32
local control of spending and, 43–45
state and local economic
development effort limited by, 5
See also Community Development
Block Grants (CDBG); Government;
Local government; Public policy;
State government
Federal taxes
on corporation income, 35
See also Corporate income taxes and
credits
Federal training programs, 41
See also Job training
Fees, on loan guarantees, 97
Financial statements
constructing, 63–64
and hypothetical firm method, 59
incorporating incentives in, 245–246
new plant financing and, 239–241,
242 (table)
Financing
of new investment, 62–63
role in state in local policy, 161
of subsidies, 6
See also General-purpose financing
programs

Firm
  benefits of incentives to, 3
  characteristics and non-tax
    incentives, 177–180
  financial statements and new plant
    financing, 239–241, 242 (table)
  location affecting modeling, 70–72
  tax and incentive evaluation and, 17
  tax burden modeling, 18
  value of incentives to, 2
  See also Manufacturing industries;
    Multistate firms
Firm size
  non-tax incentives and, 154, 207
  selection for study by, 65, 68
Firm-specific tax policies, 214–217
Fiscal policy, economic development
    efforts and, 1
Flat tax rates, 116n
Florida, fund disbursement in, 137–140
Foreign direct investment (FDI),
    importance of, 11
Fuel, sales tax on, 37

GATT. *See* General Agreement on Tariffs
    and Trade (GATT)
General Agreement on Tariffs and Trade
    (GATT), 101–102
General credits, 116n
General equilibrium technique,
    evaluating incentive impact using, 17
General Motors Saturn plant, 18
General-purpose financing programs, 40
General-use incentives, 90–91, 93, 94,
    108n22
Geographic dispersion, of states and
    cities in study, 47 (map)
Geographic information systems (GIS)
    database, 50
Geography
  incentive program targeting, 104,
    108n24
  See also Spatial distribution of
    investment returns; Spatial patterns
    of incentives

GIS. *See* Geographic information
    systems (GIS) database
Government
  financing of subsidies by, 6
  impact of economic development
    on, 1
  limitations by federal, 5
  training programs and, 41
  See also City government; Federal
    government; Local government;
    Public policy; State government
Government services, impact of
    incentives on, 7–8
Grants, 40, 85
  awarding, 95–98
  general-use, 90–91
Great Britain
  literature on impact of incentives on
    investment decisions, 107n11
  regional programs in, 29n12, 33,
    52n2
Greenville-Spartanburg airport, BMW
    and expansion of, 2–3
Gross receipts tax, Washington, 113
Growth
  impact of taxes and incentives on,
    25–26, 109
  measuring impact of taxes and
    incentives on, 13–19

Headquarters
  location of, 70–72
  of single-state firm, 106n5
High-technology industries, 27n3
Highways. *See* Infrastructure incentives
Historical information, 91, 92
Hypothetical firm model, 4, 45–49
  administration of incentives and,
    98–103
  aggregate tax measures alternative to,
    56–57
  analytical approach to, 48
  assumptions and details of operation,
    239–246
  creation of firms for, 46, 48

disaggregating results of, 82–83
evaluating incentive impact using,
    18–19
firm characteristics in study,
    66–67 (table)
life cycle of firms and, 78
for measuring impact of taxes and
    incentives on growth, 18–19, 30
measurement of profitability in,
    78–80
non-tax incentives and, 39–45,
    49–50, 83–98
operation of, 58–63
problems with, 60
program counting alternative to,
    57–58
program or tax expenditures
    alternative to, 58
simulating worth of non-tax
    incentives and, 83–98
TAIM as, 55
zero inflation assumption in, 81–82
Hysteresis effect, skill acquisition and,
    29n9

Illinois Enterprise Zone program, 23
Incentive package, 171–172
    for relocating and new plants, 6
    simulation of, 91–98
    tax-based and non-tax proportions
        of, 5
Incentive programs, overlap in, 92–93
Income
    impact of local taxes and incentives
        on, 18
    labor mobility and local distribution
        of, 8–9
    See also Corporate income taxes and
        credits
Income-net worth tax, 110
Income taxes. See Corporate income
    taxes and credits

Industrial location theory, 6–7
    See also Location; Spatial patterns of
        taxes and incentives
Industrial policy, 109
Industrial revenue bonds (IRBs), 22, 32,
    44, 52n9
Industry-specific measures, of tax
    burden, 19
Inflation, zero
    hypothetical firm effects of assuming,
        80–81, 82
Infrastructure incentives, 87–89, 94
    growth and, 30n16
    and Japanese auto plant investment, 3
    programs for, 140
    subsidies, 42–43, 172
    value of, 142
Instruments of economic development,
    2, 5–6
Interest rates
    and loan term assumptions,
        242 (table)
    See also Loans
Interlocal competition, vs. interstate
    competition, 75–78
Internal rate of return (IRR),
    hypothetical firm returns measured
        by, 79–80
Interstate comparisons, hypothetical firm
    method and, 70
Interstate competition, vs. interlocal
    competition, 75–78
Investment
    financing new, 62–63
    foreign direct, 11
    incentive-induced, 9–10
    incentives as replacement, 85
    Japanese auto plant, 3
    relocation of, 12, 13–20
    spatial reshuffling of, 9
    trouble signs for, 34
Investment decisions
    impact of incentives on, 107n11
    process of making, 45–46

Investment tax credits (ITCs), 76, 117,
119, 124n, 128, 204–205, 217
statewide, 62
Iowa, 21–22
competitive position in, 212
in TAIM study, 53n12
training programs in, 137
See also Community Economic
Betterment Account (CEBA)
IRB. *See* Industrial revenue bonds
(IRBs)
IRR. *See* Internal rate of return (IRR)
ITCs. *See* Investment tax credits (ITCs)

Job creation, 8–9, 99–100
Job growth
effective tax and incentives rates and,
185 (table)
in enterprise zones, 190
and poverty, 198
Job Opportunities and Basic Skills
(JOBS) training, 41
Jobs
loss of, 8
spending on, by locality, 24–25
See also Employment;
Unemployment
Job search theory, 29n10
Jobs Training Partnership Act (JTPA)
funds, 41, 44
Job tax credits, 77–78, 117, 128,
204–205
and employee eligibility, 246
Job training
incentives and, 40–41, 89–90, 137,
142, 172
subsidies for, 177–180
JTPA. *See* Jobs Training Partnership Act
(JTPA) funds

Knowledge base. *See* Expert systems

Labor
as business cost, 13
growth shocks from incentives and,
12

mobility of, 8–9
skill acquisition theory, 29n9
See also Job training
Lawmakers, justification of spending by,
32
"Least-cost" site, 6–7
Life cycle of firms, hypothetical firm
model criticism, 78
Linked-deposit programs, 97–98
Loan subsidy incentive, 97
Loans, 40, 85–86, 90–91
awarding, 95–98
guarantees and, 90–91, 95–98
term and interest rate assumptions,
242 (table)
Local government
adoption of economic development
instruments and, 22
benefits of economic development
programs to, 11, 13
control over spending by, 43–45
results of incentive competition, 9
Localities
comparing variations in incentive
levels across, 24–25
disaggregating results for
comparisons, 83
importance of taxes and tax
incentives compared with state
variations, 129–134,
131–132 (table)
shared benefits with nation, 11
See also Variations in economic
development incentives
Location
assumptions about, 48
of firm, plant, and headquarters,
70–72
of General Motors Saturn Plant, 18
incentives as benefit to poorer areas,
12
interstate competition and, 75–78
"least-cost" site, 6
for modeled firms, 163–171,
167–170 (figs.)
tax differences and, 204

traditional theory of, 6–7
value of investment to local residents, 7
See also Geography; Location decisions; Multistate firms; Single-state firms; Spatial distribution of investment returns; Spatial patterns of taxes and incentives
Location decisions
incentives and, 4, 13–20, 108n21
non-economic factors used in making, 27n3
Location theory
economic development policy and, 2
hypothetical firm method and, 45–46
location behavior and, 27n3
Losses, modeling of firm's financial, 52n4

Machinery, sales tax on, 37
MACRS. See Modified Accelerated Cost Recovery System (MACRS) depreciation
Manufacturing industries
selection for study, 63–70
states with greatest employment in, 50
Markets, economic development policy impact on, 10
Massachusetts
modeling in, 106n3
sales throwback and, 74–75
Mazda, Michigan incentives to, 3
Median-state approach, in TAIM model, 71–72
Mercedes-Benz, in Alabama, 1, 2, 208–211
Michigan
loan subsidy incentive in, 97
Mazda incentives, 3
tax abatements in, 23
Misallocation of resources, 28n7
Mississippi
"Balance Agriculture with Industry" program, 5
exclusion from TAIM study, 53n12

Mobility, of labor, 8–9
Modified Accelerated Cost Recovery System (MACRS) depreciation, 81, 116n, 241
Multistate Corporate Income Tax Guide, 51
Multistate firms, 60, 71, 77
firm characteristics and rankings of investment returns, 69 (table)
project returns for, 144 (table), 145–154, 146–153 (figs.)
Multiyear analysis, hypothetical firm model requirement for, 78

NASDA. See National Association of State Development Agencies (NASDA)
Nation
lack of benefits from incentives, 9
shared benefits with localities, 11
National advertising, 22
National Association of State Development Agencies (NASDA), 103, 203
Negative-sum game, competition as, 213
Net operating losses (NOL), modeling of, 35
Net present value (NPV), hypothetical firm returns measured by, 79–80
Net worth taxes
corporate income taxes and, 114–116 (table)
See also Corporate income taxes and credits
New investment
modeling assumptions on financing of, 62–63
firm's financial statements and, 239–241, 242 (table)
non-tax incentives and, 109
See also Variations in economic development incentives
New York, tax credit in, 62
NOL. See Net operating losses (NOL)
Nonbusiness income, 36, 116

Non-tax incentives, 32, 33, 55, 39–45, 172
  after-tax value of, 85
  basic tax system and, 205–206
  clawbacks and, 99–102
  compared with tax incentives, 140–142
  and competitive positions of cities and states, 206
  customized job training and wage subsidies, 40–41
  extensions to hypothetical firm method, 49–50
  and hypothetical firm model, 84–86
  impact of taxes on, 134–136
  impact on new investment, 109
  incentive programs not included, 43–45
  information availability on, 103
  infrastructure subsidies, 42–43
  programs excluded from study, 43–45
  simulating worth of, 83–98
  size of plants and, 154
  state role in defining, 161
  TAIM and, 83–86, 86 (fig.), 103–104
  value of, 134–142, 177–180
  See also Hypothetical firm model; Taxes and tax incentives
NPV. *See* Net present value (NPV)

On-the-job training, 41

Parent firm. *See* Headquarters
Payroll. *See* Corporate income taxes and credits; Payroll factor
Payroll factor, 36
  sales distributed among states and, 72–74
Per-capital expenditure, differences among localities, 24–25
Personal property, taxation of, 37, 118
Plants
  construction of, 46

financing of new, 239–241, 242 (table)
location of, 6, 70–72, 154–171
See also Firm; Firm size
Policies. *See* Public policy
Political justification, for use of revenues, 7, 32
Poverty rate
  defined, 233n
  development effort and, 22, 23
  effective tax and incentives rates and, 185 (table)
  employment growth, net return on new plant investment, and, 182 (table), 183
  investment in cities and, 188–190
  job growth and, 198
  and net returns from new plant investment (cities), 189 (table)
  value of incentives and, 199 (table)
Private investment, incentives as replacement, 85
Profitability
  measures of, 79
  value of incentive package and, 46
Profit maximizers, location of firms and, 6–7
Program counting
  as incentive analysis approach, 57–58
Program expenditures
  as incentive analysis approach, 58
Project returns
  for 16 multistate firms, 144 (table), 145–154, 146–153 (figs.)
  correlations with unemployment rates, 265–275
  impact of taxes and incentives on, 158 (table), 159 (table), 253–264
  large multistate drug firms, 147 (fig.), 151 (fig.), 158 (table), 168 (map)
  large multistate plastics firms, 149 (fig.), 153 (fig.), 159 (table), 170 (map)

multistate instruments firms,
197 (fig.)
small multistate drug firms,
146 (fig.), 150 (fig.), 158 (table),
163 (map), 164 (fig.), 165 (fig.),
167 (fig.)
small multistate soap firms,
148 (fig.), 152 (fig.), 155 (fig.),
159 (table), 169 (map)
Property taxes
abatement of, 128, 192
on business realty and personal
property, 35
calculation of, 244–245
simulation treatment of, 38–39
by state (1992), 118, 120–121 (table)
Property tax rates, 75, 76
by state, 120–121, 234–235 (table)
Public debt, subordination of, 91
Public loans, 96
and guaranteed loans, 97
Public policy, 4, 12
competitive incentives and, 32–33,
211–212
incentive competition and, 203–221
justifications for, 28n4
See also Federal government; Taxes
and tax incentives

Quasi-governmental incentives, not
included in TAIM, 45

Rate of return, on new plant investment,
197 (fig.)
Redistribution of jobs, 20, 188
See also entries under Job
Regional policy, in Great Britain, 29n12
Relocation
incentive packages for, 6
of investment, 12, 13–20
See also Location
Representative firm method. See
Hypothetical firm model

Research
on usefulness of incentives, 10–13
spatial patterns of incentives, 20–24
Reservation wage, 12, 29n10
Residence, assumptions for enterprise
zone incentives, 246 (table)
Resources
efficiency in allocation of, 10
misallocation of, 28n7
Returns on investment
in best and worst states, 161–171
among cities, 73, 186–190
city-state differences and, 204
differences after taxes in states and
cities, 171–173
enterprise zones and, 190–199
measurement over time, 78–79
among states, 176–185, 200–201
taxes, tax incentives, and spatial
distribution of, 175–201
Revenues, for new industrial investment,
7
Revolving loan funds (RLFs), 44,
108n16
RLFs. See Revolving loan funds (RLFs)
Roads and highways
funding for, 44
See also Department of
Transportation (DOT); Infrastructure
incentives
Rule-based system. See Expert systems

Sales distribution, hypothetical firm
model, 72–75
Sales factor, 74
Sales taxes
on business purchases, 35
simulation treatment of, 36–38, 52n5
variations among states, 110–112,
111–112 (table)
Sales throwback, 74–75
Saturn. See General Motors Saturn plant
SBA. See Small Business Administration
(SBA)

SBICs. *See* Small business investment companies (SBICs)

Scotland, 27n3
  incentives in, 52n2

Sector-specific tax policies, 214

SIC. *See* Standard Industrial Classification (SIC) manufacturing industries

Simulation. *See* Hypothetical firm model

Single-state firms, hypothetical firm model treatment of, 70, 77

Site Selection and Industrial Development, 5, 39, 51, 103

Sites. *See* Location

Size. *See* Firm size

Skill acquisition theory, hysteresis effect and, 29n9

Skills. *See* Job training

Small Business Administration (SBA)
  financing available through, 140
  programs of, 32

Small business investment companies (SBICs), 45

South Carolina
  BMW in, 2–3
  training programs in, 137

Spatial distribution of investment returns, 175–201
  among cities, 186–190
  enterprise zones and, 190–199
  among states, 176–185

Spatial patterns of incentives, 2, 4, 12, 27n3, 142–171, 172, 253–264
  and national benefits of competitive economic development policy, 211–212
  poor vs. wealthy communities, 4, 21–24
  standing offers and, 26
  See also Econometric technique; Location; Location theory

Standard Industrial Classification (SIC) manufacturing industries, 63–64

Standing incentive offer, 24–26, 46
  tax vs. incentive differences and, 208–211

State government
  benefits of economic development programs to, 11–13
  control over spending by, 43–45
  economic development agencies, 5–6
  economic development instruments of, 2
  efforts toward economic expansion, 22
  incentives to firms, 2
  results of incentive competition, 9

States
  characteristics of sample, 225–226 (table)
  city unemployment and, 188
  cooperative agreements among, 221
  correlations between project returns and unemployment rates for, 265–275
  data on taxes and tax incentives, 51–52
  disaggregating results for comparisons, 82–83
  economic distress and expanded incentives in, 23
  incentives and economic conditions in, 21
  incentive wars and, 220
  levels of variation in, 162–166
  local property tax rates by, 234–235 (table)
  returns on investment among, 176–185, 200–201
  sales distributed among, 72–75
  statewide investment tax credits offered by, 62
  studies of tax systems in, 59–60
  for study, 50
  taxes and tax incentives compared with city variations, 129–134, 131–132 (table)

304

See also Sales taxes; Tax credits;
Taxes and tax incentives; Variations
in economic development incentives
Subsidies
combinations of federal, state, and
locally financed, 6
infrastructure, 42–43
job training and wage, 40–41
loan, 40
to Mercedes-Benz, 209–210 (table)
provision of, 32–33
substitution and, 89
value of incentive and, 134
wage, and worker training incentives,
89–90
See also Job training
Subsidy indifference argument, 102
Substitution effects, 88
grants, loans, subsidies, and, 91
Survey technique, evaluating incentive
impact using, 14–15

TAA. *See* Trade Adjustment Assistance
(TAA)
TAIM. *See* Tax and Incentive Model
(TAIM)
Targeted Jobs Tax Credit (TJTC), 41
Targeted tax incentives, 118–119, 214–
215
Targeting geography, 104–105
Tax abatements, Michigan, 23
Tax and Incentive Model (TAIM), 4
AFTAX model and, 160
city/state selection for, 50–52
computational structure of, 247–250,
251 (fig.)
debt and tax structures and, 108n15
and hypothetical firm method, 55
incentive selection by, 91–98
industry/firm choice for, 63–70
loan costs and, 107n14
multistate vs. single-location firms,
70–72
non-tax incentives and, 49–50,
86 (fig.)

non-tax portion of, 103–104
public vs. private sector loans and, 93
results summary, 203–211
state and local discretionary
incentives and, 86
state-level targeting of, 108n24
subordination of public debt and, 91
tax treatment in, 33–39
tax vs. non-tax incentives, 32–33
Tax breaks, states and, 216–217
Tax credits
hypothetical firm model treatment of,
76
generally available, 62
See also Credits
Tax effects, hypothetical firm method
and, 55–56
Taxes and tax incentives, 5, 33–39
aggregate measures, 56–57
basic tax systems vs. tax incentives,
119–128
as business cost, 13
calculating for hypothetical firm
method, 59
compared with non-tax incentives,
140–142
competition, public policy, and,
203–221
corporate income taxes and credits,
35–36, 52n3, 113–117
correlation with unemployment, 184
credits as incentives, 6
differences between taxes and
incentives, 203–211
effective, in representative city in
each state, 135–136 (table)
efficiency and, 213–218
impact on growth, 13–19, 25–26, 109
impact on new investment, 109
importance of state vs. local,
129–134
incentive competition and, 10
income effects of, 18
interstate and interlocal competition
and, 75–78

interstate differences in business, 55
non-tax incentives and, 32, 39–45,
    52n1
property taxes and, 38–39, 118
sales tax and, 36–38, 110–113
spatial distribution of investment
    returns and, 175–201
spatial patterns of, 142–171
state system studies and, 59–60
statewide and in enterprise zones for
    distressed areas, 122–124 (table)
targeted tax incentives, 118–119
value to firm of selected features,
    125–126
variation in, 110–119
See also Enterprise zones
Tax incentives. *See* Economic
    development incentives; Tax credits;
    Taxes and Tax Incentives
Tax incidence, hypothetical firm method
    and, 60
Tax increment financing instruments
    (TIFs), 94–95
Tax policy, economic development vs.
    general tax policy, 33–35
Tax rates. *See* Effective tax rates (ETRs)
Tax subsidies, 32–33
Tax systems, neutral nature of incentives
    and, 215
Throwback rules, sales factors and, 74,
    75, 173n4
Tiebout hypothesis, 213, 215
TIFs. *See* Tax increment financing
    instruments (TIFs)
Time, measuring effects over, 78–82
Title IX, of EDA, 44
TJTC. *See* Targeted Jobs Tax Credit
    (TJTC)
Trade Adjustment Assistance (TAA), 41
Training. *See* Job training

Unemployed persons
    mobility of, 9
    See also Employees; Unemployment

Unemployment
    assumptions for enterprise zone
        incentives, 246 (table)
    effective tax and incentives rates and,
        185 (table)
    intensity of incentives and, 23
    and net return on new plant
        investment, 178–179 (table),
        187 (table), 197 (fig.)
    redistribution of jobs and, 20
    reservation wage and, 29n9
    returns among cities and, 175–190
    returns among states and, 175–185
    value of economic development
        policy in relation to, 12
    value of incentives and, 195 (table)
    See also Employment; Enterprise
        zones; Job training; Taxes and tax
        incentives
Unemployment rates, correlation with
    project returns, 265–275
Urban Development Action Grants, 22
Urban Institute, 203

Value
    administration of incentives and,
        98–103
    discretionary incentives, after-tax, 85
    of incentives, 3–4, 82, 253–264
    of non-tax incentives, 134–140
    of selected tax features, 119–128,
        125–126 (table)
    of state tax incentives vs. non-tax
        incentives, 140–142
Value-added tax, 110, 113
Variations in economic development
    incentives, 109–110
    in basic tax systems vs. tax
        incentives, 119–128
    importance of state vs. local taxes
        and tax incentives, 129–134
    non-tax incentive programs and value
        to firm, 134–142

spatial pattern of taxes and
    incentives, 142–171
in taxes and tax incentives, 110–119

Wages, taxes and, 13
Wage subsidies
    job training and, 40–41
    and worker training incentives, 89–90
Wisconsin
    modeling in, 106n3
    sales throwback and, 74–75
    taxes in, 173n3, 245
Wisconsin Department of Revenue,
    state tax system study in, 59
Workers. *See* Employees
Worth. *See* Value

Zero inflation assumption, 80–81, 82
Zero-sum process, 28n6
    state and local incentive competition
    as, 1, 9, 11

About the Institute

The W.E. Upjohn Institute for Employment Research is a nonprofit research organization devoted to finding and promoting solutions to employment-related problems at the national, state, and local levels. It is an activity of the W.E. Upjohn Unemployment Trustee Corporation, which was established in 1932 to administer a fund set aside by the late Dr. W.E. Upjohn, founder of The Upjohn Company, to seek ways to counteract the loss of employment income during economic downturns.

The Institute is funded largely by income from the W.E. Upjohn Unemployment Trust, supplemented by outside grants, contracts, and sales of publications. Activities of the Institute comprise the following elements: 1) a research program conducted by a resident staff of professional social scientists; 2) a competitive grant program, which expands and complements the internal research program by providing financial support to researchers outside the Institute; 3) a publications program, which provides the major vehicle for disseminating the research of staff and grantees, as well as other selected works in the field; and 4) an Employment Management Services division, which manages most of the publicly funded employment and training programs in the local area.

The broad objectives of the Institute's research, grant, and publication programs are to 1) promote scholarship and experimentation on issues of public and private employment and unemployment policy, and 2) make knowledge and scholarship relevant and useful to policymakers in their pursuit of solutions to employment and unemployment problems.

Current areas of concentration for these programs include causes, consequences, and measures to alleviate unemployment; social insurance and income maintenance programs; compensation; workforce quality; work arrangements; family labor issues; labor-management relations; and regional economic development and local labor markets.